DATE DUE

DE 1 03			

Demco No. 62-0549

Critical Essays on
Gabriel García Márquez

Critical Essays on
World Literature

Robert Lecker, General Editor
McGill University

Critical Essays on
Gabriel García Márquez

George R. McMurray

G. K. Hall & Co. • Boston, Massachusetts

Library of Congress Cataloging in Publication Data

Critical essays on Gabriel García Márquez.

(Critical essays' on world literature)
Includes index.
1. García Márquez, Gabriel, 1928- —Criticism
and interpretation. I. McMurray, George R. II. Series.
PQ8180.17.A73Z653 1987   863   86-33717
ISBN 0-8161-8834-3 (alk. paper)

This publication is printed on permanent/durable acid-free paper
MANUFACTURED IN THE UNITED STATES OF AMERICA

To my wife, Doris

CONTENTS

INTRODUCTION

"In about the middle of 1967, the novel *Cien años de soledad* (*One Hundred Years of Solitude*) was published in Buenos Aires, provoking a literary earthquake throughout Latin America. The critics recognized the book as a masterpiece of the art of fiction and the public endorsed this opinion, systematically exhausting new editions, which, at one point, appeared at the astounding rate of one per week. Overnight, García Márquez became almost as famous as a great soccer player or an eminent singer of boleros."[1] The preceding remarks by Mario Vargas Llosa, Peru's best writer of contemporary prose fiction, describe the initial impact Gabriel García Márquez's most famous work had on the Latin American reading public. The novel's success on an even broader international scale is evidenced by the numerous prizes it has won, the critical acclaim it has elicited throughout the western world, and its many translations, which numbered eighteen within a few months of its initial appearance. Fifteen years later, in 1982, García Márquez's international audience enthusiastically applauded the news from Stockholm that he had been awarded the Nobel Prize for literature. Although his oeuvre attains high levels of excellence both before and after *Solitude*, this undisputed masterpiece remains the most widely read of all his works.

The Colombian author's fictional world reflects above all his obsessions with Aracataca, the small town near the Atlantic coast of his native land where he was born in 1928.[2] The oldest of a telegrapher's twelve children, García Márquez spent the first eight years of his life in Aracataca in the large home of his beloved maternal grandparents, whose accounts of local legends and myths would later figure in his works. He then studied law briefly at the National University in Bogotá, after which he worked as a journalist for more than a decade before settling in Mexico City where his obsessions with Aracataca—Macondo in his first novel and several of his short stories—coalesced in the magical vision of *Solitude*. From 1967 until 1975 he resided in Spain; since then he has divided his time between Mexico and Colombia.

Prior to the appearance of his masterpiece, García Márquez's works had elicited scant critical acclaim, nor had he reached a large number of

1

readers outside his native land. Indeed, Harley D. Oberhelman states, "With the 1967 publication of *Cien años de soledad*, García Márquez passed from the ranks of obscure secondary writers of contemporary Spanish American fiction to the spotlight of critical attention and furor of public interest."[3] Although in retrospect some critics might disagree with Oberhelman's implied negative assessment of the early works, it is nevertheless certain that very few perceived the Colombian author's remarkable talent before his meteoric rise on the literary scene. Two major exceptions are Luis Harss and Barbara Dohmann, whose chapter on García Márquez in their seminal book *Los nuestros* was the most widely read panoramic view of the author's life and fiction before 1967.[4] Though marred by factual errors, this essay reveals early insights into the fabulous fictional universe still in embryonic form. The discussion below of the criticism on García Márquez follows the chronological order of his works, but it should be pointed out that most of his vast bibliography, including that dealing with his writings before *Solitude*, has appeared since his sudden fame in 1967.

Between 1947 and 1954 García Márquez published approximately a dozen short stories in the Bogotá daily, *El Espectador*. Ten of these tales, which the author "would destroy . . . if he could get his hands on them,"[5] were published without his consent in two pirate editions, *El negro que hizo esperar a los ángeles* (The black man who made the angels wait)[6] and *Ojos de perro azul* (Blue dog eyes).[7] In his *García Márquez: Historia de un deicidio* (García Márquez: History of a deicide), Mario Vargas Llosa analyzes most of these pieces, referring to them as his Colombian colleague's "prehistoria morbosa" ("morbid prehistory") — their overriding theme is death — and stressing the influence of Kafka, Faulkner, and the surrealists. According to Vargas Llosa, the best and most convincing is "Nabo, el negro que hizo esperar a los ángeles ("Nabo, the Black Man Who Made the Angels Wait"), about a black boy who loses his mind after being kicked in the head by a horse and shut up in a room for fifteen years.[8] Mary Alice Kilmer-Tchalekian treats this work in greater detail, emphasizing its Faulknerian elements, deliberate ambiguity, and early depiction of solitude.[9]

Praising the imagery of these early narratives, Gilbert Smith uses as an example "La otra costilla de la muerte" ("The Other Side of Death"), whose protagonist senses death flowing through his bones "like a river of ashes."[10] Donald McGrady bases his even greater admiration on the author's adroit manipulation of experimental techniques and imaginative delineation of tense psychic states, adding that the poetic quality of these stories adumbrates the artistic genius revealed more than a decade later in *Solitude*.[11] More negative in his assessment, John Sturrock speaks of these "ambitious but as yet uncertain and over-abstract tales,"[12] and Martin Kaplan, a reviewer for The *New Republic*, refers to them as "interesting archeology, compelling mainly because they pander to the glimmers-of-greatness triumphs of literary hindsight."[13] Echoing these judgments, Gene H. Bell-Villada writes of the "twenty-year-old adolescent shooting for the long sentence and purple rhetoric, groping for technique but coming up with forced conceits and pat endings."[14] For Raymond L. Williams the most significant aspect of the early stories is their illustration of the principal lesson García Márquez learned from Kafka, namely, that instead of mirroring the world, the writer should feel free to create another reality.[15]

In an interview with Rita Guibert, García Márquez stated that of all the books he had written, *La hojarasca* (1955) (Leaf Storm)[16] was his favorite because he felt it was his most sincere and spontaneous.[17] Although the novel was a commercial success in Colombia, selling thirty thousand copies when it first appeared,[18] the author told Raymond Williams that it drew little critical attention at that time,[19] and indeed the growing bibliography on *Leaf Storm* includes only a few items prior to the publication of *Solitude*.[20] Harss and Dohmann find this somber picture of a decaying village (Macondo) in the year 1928 "a somewhat makeshift book written in starts and spurts that . . . often fade out before reaching fulfillment." Like numerous other critics, Harss and Dohmann also allude to Faulkner's influence on *Leaf Storm*, eliciting from García Márquez the statement that when he first read Faulkner in the late 1940s, he decided he had to become a writer.[21]

García Márquez has expressed his admiration for Sophocles' tragedies on many occasions,[22] a fact which, together with the quotation from *Antigone* at the beginning of *Leaf Storm*, prompted Pedro Lastra to write one of the most illuminating studies of the Colombian's first novel. Lastra demonstrates that the moral dilemma in *Antigone* provides the structural underpinnings for *Leaf Storm*: Creon's decree to leave Polynices' body to the vultures is reflected by the determination of the citizens of Macondo to leave the doctor's corpse in his house to rot; Antigone's promise to bury her brother parallels the colonel's promise to bury the doctor; and the brothers Polynices and Eteocles in Sophocles' drama are evoked in *Leaf Storm* by the strikingly similar doctor and priest.[23]

Mario Vargas Llosa's and Graciela Maturo's comments on *Leaf Storm* are also illuminating, the former concentrating primarily on Macondo's rigid social structure,[24] and the latter on the mythical and religious symbols informing the plot.[25] Another perceptive Latin American critic, Juan Loveluck, emphasizes the possible influence of Virginia Woolf on García Márquez, comparing the static psychic time in *Orlando* with the impression of temporal paralysis in *Leaf Storm*.[26]

The reactions of U.S. reviewers to *Leaf Storm* have been mixed. Martha Duffy considers it a letdown because "One searches in vain for the raffish Macondo of *One Hundred Years of Solitude*,"[27] while Ronald De Feo, a reviewer for the *Nation*, describes it as "too long and . . . somewhat static and flat."[28] Writing for *Harper's Magazine*, Earl Shorris comes to the conclusion that *Leaf Storm* is made "as much of device as of art" and that it is more interesting for what it tells about García Márquez's development as a writer than for its intrinsic worth.[29] J. Yglesias laments the lack of humor in the novel, but he nevertheless concedes that García Márquez "found his voice from the very first."[30]

On a more scholarly note, Martha Lafollette Miller has published one of the few Jungian interpretations of *Leaf Storm*, the plot of which in her view illustrates modern man's loss of love and resultant isolation and anguish.[31] George R. McMurray perceives in García Márquez's winding, complex sentences, sprinkled with hypnotic repetitions, abrupt syntactic thrusts, and parenthetic insertions, an affinity with Faulkner's involuted style.[32] The unresolved plot threads are viewed by Frank Dauster as reflections of an ambiguous reality the author deliberately sought to depict.[33]

Most of the critical articles on *El coronel no tiene quien le escriba* (1961) (No one writes to the colonel),[34] like those on the early short stories and *Leaf Storm*, were published after *Solitude*. Written in 1956 while the author was living in Paris without a job, this poignant portrait of an aging, impoverished colonel struggling to survive in a Colombian backwater is an offshoot of *La mala hora* (*In Evil Hour*), which García Márquez began and then abandoned in order to focus entirely on one of his characters. Thus, Angel Rama has advised that the two works be read in succession because "they are definitely one single novel."[35] In their discussion of *Colonel*, Harss and Dohmann admire the pared-to-the-bone, Hemingwayesque style which demonstrates that "clarity, precision, understatement, a deceptive simplicity, seduce where rhetoric never could." The principal focus of these two critics, however, is the character of the colonel, whom they consider to be one of the most endearing in Latin American fiction.[36]

Writing for the prestigious but now defunct Argentine journal *Sur*, Fryda Schultz de Mantovani also focuses on García Márquez's concise style "stripped of grandiloquence,"[37] while Robert G. Mead, Jr., in the *Saturday Review*, extols the "glints of humor" woven into the "small, simple tapestry of a life [the colonel's] that is rich in human values."[38] The artistic merits and the elements of hope in *Colonel* are most enthusiastically proclaimed by James R. Frakes and David Haworth, the former lauding "the rare combination of grace and vibrancy" in the style of "this Colombian virtuoso," whose "every scene, every gesture sings life and denies death,"[39] and the latter describing the novelette as a "masterly picture of despair and optimism" that "dazzles with powerful effect."[40]

The first critic to discuss in detail the political aspects of *Colonel* is Mario Vargas Llosa, who points out how oblique allusions to the curfew, the censored press, and the underground newsletter are unobtrusively injected into the text to create tension and suggest the ambience of *la violencia*, the civil war that wracked Colombia from 1948 until the early

1960s.[41] Like Harss and Dohmann, Earl Shorris comments on the poignance of the aging protagonist who "is almost unbearably human" and, elaborating on one of the major themes, adds that the old man's final despairing utterance ("Shit") illustrates Heidegger's statement that "the loss of all hope does not deprive human reality of its possibilities; it is simply a way of *being* toward these same possibilities."[42] George R. McMurray underscores the threat of *la violencia* in the midst of which the colonel emerges as an absurd hero doggedly resisting adversity.[43] Although some may disagree, Raymond L. Williams believes that *Colonel* is basically a political novel, but that because the characters scrupulously avoid the subject of politics, the theme is implied rather than articulated.[44]

In 1961 García Márquez was awarded the Esso Literary Prize for his manuscript of *La mala hora* (*In Evil Hour*), which was published in Spain the following year. The author rejected the edition, however, because the editor took the liberty of changing certain expressions in the manuscript in order to preserve the "purity" of the language. Four years later, in 1966, this novel about the ravages of *la violencia* on a small town appeared in Mexico in its original form.

Written immediately after the first edition was printed in Spain, Ernesto Volkening's article "A propósito de *La mala hora*" (About *In Evil Hour*), isolates praiseworthy elements — the masterful, symbolic characterization of the mayor, for example — but Volkening dislikes the loose, fragmented structure and the open ending that in his opinion leaves the reader unsatisfied.[45] Like several other early critics, he mistakenly assumes the setting to be Macondo; in reality, the action of both *Colonel* and *In Evil Hour* occurs in an unnamed town, probably Sucre, further inland from the coastal region where Macondo is located.[46] In his study of *la violencia* in Colombian fiction, Robert Kirsner concludes that in view of its bitter tone and the devastating events it depicts, *In Evil Hour* raises serious doubts about the nation's ability to build a durable peace "on the rubble of human destruction."[47]

The well-known Mexican critic Emmanuel Carballo sees *In Evil Hour* as an "X-ray of Colombia," García Márquez's novel that best comes to grips with the political situation there.[48] More concerned with form, Alicia M. Alonso finds the unadorned style and cinemagraphic technique effective for achieving dramatic impact but scarcely appropriate for the delineation of character.[49] Vargas Llosa takes a more imaginative stance, viewing the plot as a dramatization of the conflict between reality (political oppression) and imagination (the slanderous lampoons appearing on the doors of houses belonging to upper-class citizens).[50] George R. McMurray points out that the disjointed montage structure of *In Evil Hour* serves to spatialize time and thus capture simultaneously the crisscrossing currents of resentment dividing the community.[51]

One of the U.S. authors most fascinated with García Márquez's oeuvre, Robert Coover reveals ambivalent reactions to *In Evil Hour*, praising its wit, imaginative richness, and comic exaggeration on the one hand, but, on the other, lamenting that the clash between the real and the imaginary (echoing Vargas Llosa, he believes the novel can be read as a parable about the power of art) is never satisfactorily resolved.[52] Mary E. Davis finds numerous subtle allusions to other literatures, a case in point being the lampoons which she views as a modern version of the Greek chorus.[53] Mikhail Bakhtin's theory of heteroglossia, or the presence of a variety of "languages" in a given text, serves as a starting point for Raymond L. Williams's analysis of social disintegration caused by the mysterious events.[54]

The political and social implications of *Los funerales de la Mamá Grande* (1962) (*Big Mama's Funeral*),[55] García Márquez's first collection of short fiction, are emphasized in early reviews including those by Federico Álvarez and Alberto Dallal.[56] Although Harss and Dohmann give scant attention to this work, dismissing the title story about the death of a feudal matriarch and its aftermath as a "rather specious" parody of the official rhetoric of Colombian journalism, their discussion of the other pieces in the volume does bring into proper focus the close relationship between the characters' inner lives and their physical milieux.[57] Even less impressed by these tales, Emmanuel Carballo sees them as "fragments or chapters that didn't fit into his novels."[58] while Jaime Tello, who reviewed the collection after having read *Solitude*, calls them "a disappointment" and, except for "Big Mama's Funeral," "without significant interest or importance."[59] In general, U.S. critics have shown far greater appreciation than their Latin American counterparts for *Funeral*. James E. Frakes, for example, refers to the eight pieces as "gems of obliquity" or "hilarious social farces whose inflated mocking style and tone fit the content like young skin." Frakes ecstatically concludes, "He [García Márquez] is an absolute master."[60] Robert G. Mead, Jr., praises the author's ability to enable his readers to "intuit the mysterious inner lives of his characters through their laconic utterances, their actions, and their emotions."[61]

The thrust of Vargas Llosa's lengthy examination of *Funeral* is that these tales, which range from the objective realism of "La siesta del martes" (Tuesday siesta), the account of an impoverished woman's visit to her son's grave, to the hyperbolic, mythical "Big Mama's Funeral," illustrate a gradual progression toward the fantasy that prevails in much of García Márquez's subsequent work.[62] Roger Peel also comments on the sharp contrast between the above-mentioned stories, but he believes the author's purpose throughout is to escape the rhetoric that dominated previous Latin American writing.[63] Focusing only on "Big Mama's Funeral," Judith A. Goetzinger demonstrates that the narrator, a kind of folk chronicler, represents the popular imagination whose subjective vision of reality creates an aura of myth and whose irony and fantasy convey the overriding theme of social and moral decay.[64]

Frank Dauster divides the tales of *Funeral* into two types: those reminiscent of Hemingway's direct, objective style, and those representing "a crack in the wall of reality" through which a skewed world vision gradually comes into view.[65] According to Robert Coover, the "comic hyperbole and mock-mythologizing of 'Big Mama's Funeral' contrast sharply with the objective sobriety" of much of the author's previous fiction, suggesting that he "may have felt himself trapped in some kind of cul-de-sac" and needed to return to his roots in Macondo.[66] In still another discussion of the mythical elements in this tale, Robert Sims draws an analogy between the *bricoleur* or handyman, who makes use of whatever raw materials he can find in order to complete his task, and the mythmaker (the anonymous narrator of the story), who incorporates shards of fact and fantasy into his chronicle.[67] The protagonist of "La prodigiosa tarde de Baltazar" (Balthazar's marvelous afternoon), García Márquez's popular tale about a carpenter who constructs a fabulous bird cage, is seen by George R. McMurray as the artist alienated and victimized by bourgeois values,[68] whereas David William Foster, guided by the principles of structuralism, demonstrates that as a result of the author's adroit manipulation of distancing techniques, the reader and narrator become accomplices in their ironic view of the naive Balthazar.[69]

Approximately a year before the publication of *Solitude* (1967) Mexico's best-known writer of fiction, Carlos Fuentes, having read the first three chapters of the novel in rough draft, declared it "absolutely masterful" and went on to say, "Macondo is transformed into a universal territory, into a history of the origins and destiny of all human time and of the dreams and desires with which men save or destroy themselves."[70] Immediately after its publication the novel was greeted by an avalanche of reviews throughout the Spanish-speaking world ranging in tone from favorable to euphoric,[71] and three years later, when the English translation appeared, reviewers were equally impressed.[72] In this same year (1970) critic Wolfgang A. Luchting expressed the feelings of many readers and academics in the following terms: "Whatever one reads or hears about it [*Solitude*] reveals . . . an underlying helplessness in the face of this intensely alive work, a kind of embarrassed secret admission of critical arms thrown away, and of an at first hesitant, then joyful abandon to the seductive powers of the novel."[73] Though perhaps valid at the time it was written, Luchting's reference to "critical arms thrown away" seems highly ironic in retrospect; indeed, between 1967 and 1984 the *MLA International Bibliography* lists no fewer than 285 scholarly publications, including doctoral dissertations, dealing with García Márquez's masterpiece. Obviously, only a small fraction of this huge volume of criticism can be referred to in the present survey.

Of the book-length studies by a single author dealing with *Solitude*, the following are judged to be the most significant: *García Márquez o el olvidado arte de contar* (García Márquez or the forgotten art of storytelling), by Ricardo Gullón, an analysis of narrative art and technique as applied to *Solitude*;[74] *Las claves del mito en García Márquez* (The keys to myth in García Márquez), by René Jara Cuadra and Jaime Mejía Duque, in which myth is seen as an instrument for ordering and humanizing a chaotic and brutal fictional world;[75] *"Cien años de soledad": Una interpretación* (*One Hundred Years of Solitude:* An interpretation), by Josefina Ludmer, a post-structuralist, Freudian treatment of the novel;[76] *El espejo hablado: Un estudio de "Cien años de soledad* (The talking mirror: a study of *One Hundred Years of Solitude*), by Suzanne Jill Levine, which brings to light poetic similarities between *Solitude* and works by Borges and Virginia Woolf;[77] and *La función de la historia en "Cien años de soledad"* (The function of history in *One Hundred Years of Solitude*), by Lucila Ines Mena, demonstrating that many of the "fantastic" events of the novel are solidly based on the political and historical realities of Colombia.[78] Mention should also be made of a special issue of the journal *Explicación de Textos Literarios* dedicated entirely to *Solitude*.[79]

The following studies indicate the broad spectrum of interpretations García Márquez's masterpiece has elicited. "Novedad y anacronismo de *Cien años de soledad*," (Novelty and anachronism of *One Hundred Years of Solitude*), by Uruguayan critic Emir Rodríguez Monegal, introduces the reader to the innovative elements of the novel which, because of its development of plot and character, seemed anachronistic in the experimental decade of the 1960s.[80] Another introductory article, "A propósito de *Cien años de soledad* (About *One Hundred Years of Solitude*), by Isaís Lerner, touches briefly on specifics such as the treatment of time and the use of paradox and hyperbole.[81] Adalbert Dessau is one of the first to concentrate on solitude as a major theme, not only in *Solitude*, but also in other works by the Colombian author.[82] Gregory Lawrence sees this condition as the equivalent of Marxist alienation,[83] while Paul Hedeen draws parallels between García Márquez's solitary figures and Octavio Paz's psychological portrait of the Mexican.[84] The curse of incest plaguing the Buendías comes under the scrutiny of Suzanne Jill Levine, who finds this anti-social behavior a manifestation of their isolation and a major cause of their solitude.[85]

Mario Vargas Llosa emphasizes the novel's representation of a total literary experience encompassing the historical and mythical, the logical and fantastic, the tragic and humorous, and the individual and collective; also treated in his exhaustive analysis are the various literary techniques designed to reinforce the impression of totality.[86] *Solitude* as an example of magical realism is examined by Vicente Cabrera and Luis González del Valle, who conclude that because the fusion of reality and fantasy enhances aesthetic effect, "artistic realism" is a more appropriate term for this type of fiction.[87] The creation of a hallucinatory, fictive reality reminiscent of Borges is elucidated by the Chilean D.P. Gallagher who, in addition, delineates the roles of Colombian history and cyclical time in García Márquez's mythical universe.[88]

Gallagher's consideration of time as a major theme of the novel in question is shared by numerous other critics. Patricia Tobin, for example, analyzes the Colombian author's revolt against the inexorable lineality that has governed Western thinking about time, history, and the structuring of fiction.[89] Djelal Kadir finds similarities between the Italian philosopher Giambattista Vico's ontogeny of history and the development and decay of civilization in *Solitude*.[90] Another approach to the subject of time is that of Lois P. Zamora, who sees *Solitude* as a "monumental fiction of succession and ending," "a fiction of temporal fulfillment," humanized by an author whose perspective is mythical, eschatological, and apocalyptic.[91] Robert Paoli stresses circular time, but he alone relates it to irreverent, carnivalesque episodes of popular culture, which generate momentum by alternating with diametrical opposites.[92]

In his analysis of José Arcadio Buendía's character, Floyd Merrel traces a series of analogies between the restless patriarch's quest for knowledge and Western man's archetypal struggle to understand his environment.[93] Similarities and differences between *Solitude* and Joseph Conrad's *Nostromo*, which also has a Latin American setting, are brought out by Jean Franco, who views *Nostromo* as the realistic, bourgeois novel par excellence, and *Solitude* as the representation of a fantastic world vulnerable to harsh reality.[94] Doris Kay Rolfe offers a detailed study of tone and structure in which she points out that *Solitude* does not follow modernist patterns, but rather those of literary tradition, namely, fantasy, epic adventure, and omniscient narration.[95] The novel's mythical underpinnings are revealed by two very different critics: Katalin Kulin, who finds meanings in archetypal motifs,[96] and Alfonso de Toro, a structuralist who examines linguistic codes and compositional organization to arrive at similar conclusions.[97] In his essay, "Ideology and Deconstruction in Macondo," José David Saldívar considers Marxism and Biblical myth as the two major influences on the novel which in his view emerges as a metaphor of Latin American isolation and alienation.[98] Emilio García also deals with the theme of alienation, but he believes that its causes are more existential than political or historical.[99]

García Márquez's collection of seven stories entitled *La increíble y triste historia de la cándida Eréndira y de su abuela desalmada (The Incredible and Sad Tale of Innocent Eréndira and Her Heartless Grandmother)* appeared in 1972 and, as mentioned previously, four of these stories were published that same year in *Leaf Storm and Other Stories*. Six years later, in 1978, the remaining three, including the title story, were translated in *Innocent Eréndira and Other Stories*. The first critic to treat any of these tales extensively is Mario Vargas Llosa, who read five of them in literary journals before finishing his monograph in 1971. Vargas Llosa's overall view is that after the total reality, i.e., the ingenious fusion of objective reality and fantasy, in *Solitude*, García Márquez's subsequent fiction represents the "hegemonía" (hegemony) of fantasy in his imaginary universe.[100] Of the initial reviews, those written by U.S. critics are generally more enthusiastic than those of their Latin American colleagues, perhaps because of the recent resounding success of *Solitude* in English.

For Peter S. Prescott, a reviewer for *Newsweek*, García Márquez seems to say, "The world contains mysteries that we need and can easily live with, but also miracles that we cannot understand, that speak for forces unknown to men."[101] Ronald De Feo reserves special praise for "El ahogado más hermoso del mundo" ("The Handsomest Drowned Man in the World") and "Un señor muy viejo con unas alas enormes" ("A Very Old Man with Enormous Wings"), stating that "when García Márquez tells us about a drowned man who is washed up on a beach one day, or an old angel who is driven into a village by a storm, we suspend our disbelief. García Márquez always includes details that give reality to the fantasy, help us believe in the unbelievable."[102] Also preferring "The Handsomest Drowned Man in the World," V.S. Pritchett reads this tale as a celebration of the myth-making process, a fable about a dead god, written in subtle, "springy" prose that "easily leaps into the comical and the exuberant."[103] Going beyond the superficial review, Marta Morello Frosch's scholarly essay demonstrates that fantasy does not dominate in these stories, as Vargas Llosa asserts, but rather that reality is incorporated into fantasy, making wonders a part of everyday life. Thus, an angel with wings becomes an ordinary being, a drowned man becomes a member of the community, and the ghost ship in "El último viaje del buque fantasma" ("The Last Voyage of the Ghost Ship") is ultimately transformed into a real vessel that comes crashing ashore.[104]

Robert Coover, who obviously has a good command of Spanish, observes that "El mar del tiempo perdido" ("The Sea of Lost Time"), about a series of fantastic occurrences in a poverty-ridden seaside village after the arrival of a gringo philanthropist, is narrated in the same convincing voice that makes *Solitude* believable.[105] A major focus of Gilbert Smith is "Muerte constante más allá del amor" ("Death Constant Beyond Love"), which he calls "a precise, imaginative presentation of the death experience of a man who has spent his life in the self-imposed isolation of a political career."[106] Basing his discussion on archetypes and Northrop Frye's system of ironic and romantic plots, James J. Alstrum analyzes the title story—about a young girl's revenge after years of exploitation by her grandmother—as a subversion of the heroic myth.[107] Antonio Rojo Benítez and Hilda O. Benítez treat this same piece in greater detail, describing Eréndira as the anima of Ulises, her lover, and the latter's ultimate defeat as his symbolic castration and return to the Mother Uroboros. Eréndira's manipulation of Ulises and subsequent flight, moreover, represent not only her emergence from the unconscious state, but also her rebellion against the patriarchal order by which she has been victimized.[108] John Sturrock calls all the stories in the English collection "makeweights" except for "Innocent Eréndira," which he refers to as a "nasty fairy tale" about Marxist exploitation, the grandmother representing the capitalist and Eréndira the oppressed victim who ultimately rebels.[109]

"The Handsomest Drowned Man in the World" is extolled by George R. McMurray as a dramatization of purification and rebirth, themes suggested by the dead man's gifts of beauty, hope, and solidarity to a community steeped in inertia.[110] Lida Aronne-Amestoy takes a similar approach, concluding that the structure and archetypal symbols of this tale suggest the re-creation of the Utopian ideal.[111] Aided by the theories of Mikhail Bakhtin, Rosalba Campra demonstrates how meaning evolves from structural organization, a case in point being "The Last Voyage of the Ghost Ship," which can be read as an example of the surrealist's attempt to make the temporal and spatial constructs of a dream coincide with those of the real world.[112]

El otoño del patriarca (1975) (*The Autumn of the Patriarch*) did not receive the unanimous acclaim expressed by the reviewers of *Solitude* and, like *Innocent Eréndira and Other Stories*, this sophisticated depiction of an aging dictator trapped in labyrinthian solitude was better understood and more enthusiastically welcomed in the United States than in Latin America or Spain. Writing for *El Nacional*, a Mexican newspaper, Elena Urrutia finds the book "dazzling" at times, but also "annoying," "disgusting," and sprinkled with almost insurmountable hurdles for the reader.[113] Another Mexican critic, Leopoldo Peniche Vallado, dislikes García Márquez's break with literary tradition and compares *Patriarch* unfavorably with *Solitude*.[114] W. Clemons, a reviewer for *Newsweek*, is ambivalent, his assessments ranging from "a heartbreaking disappointment" and "static and suffocating" to "an extended piece of magnificent writing."[115] More perceptive, Luys A. Diez draws some valid parallels between the novel and Latin American reality and, in his commentary on García Márquez's style, asserts that "the monolithic paragraphs, nearly devoid of periods, compel us further into the labyrinth of prose until we are suddenly helpless, caught and controlled by the writer, our dictator."[116] The conclusion drawn by Kessel Schwartz is that the author uses the oneiric, symbolic, temporal and atemporal to create ambiguity and obfuscate reality.[117]

Gregory Rabassa, the English translator, describes the stylistic density of *Patriarch* as follows: "The impression one has after finishing this novel is that of having read a fat tome of over a thousand pages; but this concision . . . is what has made all of García Márquez's narration so unique and perfect."[118] Focusing on the elements of protest, William Kennedy calls the book "a supreme polemic, a spiritual exposé, an attack against any society that encourages or even permits such a monstrosity."[119] Paul West's note in *Review* is perhaps the most inspired: "What is supremely interesting here, and more so than anything in *One Hundred Years of Solitude*, is García Márquez's *modus operandi*, which a merely cursory description would have to call a voluptuous, thick, garish centripetal weaving and re-weaving of quasi-narrative motifs that figure now as emblems, now as salient samples of all the stuff from which the world is made (at least the Caribbean one)."[120]

Surely one of the most negative statements is that of Brian J. Mallet who, writing in the Spanish journal *Arbor*, classifies *Patriarch* as "tedious," "chaotic," and freighted with interminable sentences "longer than the Magdalena River."[121] On the other hand, Elizabeth Langhorne declares in the *Virginia Quarterly Review* that García Márquez belongs to a distinguished line of technical experimenters including Proust, Faulkner, and Virginia Woolf, adding that "his feats of sleight of hand [are] so sure and so dazzling, that we must recognize him at once as an original talent."[122] Juan M. Lipski analyzes the structure of the novel in terms of semiotics, concentrating primarily on the role of dialogue and the constantly shifting point of view.[123] Another of the relatively few structuralist approaches is that of Raymond L. Williams who bases his study of the novel's complex organization on four levels of apertures: the opening of the original situation, the opening of the sentence length, the opening of narrative forms, and the opening of a "seen" reality.[124] Although Kurt Levy eschews the technical language of structuralism, he too delineates various levels of reality in *Patriarch*: the philosophical, the political, and the psychological, all of which gain immediacy through the author's figurative style and skillful manipulation of the point of view.[125] After pointing out parallels between the Patriarch and real political figures, Regina Janes concludes that García Márquez's portrait represents a composite of many dictators, and the Patriarch's anonymity and extraordinary longevity (between 107 and 232 years), the universality of the political despot.[126]

Michael Palencia-Roth believes that because the Patriarch is not presented directly, but rather through the utterances of unidentified, unreliable narrators, he emerges as a larger-than-life, mythical figure, more invented than real.[127] In her lengthy treatment of *Patriarch* as an example of innovative art, Martha L. Canfield uses Roland Barthes's theory of the differences between the literature of pleasure and the literature of enjoyment—the former traditional and the latter avant-garde—to trace the evolution of the Patriarch from charismatic hero to brutal tyrant and doddering, solitary old man.[128] Patricia Tobin's approach to *Patriarch* is similar to Canfield's, her focus being the wake of destruction left by the Patriarch and García Márquez's sacrifice of unity, consistency, and continuity in order to fully develop his subject matter.[129]

A tale based on a gruesome murder that occurred in the Colombian town of Sucre in 1951, *Crónica de una muerte anunciada* (1981) (*Chronicle of a Death Foretold*), like *Patriarch*, was met by a meld of acclaim and negative criticism. Writing for *Vuelta*, the Mexican literary journal, Aurelio Asiain lauds the tight fabric woven by the various plot threads, but nevertheless feels that for the little it has to say, the book is longer than necessary.[130] One of the most negative reviews is that of Joshua Gilder, who reveals a lack of understanding when he asserts in the *Wall Street Journal* that *Chronicle* is a "simplistic story of social determinism" with unconvincing characters and an unmistakeable didactic political message.[131] Adelaida López de Martínez sees the novel as a perfect blend of journalism and literature and, like many other reviewers, emphasizes the primitive code of honor precipitating the main event.[132] Leonard Michaels convincingly describes *Chronicle* as a metaphysical detective story replete with painful ironies and unresolved mysteries; he also judges the graphically depicted murder to be one of the most "powerfully rendered in modern literature."[133] In her essay, "Truth Is Stranger Than Fact," Edith Grossman traces the creative process of the novel (the author-narrator records the testimony of numerous witnesses twenty-seven years after the crime) which she sees as an invented parody of romance with "uncommon blendings of fantasy, fable, and fact."[134] John L. Conlon echoes some of Grossman's assertions, pointing out that García Márquez's preoccupation with the act of reordering experience emerges as the book's unifying theme.[135] An entirely different interpretation is provided by the Uruguayan critic Ángel Rama, who draws parallels between *Chronicle* and Greek tragedy: the more-than-likely innocent Santiago Nasar is seen as a sacrificial victim of the entire community, whose collective recollection of events plays a role analogous to that of the chorus.[136]

Richard Predmore repeats the above-mentioned remarks on the primitive code of honor, but in addition his essay exposes the moral deficiencies of the society portrayed, namely, the double sexual standard, the crass materialism (Angela Vicario is virtually bought by her wealthy fiancé) and the absurd tradition of raising girls to marry, suffer, and thus contribute to the happiness of their mates.[137] In contrast to Predmore, Raymond L. Williams concentrates on the literary elements of *Chronicle*, that is, how the author utilizes journalistic techniques and dreams, premonitions, and symbols to blur the line between fact and fiction.[138] Analyzing the novel as a parody of the rigid conventions of the detective genre, Isabel Álvarez-Borland labels it a perfect model of the "hermeneutic tale," "a questioning structure rather than an answer-providing construct."[139] Myrna Solotorevsky extols *Chronicle* as an irreverent text which utilizes hyperbole to undermine the objectivity characteristic of the chronicle and irony to destroy the hallowed myths.[140] Still another similar treatment is that of Dona M. Kercher, for whom the tragic chain of events represents an absurd parody of Golden Age drama and, in its denouement, of improbable romantic fiction.[141] In her study of the novel's structure, Lois Parkinson Zamora discovers paradigms of apocalyptic literature with its alternating rhythms of civilization, decay, and cataclysm which shape the plot and, at the same time, satisfy the very human desire for conclusions.[142]

Since the publication of *Solitude* García Márquez has given dozens of interviews, not because he enjoys being a public figure but, as he told Armando Durán, because he himself was a journalist for many years and would feel disloyal if he said no to a fellow journalist. He also told Durán that by granting numerous interviews, he hoped the public would tire of him and no longer consider him newsworthy.[143]

The most extensive of the bibliographies on García Márquez's works to date is Margaret Eustella Fau's *Gabriel García Márquez: An annotated Bibliography, 1947–1979.*[144]

With reviews and critical essays spanning the period from the early 1960s to the present, this collection displays a diversity of attitudes toward Gabriel García Márquez and an array of insights into his writings, thus enabling the reader to see the man and his works from a variety of perspectives. In "William Faulkner and Gabriel García Márquez: Two Nobel Laureates," Harley D. Oberhelman discusses the most important single literary influence on the Colombian author's oeuvre. Focusing on what many critics consider García Márquez's first major work, Richard D. Woods's "Time and Futility in the Novel *El coronel no tiene quien le escriba*" demonstrates how the leitmotifs of monotony and death reflect an atmosphere devoid of hope during *la violencia* of the 1950s. In his essay "The Threat of '*La Violencia*,'" George R. McMurray takes a very different approach to this masterful novelette, defining it as an optimistic portrait of a lovable, absurd hero struggling against overwhelming odds. "Lampooning Literature: *La mala hora*," by Wolfgang A. Luchting, treats the slanderous messages aimed at upper-class citizens as a metaphor of protest literature denouncing political oppression and exacerbating civil strife. In "The Double Inscription of the *Narrataire* in 'Los funerales de la Mamá Grande,'" David William Foster views this fanciful tale as a metanarrative that functions on two levels: the first straightforward, directed to the implied reader (*narrataire*) of the folk narrative; and the second self-ironizing and self-critical, directed to the more sophisticated implied reader (*narrataire*) capable of gauging the distance between official history, folk legend, and demythifying literature. Four essays deal with *One Hundred Years of Solitude*: D. P. Gallagher's "Gabriel García Márquez," which treats myth, cyclical time, and other literary elements the Colombian shares with his Spanish American colleagues; Ricardo Gullón's "García Márquez or the Forgotten Art of Storytelling," which concentrates on tone, rhythm, motif, and hyperbole as traditional narrative techniques the author revives and refurbishes; Biruté Ciplijauskaité's "Foreshadowing as Technique and Theme in *One Hundred Years of Solitude*," which demonstrates how the ingenious use of dreams, premonitions, and fantasy enhances the novel's structural and thematic unity; and Emir Rodríguez Monegal's "*One Hundred Years of Solitude*: The Last Three Pages," which defines the masterful climactic ending as a temporal version of Borges's spatial Aleph. In his essay entitled "Gabriel García

Márquez's 'Eréndira' and the Brothers Grimm," Joel Hancock discovers that the archetypal plots, characters, and motifs in fairy tales such as "Sleeping Beauty," "Snow White," and "Little Red Ridinghood" reappear in this highly acclaimed novella. Another of the Colombian's most famous tales is the subject of Mary E. Davis's essay, "The Voyage beyond the Map: 'El ahogado más hermoso del mundo,'" which examines the poetic resonances of myth enriching the literary texture of an inspiring fantasy. Julio Ortega's *"The Autumn of the Patriarch*: Text and Culture" utilizes the theories of Roland Barthes to study García Márquez's most complex book as a composite of political, historical, popular, mythical and literary codes. "The Sleep of Vital Reason in García Márquez's *Crónica de una muerte anunciada*," by Arnold M. Penuel, demonstrates that this deceptively facile mélange of fiction and reportage, dismissed by some critics as without significance, is in reality a complex, universal dramatization of traditional and timely themes. Finally, in "García Márquez and the Novel," Gene H. Bell-Villada pinpoints the Nobel laureate's position in the world today as one of the most talented and influential fiction writers, one who has broken out of the claustrophobic atmosphere created by French and American letters, reopened literary doors and windows, and given his readers a vast panorama of human experience.

. . .

All translations of quotations in Spanish are the editor's.

. . .

For smoothing the editorial way, my thanks go to: my wife, Doris; Judy Berndt; Barbara Branstad; Martin Bucco; Athenaide Dallett; Ron De Waal; Doug Ernest; Kathy Graybill; Stephen Green; Dorothy Haddad; Marge Hill; Robert Lecker; Harley Oberhelman; Richard Stevens; Emily Taylor; and Colleen Thornton.

GEORGE R. MCMURRAY

Colorado State University

Notes

1. Mario Vargas Llosa, "García Márquez: From Aracataca to Macondo," *70 Review* (Center for Inter-American Relations, 1971):129.

2. García Márquez's father told Harley D. Oberhelman that his famous son, Gabito, was born in 1927, and the author himself has admitted that he is uncertain about the date of his birth. See Harley D. Oberhelman, "Gabriel Eligio García habla de Gabito" [Gabriel Eligio García talks about Gabito], *Hispania* 61, no. 3 (September 1978):541–42.

3. Harley D. Oberhelman, "William Faulkner and Gabriel García Márquez: Two Nobel Laureates." Published for the first time in this volume.

4. Luis Harss and Barbara Dohmann, "Gabriel García Márquez, o la cuerda floja," in *Los nuestros* (Buenos Aires: Editorial Sudamericana, 1966), 381–419. The English translation of *Los nuestros* is *Into the Mainstream: Conversations with Latin-American Writers* (New York: Harper & Row, 1967). The chapter in question bears the English title "Gabriel García Márquez, or the Lost Chord," 310–41.

5. Harss and Dohmann, *Los nuestros*, 314.

6. Gabriel García Márquez, *El negro que hizo esperar a los ángeles* (Montevideo: Ediciones Alfil, 1972).

7. Gabriel García Márquez, *Ojos de perro azul* (Rosario, Argentina: Equiseditorial, 1972).

8. Mario Vargas Llosa, *García Márquez: Historia de un deicidio* (Barcelona: Barral Editores, 1971), 217–30.

9. Mary Alice Kilmer-Thalekian, "Nabo, el negro a quien García Márquez hizo volar" (Nabo, the black man García Márquez made fly), *Journal of Spanish Studies: Twentieth Century* 6, no. 1 (Spring 1978):35.

10. Gilbert Smith, review of *Innocent Eréndira and Other Stories*, in *Magill's Literary Annual* (Englewood Cliffs, New Jersey: Salem Press, 1978): 321. "The Other Side of Death" is in both pirated editions of García Márquez's stories. Nine of the early tales appear in translation in *Innocent Eréndira and Other Stories*, whose title story was not published in Spanish until 1972.

11. Donald McGrady, "Acerca de una colección desconocida de relatos por Gabriel García Márquez," (About an unknown collection of stories by Gabriel García Márquez), in *Gabriel García Márquez*, ed. Peter G. Earle (Madrid: Taurus Ediciones, 1981), 60–80. This collection includes twenty essays, most by well-known critics.

12. John Sturrock, "Shorter Márquez: *Innocent Eréndira and Other Stories*," *New York Times Book Review* 83, 16 July 1978, 3.

13. Martin Kaplan, review of *Innocent Eréndira and Other Stories*," *New Republic* 179 (26 August 1978):45.

14. Gene H. Bell-Villada, "Precious and Semi-Precious Gems: *Innocent Eréndira and Other Stories*, *Review* 24 (Center for Inter-American Relations, 1979):99.

15. Raymond L. Williams, *Gabriel García Márquez* (Boston: Twayne Publishers, 1984), 14. This monograph treats García Márquez's life and development as a writer from the early stories through *Chronicle of a Death Foretold*. It also includes a chapter on his early journalistic articles.

16. Translated in *Leaf Storm and Other Stories*. The six stories in this volume include four from *La increíble y triste historia de la cándida Eréndira y de su abuela desalmada* [*The Incredible and Sad Tale of Innocent Eréndira and Her Heartless Grandmother*] and two written prior to *Leaf Storm*.

17. Rita Gulbert, *Seven Voices* (New York: Alfred A. Knopf, 1973), 326.

18. Harss and Dohmann, *Los nuestros*, 322.

19. Williams, *Gabriel García Márquez*, 9.

20. Two early and generally favorable reviews of *Leaf Storm* are: Alonso Ángel Restrepo, review of *La hojarasca*, *Revista Universidad de Antioquia* (Colombia) 31, no. 122 (June–August 1955):542–45; and Ariel Dorfman, "La vorágine de los fantasmas" (The vortex of the phantoms), *Ercilla* (Chile) 1617 (1 June 1956):34.

21. Harss and Dohmann, *Los nuestros*, 322.

22. Two of the numerous references to García Márquez's readings of Sophocles appear in Vargas Llosa's *Historia de un deicidio*, 156, and in Armando Durán's "Conversations with Gabriel García Márquez," *70 Review* (Center for Inter-American Relations, 1971):112.

23. Pedro Lastra, "La tragedia como fundamento estructural en *La hojarasca*"

(Tragedy as the structural foundation in *Leaf Storm*), in *Nueve asedios a Gabriel García Márquez* (Nine approaches to Gabriel *García Márquez*) (Santiago de Chile: Editorial Universitaria, 1969), 38–51. This collection contains essays by nine well-known critics.

24. Vargas Llosa, *García Márquez: Historia de un deicidio*, 243–91.

25. Graciela Maturo, *Claves simbólicas de Gabriel García Márquez* (Symbolic keys to Gabriel García Márquez) (Buenos Aires: F. García Cambeiro, 1972), 65–88.

26. Juan Loveluck, "Gabriel García Márquez, narrador colombiana" (Gabriel García Márquez, a Colombian narrator), in *Nueve asedios a Gabriel García Márquez*, 52–73.

27. Martha Duffy, "Back to Macondo: *Leaf Storm and Other Stories,*" *Time* 99 (13 March 1972):86.

28. Ronald De Feo, "Portents, Prodigies, Miracles," *Nation* 214 (15 May 1972):634.

29. Earl Shorris, "Gabriel García Márquez: The Alchemy of History," *Harper's Magazine* 244 (February 1972):102.

30. J. Yglesias, review of *Leaf Storm and Other Stories*, *Atlantic Monthly* 230 (August 1972):86.

31. Martha Lafollette Miller, "La angustia en tres novelas contemporáneas latinoamericanas" (Anguish in three contemporary Latin American novels), *Journal of Spanish Studies* 2, no. 3 (Winter 1974):137–55.

32. George R. McMurray, *Gabriel García Márquez* (New York: Frederick Ungar, 1977), 18–19. This monograph discusses the author's life and development as a writer from the early stories through *The Autumn of the Patriarch*.

33. Frank Dauster, "Ambiguity and Indeterminacy in *La hojarasca,*" *Latin American Literary Review* 13, no. 25 (January–June 1985): 24–28. This special issue contains twelve articles by well-known critics on García Márquez's writings.

34. Published in *No One Writes to the Colonel and Other Stories*.

35. Angel Rama, "Un novelista de la violencia americana" (A novelist of American violence), in *Homenaje a Gabriel García Márquez: Variaciones interpretativas en torno a su obra* (In honor of Gabriel García Márquez: Various interpretations of his work), ed. Helmy Giacoman (Long Island City, New York: Las Americas Publishing Co., 1972), 66. This festschrift contains seventeen essays on García Márquez's works through *One Hundred Years of Solitude*.

36. Harss and Dohmann, *Los nuestros*, 324–26.

37. Fryda Schultz de Mantovani, review of *El coronel no tiene quien le escriba,*" *Sur* 313 (July–August 1968):90.

38. Robert G. Mead, Jr., review of *No One Writes to the Colonel and Other Stories,*" *Saturday Review* 51 (December 1968):26.

39. James R. Frakes, "Density Clarified: *No One Writes to the Colonel and Other Stories*, *New York Times Book Review*, 29 September 1968, 56.

40. David Haworth, "Gland Manor. *No One Writes to the Colonel and Other Stories,*" *New Statesman* 82 (16 July 1971):89.

41. Vargas Llosa, *Historia de un deicidio*, 308–12. According to Vargas Llosa, García Márquez greatly admires Albert Camus's novel *The Plague*. Just as Camus concentrates on the psychological reactions of the survivors rather than on the ravages of the epidemic, García Márquez prefers to describe the atmosphere of terror engendered by *la violencia* rather than the brutalities it produces.

42. Shorris, "Gabriel García Márquez: The Alchemy of History," 98–100.

43. McMurray, *Gabriel García Márquez*, 23–28.

44. Williams, *Gabriel García Márquez*, 57–59.

45. Ernesto Volkening, "A propósito de *La mala hora,*" *Eco. Revista de Cultura de Occidente* 7, no. 4 (August 1963):294–304.

18   Critical Essays on Gabriel García Márquez

46. *La violencia* was generally a more serious problem in the interior of the country than along the coast.

47. Robert Kirsner, "Four Colombian Novels of *La Violencia*," *Hispania* 44, no. 1 (March 1966):70–74.

48. Emmanuel Carballo, "Gabriel García Márquez: Un gran novelista americano" [Gabriel García Márquez: A great American novelist), *Revista de la Universidad de México* 13, no. 3 (November 1967):14.

49. Alicia M. Alonso, review of *La mala hora, Sur* 314 (September–October 1968):91–92.

50. Vargas Llosa, *Historia de un deicidio*, 421–56.

51. McMurray, *Gabriel García Márquez*, 37–38.

52. Robert Coover, "The Gossip on the Wall," *New York Times Book Review*, 11 November 1979, 3, 30.

53. Mary E. Davis, review of *In Evil Hour, Review* 30 (September–December 1981): 78–79.

54. Williams, *Gabriel García Márquez*, 66–68.

55. *Los funerales de la Mamá Grande* has never appeared as a separate book in English; rather, it has been incorporated into *No One Writes to the Colonel and Other Stories*. The title story in Spanish has been translated as "Big Mama's Funeral."

56. Federico Álvarez, "Gabriel García Márquez: *Los funerales de la Mamá Grande*," *Revista de la Universidad de México* 17, no. 3 (November 1962):31; Alberto Dallal, "García Márquez y la realidad colombiana" (García Márquez and Colombian reality), *Revista Mexicana de Literatura* nos. 3–4 (March–April 1963):63–64.

57. Harss and Dohmann, *Los nuestros*, 329.

58. Carballo, "Gabriel García Márquez: Un gran novelista americano," 30.

59. Jaime Tello, review of *Los funerales de la Mamá Grande*, in *Recopilación de textos sobre Gabriel García Márquez*) (Compilation of texts on Gabriel García Márquez) (Havana: Casa de las Américas, 1969), 98–99. This volume contains articles, reviews, and comments by fifty critics.

60. See note 39 above.

61. See note 38 above.

62. Vargas Llosa, *Historia de un deicidio*, 345–419.

63. Roger Peel, "The Short Stories of Gabriel García Márquez," *Studies in Short Fiction* 8, no. 1 (Winter 1971):161.

64. Judith A. Goetzinger, "The Emergence of a Folk Myth in 'Los funerales de la Mamá Grande,' " *Revista de Estudios Hispánicos* 6, no. 2 (May 1972):238–39.

65. Frank Dauster, "The Short Stories of García Márquez," *Books Abroad* 47, no. 3 (Summer 1973):466–70. This issue contains nine essays on García Márquez's works.

66. Robert Coover, "The Master's Voice," *American Review* 26 (November 1977):375.

67. Robert Sims, "The Creation of Myth in García Márquez's 'Los funerales de la Mamá Grande,' " *Hispania* 61, no. 1 (March 1978):16.

68. George R. McMurray, "The Spanish American Short Story from Borges to the Present," in *The Latin American Short Story*, ed. Margaret Sayers Peden (Boston: Twayne Publishers, 1983), 117–18.

69. David William Foster, "García Márquez and the *Ecriture* of Complicity: 'La prodigiosa tarde de Baltazar,' " in his *Studies in the Contemporary Spanish American Short Story* (Columbia: University of Missouri Press, 1979), 48–50.

70. Carlos Fuentes, "García Márquez. *Cien años de soledad*," *Siempre* (Mexico) 679 (29 June 1966):vii.

71. The best of these include the following: Roberto Burgos Cantor, review of *Cien años de soledad*, *El Espectador* (Bogotá), 24 September 1967, 17; Ángel Rama, "Introducción a *Cien años de soledad*," *Marcha* (Montevideo) 1368 (2 September 1967):31; Marco Rodríguez Fernández, "*Cien años de soledad*, de Gabriel García Márquez," *La Nación* (Santiago, Chile), 26 August 1967, 5.

72. *70 Review* (Center for Inter-American Relations, 1971) contains a good selection of reviews and articles in English from publications in the United States, France, Portugal, Germany, and Italy.

73. Wolfgang A. Luchting, "Gabriel García Márquez: The Boom and the Whimper," *Books Abroad* 44, no. 1 (Winter 1970):27.

74. Ricardo Gullón, *García Márquez o el olvidado arte de contar* (Madrid: Taurus, 1970). The article by Gullón reprinted in this volume is a shortened version of his book.

75. René Jara Cuadra and Jaime Mejía Duque, *Las claves del mito en García Márquez* (Valparaíso, Chile: Ediciones Universitarias de Valparaíso, 1972).

76. Josefina Ludmer, "*Cien años de soledad*": *Una interpretación* (Buenos Aires: Editorial Tiempo Contemporáneo, 1972).

77. Suzanne Jill Levine, *El espejo hablado: Un estudio de "Cien años de soledad"* (Caracas: Monte Ávila, 1975).

78. Lucila Inés Mena, *La función de la historia en "Cien años de soledad"* (Barcelona: Plaza y Janés, 1979).

79. Francis E. Porrata and Fausto Avendaño, eds., *Explicación de "Cien años de soledad*," *de García Márquez* (Explication of *One Hundred Years of Solitude*, by García Márquez) (Sacramento, California: *Explicación de Textos Literarios*, 1976). This volume contains nineteen essays on *One Hundred Years of Solitude* and an extensive bibliography on all of García Márquez's works.

80. Emir Rodríguez Monegal, "Novedad y anacronismo de *Cien años de soledad*," *Revista Nacional de Cultura* (Caracas) 29, no. 185 (July–September 1968): 3–21. This critic delineates the salient features of *One Hundred Years of Solitude* in "La hazaña de un escritor" (The deed of a writer), *Visión* (Mexico) 37, no. 2 (18 July 1969):27–31.

81. Isaís Lerner, "A propósito de *Cien años de soledad*," *Cuadernos Americanos* 162, no. 1 (January–February 1969):186–200.

82. Adalbert Dessau, "El tema de la soledad en las novelas de Gabriel García Márquez" (The theme of solitude in the novels of Gabriel García Márquez), in *El ensayo y la crítica en Iberoamérica* (The essay and criticism in Latin America), eds. Kurt L. Levy and Keith Ellis (Toronto: University of Toronto, 1970), 209–14.

83. Gregory Lawrence, "Marx in Macondo," *Latin American Literary Review* 2, no. 4 (1974): 49–57.

84. Paul M. Hedeen, "Gabriel García Márquez's Dialectic of Solitude," *Southwest Review* 68, no. 4 (Autumn 1983):350–64.

85. Suzanne Jill Levine, "La maldición del incesto en *Cien años de soledad*" (The curse of incest in *One Hundred Years of Solitude*), *Revista Iberoamericana* 37, nos. 76–77 (July–December 1971):711–24. Gordon Brotherston goes a step further, finding in the Buendías' solitary nature and physical isolation major causes of their tragic fate. (See Gordon Brotherston, "An End to Secular Solitude," in his *The Emergence of the Latin American Novel* (Cambridge: Cambridge University Press, 1977), 122–35.

86. Vargas Llosa, *Historia de un deicidio*, 479–615.

87. Vicente Cabrera and Luis González del Valle, *La nueva ficción hispanoamericana a través de M.A. Asturias y G. García Márquez* (The new Spanish American fiction in the works of M.A. Asturias and G. García Márquez) (New York: Eliseo Torres, 1972), 11–31. Other treatments of magical realism include Stephen Hart's "Magical Realism in Gabriel García Márquez's *One Hundred Years of Solitude*," *Inti* nos. 16–17 (Fall 1982–Spring

1983):37–52, which bases the differences between surrealism and magical realism on their degree of familiarity with the realist mode — nonexistent in the former but very much alive in the latter; and Chilean critic Ariel Dorfman's "La muerte como acto imaginativo en *Cien años de soledad*" (Death as an imaginative act in *One Hundred Years of Solitude*), in *Homenaje a García Márquez*, 105–39, which explains how magical phenomena occurring at the time of death define forever the essence of the leading characters.

88. D. P. Gallagher, *Modern Latin American Literature* (London: Oxford University Press, 1973), 144–63.

89. Patricia Tobin, "García Márquez and the Subversion of the Line," *Latin American Literary Review* 2, no. 4 (1974):39–48.

90. Djelal Kadir, "The Architectonic Principle of *Cien años de soledad* and the Vichian Theory of History," *Kentucky Romance Quarterly* 24, no. 3 (1977): 251–61.

91. Lois P. Zamora, "The Myth of Apocalypse and Human Temporality in García Márquez's *Cien años de soledad* and *El otoño del patriarca*," *Symposium* 32, no. 4 (Winter 1978):341–42.

92. Roberto Paoli, "Carnavalesco y tiempo cíclico en *Cien años de soledad*" (Carnival-esque and cyclical time in *One Hundred Years of Solitude*), *Revista Iberoamericana* 50, nos. 128–129 (July–December 1984):979–98. This issue contains a section of eight articles on García Márquez's works. Additional treatments of time are William L. Siemen's "Tiempo, entropía y la estructura de *Cien años de soledad*" (Time, entropy and the structure of *One Hundred Years of Solitude*) in *Explicación de "Cien años de soledad*," 359–71, which demonstrates how, in the final lines of the novel, present, past, and future coalesce in a single infinitesimal point; George R. McMurray's " 'The Aleph' and *One Hundred Years of Solitude*: Two Microcosmic Worlds," *Latin American Literary Review* 13, no. 25 (January–June 1985): 55–64, a comparison of Borges's famous tale and the Colombian masterpiece, the former emerging as a metaphor of literature and the latter as a metaphor of all human experience; and John P. McGowan's "*A la Recherche du Temps Perdu* in *One Hundred Years of Solitude*," *Modern Fiction Studies* 28, no. 4 (Winter 1982–1983):557–67, which concludes that while the French author evokes the past as a means of conquering death, García Márquez envisions the past sliding further and further away, accentuating solitude and nostalgia.

93. Floyd Merrel, "José Arcadio Buendía's Scientific Paradigms: Man in Search of Himself," *Latin American Literary Review* 2, no. 4 (1974):59–70.

94. Jean Franco, "The Limits of the Liberal Imagination: *One Hundred Years of Solitude* and *Nostromo*," *Punto de Contacto / Point of Contact* 1, no. 1 (December 1975):4–16.

95. Doris Kay Rolfe, "Tono y estructura de *Cien años de soledad*" (Tone and structure of *One Hundred Years of Solitude*), in *Explicación de "Cien años de soledad*," 259–82.

96. Katalin Kulin, *Creación mítica en la obra de García Márquez* (Mythic creation in the work of García Márquez) (Budapest: Akadémia Kiadá, 1980), 195–205.

97. Alonso de Toro, "Estructura narrativa y temporal en *Cien años de soledad*" (Narrative and temporal structure in *One Hundred Years of Solitude*), *Revista Iberoameri-cana* 50, nos. 128–129 (July–December 1984):957–78.

98. José David Saldívar, "Ideology and Deconstruction in Macondo," *Latin American Literary Review* 13, no. 25 (January–June 1985):29–43.

99. Emilio García, "La noción existencial del absurdo en *Cien años de soledad*" (The existential notion of the absurd in *One Hundred Years of Solitude*), *Inti* nos. 16–17 (Fall 1982–Winter 1983):125–34. Dedicated entirely to García Márquez, this issue contains fifteen articles and a bibiography on his works.

100. Vargas Llosa, *Historia de un deicidio*, 617–40.

101. Peter S. Prescott, "Miracles and Mysteries: *Leaf Storm and Other Stories*," *Newsweek* 79 (28 February 1972):88.

102. Ronald De Feo, "Portents, Prodigies, Miracles: *Leaf Storm and Other Stories,*" *Nation* 214 (15 May 1972):632.

103. V.S. Pritchett, "A Ruined Arcady: *Leaf Storm and Other Stories,*" *New Statesman* 85 (9 February 1973):200.

104. Marta Morello Frosch, "The Common Wonders of García Márquez's Recent Fiction," *Books Abroad* 47, no. 3 (Summer 1973):496–501.

105. Coover, "The Master's Voice," 383.

106. Smith, review of *Innocent Eréndira and Other Stories,* 320.

107. James J. Alstrum, "Los arquetipos en 'La increíble y triste historia de la cándida Eréndira y de su abuela desalmada,' de Gabriel García Márquez" (Archetypes in "Innocent Eréndira" by Gabriel García Márquez), *Proceedings of the Pacific Northwest Conference on Foreign Languages* 29, no. 1 (1978):140–42.

108. Antonio Rojo Benítez and Hilda O. Benítez, "Eréndira liberada: La subversión del mito del macho occidental" (Liberated Eréndira: The subversion of the myth of the western macho), *Revista Iberoamericana* nos. 128–129 (July–December 1984):1057–76.

109. See note 12 above.

110. McMurray, "The Spanish American Short Story," 130.

111. Lida Aronne-Amestoy, "Fantasía y compromiso en un cuento de Gabriel García Márquez" (Fantasy and commitment in a story of Gabriel García Márquez), *Symposium* 38, no. 4 (Winter 1984–1985):287–97. The role of imagination as a liberating force is stressed by Raymond L. Williams in virtually every story, but especially in "The Handsomest Drowned Man in the World" (Williams, *García Márquez,* 92–109).

112. Rosalba Campra, "Las técnicas del sentido en los cuentos de Gabriel García Márquez" (The Techniques of meaning in the stories of Gabriel García Márquez), *Revista Iberoamericana* nos. 128–129 (July–December 1984):937–55.

113. Elena Urrutia, review of *El otoño del patriarca,* *El Nacional* ("Revista Mexicana de Cultura"), 3 August 1975, 6.

114. Leopoldo Peniche Vallado, "*El otoño del patriarca*: Valores novelísticos en desequilibrio" (*The Autumn of the Patriarch*: Novelistic values in disequilibrium), *Cuadernos Americanos* 207, no. 4 (July–August 1976):220–23.

115. W. Clemons, review of *The Autumn of the Patriarch,* *Newsweek* 88 (8 November 1976):104–5.

116. Luys A. Diez, "The Museum of Horrors: *The Autumn of the Patriarch,*" *Nation* 223 (25 December 1976):695–96.

117. Kessel Schwartz, review of *The Autumn of the Patriarch,* *Hispania* 59, no. 3 (September 1976):557. Seymour Menton also examines the novel's pervasive ambiguity in "Ver para no creer: *El otoño del patriarca*" (To see in order not to believe: *The Autumn of the Patriarch*), *Caribe* 1, no. 1 (Spring 1976):5–28.

118. Gregory Rabasa, review of *The Autumn of the Patriarch,* *Books Abroad* 50, no. 2 (Spring 1976):371.

119. William Kennedy, review of *The Autumn of the Patriarch,* *New York Times Book Review,* 31 October 1976, 6.

120. Paul West, "The Posthumous Present: *The Autumn of the Patriarch,*" *Review* 18 (Center for Inter-American Relations) (Fall 1976):76.

121. Brian J. Mallet, "Los funerales del patriarca que no quiere morir" (The funeral of the patriarch who refuses to die), *Arbor* 97, no. 377 (May 1977):56–58.

122. Elizabeth Langhorne, "Of Time and the Patriarch: *The Autumn of the Patriarch,*" *Virginia Quarterly Review* 53, no. 2 (Spring 1977):366.

123. Juan M. Lipski, "Embedded Dialogue in *El otoño del patriarca,*" *American Hispanist* 2, no. 14 (1977):9–12.

124. Raymond L. Williams, "The Dynamic Structure of García Márquez's *El otoño del patriarca*," *Symposium* 32, no. 1 (Spring 1978):56–75.

125. Kurt Levy, "Planes of Reality in *El otoño del patriarca*," in *Studies in Honor of Gerald E. Wade*, eds. Sylvia Bowman et al. (Madrid: José Porrúa Turanzas, 1979), 133–41.

126. Regina Janes, *Gabriel García Márquez: Revolutions in Wonderland* (Columbia: University of Missouri Press, 1981), 93. This monograph traces García Márquez's life and development as a writer, giving special emphasis to *One Hundred Years of Solitude* and *The Autumn of the Patriarch*.

127. Michael Palencia-Roth, "El círculo hermenéutico en *El otoño del patriarca*" (The hermeneutical circle in *The Autumn of the Patriarch*), *Revista Iberoamericana* nos. 128–129 (July–December 1984):999–1016.

128. Martha L. Canfield, "El patriarca de García Márquez: Padre, poeta, tirano" (García Márquez's patriarch: Father, poet, tyrant), *Revista Iberoamericana* nos. 128–129 (July–December 1984):1017–56.

129. Patricia Tobin, "The Autumn of the Signifier: The Deconstructionist Moment of García Márquez," *Latin American Literary Review* 13, no. 25 (January–June 1985):65–78.

130. Aurelio Asiain, review of *Crónica de una muerte anunciada*, *Vuelta* 58 (September 1981):32–33.

131. Joshua Gilder, "The Nobel Cause of South America's Arthur Miller," *Wall Street Journal*, 18 May 1983, 34.

132. Adelaida López de Martínez, review of *Crónica de una muerte anunciada*, *Chasqui* 10, nos. 2–3 (February–May 1981):70–72. Other reviews and articles emphasizing the primitive code of honor are: D. Keith Mano, "A Death Foretold," *National Review*, 10 June 1983, 699–700; Jonathan Yardley, "García Márquez and the Broken Mirror of Memory," *Book World* 13 (27 March 1983):3; and Leonor Álvarez Ulloa, review of *Crónica de una muerte anunciada*, *Crítica Literaria* 4 (1982):183.

Additional reviews underscoring this novel's blend of journalism and fiction include: Gregory Rabassa, "García Márquez's New Book: Literature or Journalism?," *World Literature Today* 56, no. 1 (Winter 1982):48–51; and Germán D. Carrillo, review of *Crónica de una muerte anunciada*, *Revista Iberoamericana* nos. 123–124 (April–September 1983):647–48.

133. Leonard Michaels, "Murder Most Foul and Comic," *New York Times Book Review*, 27 March 1983, 1, 36–37.

134. Edith Grossman, "Truth is Stranger Than Fact," *Review* 30 (Center for Inter-American Relations, September–December 1981):71–73.

135. John L. Conlon, review of *Chronicle of a Death Foretold*, in *Magill's Literary Annual* (1984):165.

136. Angel Rama, "García Márquez entre la tragedia y la policial o crónica y pesquisa de la *Crónica de una muerte anunciada*" (García Márquez between tragedy and detective story or newspaper account and inquiry in *Chronicle of a Death Foretold*), *Sin Nombre* 13, no. 1 (October–December 1982):7–27.

137. Richard Predmore, "El mundo moral de *Crónica de una muerte anunciada*" (The Moral World of *Chronicle of a Death Foretold*), *Cuadernos Hispanoamericanos* no. 390 (December 1982):703–12.

138. Williams, *García Márquez*, 135–40.

139. Isabel Álvarez-Borland, "From Mystery to Parody: (Re)readings of García Márquez's *Crónica de una muerte anunciada*," *Symposium* 38, no. 4 (Winter 1984–1985):278.

140. Myrna Solotorevsky, "*Crónica de una muerte anunciada*, la escritura de un texto irreverente" (*Chronicle of a Death Foretold*, the writing of an irreverent text), *Revista Iberoamericana* nos. 128–129 (July–December 1984):1077–91.

141. Dona M. Kercher, "García Márquez's *Chronicle of a Death Foretold*: Notes on

Parody and the Artist," *Latin American Literary Review* 13, no. 25 (January–June 1985):90–103.

142. Lois Parkinson Zamora, "Ends and Endings in García Márquez's *Chronicle of a Death Foretold," Latin American Literary Review* 13, no. 25 (January–June 1985):104–16.

143. Armando Durán, "Conversations with Gabriel García Márquez," 109–10. Other important interviews are the following: Miguel Fernández-Braso, *Gabriel García Márquez: Una conversación infinita* (Gabriel García Márquez: An endless conversation) (Madrid: Editorial Azur, 1969); William Kennedy, "The Yellow Trolley Car In Barcelona and Other Visions: A Profile of Gabriel García Márquez," *Atlantic* 231, no. 1 (January 1973): 50–59; Rita Guibert, "Gabriel García Márquez," in her *Seven Voices* (New York: Alfred A. Knopf, 1973), 305–37; Plinio Apuleyo Mendoza, *El olor de la guayaba: Conversaciones con Gabriel García Márquez* (The aroma of the guava: Conversations with Gabriel García Márquez) (Bogotá: Editorial Oveja Negra, 1982); Marlisse Simmons, "Love and Age: A Talk With García Márquez," *New York Times Book Review*, 7 April 1985, 1, 18–21.

144. Margaret Eustella Fau, *Gabriel García Márquez: An Annotated Bibliography, 1947–1979* (Westport, Conn.: Greenwood Press, 1980). Though marred by errors and omissions, Fau's bibliography is a useful research tool. Shorter bibliographies include: Vargas Llosa, *Historia de un deicidio*, 643–64; Roseanne B. de Mendoza, "Bibliografía de y sobre Gabriel García Márquez" (Bibliography of and on Gabriel García Márquez), *Revista Iberoamericana* 41, no. 90 (January–March 1975):107–43; Francisco E. Porrata, and Fausto Avendaño, eds., *Explicación*, 381–98; Peter Earle, ed., *García Márquez*, 285–94; Luis B. Eyzaguirre and Carmen Grullón, "Gabriel García Márquez, contribución bibliográfica: 1955–1984" (Gabriel García Márquez, bibliographical contribution: 1955–1984), *Inti* nos. 16–17 (Fall 1982–Spring 1983):175–93.

Reviews

Back to Macondo

Martha Duffy*

Colombian Writer Gabriel García Márquez's only novel, *One Hundred Years of Solitude*, was a seismic literary event in Latin America when first published in 1967. Translated three years later, it received awestruck notices in the U.S., and has continued to attract not so much readers as proselytizers. The chronicle of an enchanted town called Macondo, it is a "good read" in the Dickensian sense: it has abundant life, a tangle of characters and plots, all supported by a clear moral viewpoint.

The new book, which contains a novella and six stories, is in most ways a letdown. "*Leafstorm*," the long work, is also about Macondo, but it is an early, earnest exercise in which three narrators — a boy, his mother and his grandfather — recall the old man's efforts to give a decent burial to an outcast whom the town wants to leave to the vultures.

It is filled with undifferentiated nostalgia — for old values, old vitality, old civility. One searches in vain for the raffish Macondo of *One Hundred Years of Solitude* — modeled on the banana boom town of Aracataca, where the author was born. Macondophiles will at least learn some new bits and pieces about the place. The action starts with a note from Colonel Aureliano Buendía, the great revolutionary warrior who returns in *Solitude*, and the recluse Rebeca also makes an ectoplasmic appearance.

But García Márquez, who is now 43, obviously came to terms with his great gifts after he had finished "*Leafstorm*." He has acknowledged that reading Faulkner and making a pilgrimage through Yoknapatawpha country helped him to enrich his own private literary property and see its mythic possibilities. At any rate he developed from a cautious, limited craftsman into a prodigal fabulist with total command in his protean imagination.

It is in the more recent short stories included here that one finds the authentic García Márquez in the humor, the color and detail, the easy access to magic balanced by harder ironies. In "*The Handsomest Drowned*

*Reprinted from *Time*, 13 March 1972, 84–86. Copyright 1972 Time Inc. All rights reserved. Reprinted by permission from *Time*.

Man in the World," ostensibly written for children, the inhabitants of a fishing village discover a magnificent corpse on the beach, and in marveling at its splendor come to recognize the meanness of their own lives. In another story, a flea-bitten old angel makes a mysterious appearance.

"*Blacamán the Good, Vendor of Miracles*" is a wicked little fable about an itinerant worker of cures and exactly how he acquired his specialty. Blacamán is the kind of brazen fellow García Márquez obviously enjoys. The only thing he refuses to do is raise the dead, because, he says, "They're murderous with rage at the one who disturbed their state." He knows better, however. Offered the road to sainthood, he declines: "The truth is that I'd gain nothing by being a saint after being dead; an artist is what I am." And he actually manages to live forever.

[Review of *Leaf Storm and Other Stories*]

Alfred Kazin*

When Gabriel García Márquez's utterly original *One Hundred Years of Solitude* came out here in 1970, I read it — I experienced it — with the same recognition of a New World epic that one feels about *Moby Dick*. Whatever else you can say about contemporary American novels, they are generally overpopulated and personally too scornful to remind the reader that ours was, until very recently, a New World. This is a subject, a climate of feeling, that requires a virtually empty continent, a powerful sense of wonder at how little men change even in the most bizarre moments of discovering a "Nature" beyond the usual conceptions of Nature, one or two characters who are too big for the society they are trying to create.

Above all, the "New World" as a subject requires an indifference to the ordinary laws of space, time and psychology that enforce realism. No one who has read *One Hundred Years of Solitude* will ever forget the sensation of tripping on sentences that in the most matter-of-fact way described what happens under the pressure cooker of total "newness." Verily, there has been nothing to compare the New World with but the New World itself.

Gabriel García Márquez comes from Colombia, a country whose 20th-century history has been dominated by the civil wars that are the background of everything he writes. His great novel was first published in Argentina, and he now lives in Barcelona. Unlike the subtle but timid Borges, who comes out of a library and may be remembered as the Washington Irving of Latin America, Márquez — born in 1928 — reflects

*Reprinted from *New York Times Book Review*, 20 February 1972, 1, 14–16. Copyright © 1972 by The New York Times Company. Reprinted by permission.

the incessant ironies of post-imperialist national development. He has extraordinary strength and firmness of imagination and writes with the calmness of a man who knows exactly what wonders he can perform. Strange things happen in the land of Márquez. As with Emerson, Poe, Hawthorne, every sentence breaks the silence of a vast emptiness, the famous New World "solitude" that is the unconscious despair of his characters but the sign of Márquez's genius. I am guessing but I wonder if the outbreak of creative originality in Latin America today, coming after so many years of dutifulness to Spanish and French models, doesn't resemble our sudden onrush of originality after we had decided really to break away from the spell of England.

However, Márquez is not a Protestant romantic of the time when it seemed that *all* the world would soon be new. He is a dazzlingly accomplished but morally burdened end-product of centuries of colonialism, civil war and political chaos; a prime theme in all his work is the inevitability of incest and the damage to the germ plasm that at the end of his great novel produces a baby with a pig's tail. He always writes backwards, from the end of the historical cycle, and all his prophecies are acerb without being gloomy. The farcically tragic instability and inhumanity of the continent where Nature is still too much for man and where the Spanish conquest is still unresolved, dominate his work. What makes his subject "New World" is the hallucinatory chaos and stoniness of the Colombian village, Macondo, through which all history will pass. What makes Márquez's art "New World" is the totally untraditionalist unhindered technique behind this vision of the whole—from the white man's first scratches in the jungle to the white man's inability to stave off the sight of his own end.

Leaf Storm and Other Stories was Márquez's first book, begun when he was 19. In some of these beautiful early stories—"The Handsomest Drowned Man in the World," "A Very Old Man With Enormous Wings," "The Last Voyage of the Ghost Ship,"—Márquez's typical double vision of the natural world as inherently a fable, a story to be told and retold rather than something "real," expresses itself with perfect charm. The handsomest drowned man is a native of a fishing village who in death becomes super-large and magnificent, a young god, until he is recognized by his old neighbors. The very old man with enormous wings is an angel who wearily sinks to earth in a poor village and is treated as some bothersome fowl until he clambers off again. A young man constantly sees a great trans-Atlantic liner sinking before his eyes, but no one else can see it or find any record of this liner being on the high seas.

In each of these stories Márquez takes a theme that in a lesser writer would seem "poetic," a handsome conceit lifted out of a poem by Wallace Stevens but then stopped dead in its narrative tracks. Márquez manages to make a story out of each of these—not too ambitious, but just graceful enough to be itself. He succeeds because these are stories about wonders, and the wonders become actions. Márquez as a very young man was already committed to the subject of creatures working out *all* their destinies. In every Márquez work a whole historical cycle is lived through, by character after character. And each cycle is like a miniature history of the world from the creation to the final holocaust. Márquez is writing that history line by line, very slowly indeed in each piece of writing (the slowness of pace is part of his manner, his mystique; he sees things in a long-held, eerily powerful light).

The upsetting narrative sequence may remind us of the subtlest imaginations of the 20th-century. But I would guess that Márquez owes this technique to his vision of the mad repetitiousness of history in his country. A harsh mysteriously arid peasant village like Macondo experiences everything in his work, over and over again, like those characters in *One Hundred Years of Solitude* who promptly reappear after dying.

The title story itself encompasses so much of the perverse, insistent, weirdly lasting solitude that Faulkner describes that you realize what a bond exists between "American" writers, North and South, whose common experience is of a refractory landscape always too much for the most complicated persons who try to find shelter in it. A French doctor mysteriously appears one day in 1903 in the village of Macondo with a letter of "recommendation" from Colonel Aureliano Buendía. (Colonel Buendía will be a major figure in *One Hundred Years of Solitude* and another colonel, who takes in the French doctor, may be a first sketch of the fantastic José Arcádio Buendía who also married his first cousin.) But in "Leaf Storm" this colonel is a kindly old man who originally settled in the village as a refugee from the civil wars and lives there with his second wife, his daughter Isabel by his first wife, and his grandson.

The doctor is a queer one. He wears his belt outside the loops in his pants and his trunk holds two cheap shirts, a set of false teeth obviously not his own, a portrait, a formulary and some old French newspapers. When the colonel's wife hospitably asks what he would like to eat, he says "Grass" and explains "in his parsimonious ruminant voice: 'Ordinary grass, ma'am. The kind that donkeys eat.' "

The doctor earns the colonel's lasting gratitude by curing him of an illness. But later, when violence breaks out in the town and some wounded men are placed outside the doctor's door so that he can tend to them, he refuses even to go out to them on the grounds that he has forgotten medicine. "And he kept the door closed. . . . the anger turned into a collective disease which gave no respite to Macondo for the rest of his life."

The refusal somehow becomes the most important event in the town's history. Although a banana company establishes itself in Macondo and for a number of years excites and disturbs the inhabitants with visions of industrialization and prosperity before it leaves like a "leaf storm," the marvelous thing about the story is not the outward happening but the bond of hatred and silence that exists between the doctor and the town.

They mentally, obsessively feed on each other. The kindly colonel, his daughter and grandson, who interweavedly relate the story, reflect in their stolid descriptions and reflections a sense of the ominousness that the doctor has brought to Macondo, and with which he colors all human relationships.

In 1928 the doctor hangs himself from a beam in his house. The colonel is the only person in town who will cut him down and bury him; the town officials try to balk the stranger even in death, refuse a death certificate and defy the colonel to get a coffin to put the doctor in and to follow him to the cemetery. The Márquez touch: The coffin has to be opened again to put in a single shoe left on the bed. The town official refusing to give permission for burial, goes through the motions of hanging himself to prove that the doctor couldn't *really* have hanged himself. "When he gets to the coffin, he turns on his heels, looks at me, and says: 'I'd have to see him hanging to be convinced.' "

The colonel says: "I would have done it. I would have told my men to open the coffin and put the hanged man back up again the way he was until a minute ago. . . . Even though the act of moving a corpse who's lying peacefully and deservedly in his coffin is against my principles, I'd hang him up again just to see how far this man will go."

At the end the colonel finally gets the coffin out of the house and on its way to the cemetery. The town remains implacable, "lunching on the smell," of the stranger in death. The slow working out of the stranger's unfathomable life finally becomes a type of the strangeness and solitude that Macondo itself represents without knowing it. "By that time the banana company had stopped squeezing us and had left Macondo with the rubbish of the rubbish they'd brought with them. And with them went the leaf storm, the last traces of what prosperous Macondo had been like in 1915. A ruined village was there . . . occupied by unemployed and angry people who were tormented by a prosperous past and the bitterness of an overwhelming and static present."

For Sustenance: Hope   Robert G. Mead, Jr.*

In the October 1968 *Atlantic Monthly* Professor Lionel Trilling of Columbia University is reported to have said, in response to student David Shapiro's request for the teaching of Latin American and African literature, "Well, Mr. Shapiro, I've read this Latin American literature. It has, I think one might say, an anthropological interest." Shapiro, exasperated, flashed back. "This is a kind of Promethean contempt and irrelevance."

*Reprinted from *Saturday Review*, 21 December 1968, 26. © 1968 *Saturday Review* magazine. Reprinted by permission.

One can keep his cool while reading this exchange, and yet, if he knows something about the vast corpus of New World writing in Spanish and Portuguese and the minute portion of it available in English, he cannot help sympathizing with Mr. Shapiro. Really, until much more of it is available in translation, American critics ought to avoid sweeping generalizations about Latin American literature, especially if their remarks can be construed as irrelevant and contemptuous.

I am happy to report, in view of the above, that even jaundiced readers and critics of Latin American writers are likely to find this collection of nine stories by the Colombian Gabriel García Márquez, originally published in 1961–1962, to be of more than "anthropological interest." The appearance of this book, his first available in English, and the publication next year of his novel *100 Years of Solitude*, will secure a place for García Márquez among the growing constellation of Latin American authors who are familiar to U.S. readers. He is already well known in Spanish-speaking countries and increasingly successful in Europe.

The book introduces the reader to the microcosmic world of Macondo, ostensibly a sleepy, hot, coastal town in which nothing ever happens, a perfect habitat for what one of the minor characters describes as the European stereotype of the South American: "a man with a moustache, a guitar, and a gun." But in truth Macondo exists only in the fantasy of the author, a town which he himself admits is born of his nostalgia for the life he lived as a young boy more than thirty years ago in a vanished Colombia, under the tutelage of his grandfather, clearly the prototype of the Colonel in the title story.

"No One Writes to the Colonel" is a tale of dignity in old age. The Colonel, slowly starving to death at seventy-five, is borne up through every adversity by his innate belief in human worth, by his hope of receiving a long-overdue military pension, and by his dream of an imminent victory to be won by the fighting cock he owns. As he says regarding hope: "You can't eat it, but it sustains you." However, he is never maudlin, and García Márquez weaves many glints of humor into the small, simple tapestry of a life that is rich in human values. Readers will not soon forget the Colonel or his wife, a bedrock realist who understands her man.

The key to the meaning of the book, which is to say García Márquez's image of Colombian life as viewed from Macondo, is found in "Big Mama's Funeral," the last piece in the collection. Big Mama, whose family has dominated the region for two centuries, dies a virgin at ninety-two, and the whole town, the President of Colombia, and even the Pope attend her funeral. An era has closed. The event entails more pomp than any other happening in Macondo's history except for the traditional celebration of Big Mama's birthday during her seven decades of supremacy.

In other stories we glimpse a thief who is jailed for a theft he didn't commit, a dentist who avenges himself upon a patient, Macondo's mayor and his political enemy, and a mother who braves the town's hostility as she walks through the streets carrying flowers for the grave of her son who has been executed as a criminal. All the stories communicate incidents in the lives of humble (and a few rich) townspeople, all of whom have been deeply affected by the long and bloody political strife between the liberals and the conservatives in Colombia. But politics are merely a background for García Márquez, who is concerned mainly with the mysterious inner lives of his characters, lives we intuit briefly through their laconic utterances, their actions, and their emotions.

The author's style, unusual for a contemporary Latin American writer, is well suited to his purpose. It has serenity, understatement, and compassion, and is flecked with wry humor. García Márquez possesses a special felicity for deft, succinct characterization and evocative description. His short book will have a more lasting effect on many readers than numerous longer ones.

[Review of *No One Writes to the Colonel and Other Stories*]   Alberto J. Carlos*

Gabriel García Márquez is one of the most important contemporary Latin American writers. Along with such notable novelists as Mario Vargas Llosa, Julio Cortázar, Juan Carlos Onetti, and Carlos Fuentes, the forty-year-old Colombian García Márquez is responsible for the extraordinary attention that Latin American literature has of late been receiving both in North America and Europe. García Márquez has written three novels and one volume of short stories.

No One Writes to the Colonel and Other Stories includes all the short stories that appeared in *Los funerales de Mamá Grande* (Xalapa, Mexico, 1962) as well as "No One Writes to the Colonel," a longer narrative published separately in 1961. Although apparently not concerned with the most recent narrative techniques, García Márquez tells his stories in quite an extraordinary manner. He sometimes omits important details so that the reader is obliged to imagine entire scenes and even the dénouement of several stories. His fiction is usually compact and unassuming; yet some of the narratives have implications that require careful study.

It would appear that the young Colombian is not interested in denouncing social injustices; however, his stories indirectly expose the inherent injustice of a particular provincial society and the blatant corruption of its petty officials. The seventy-five-year-old colonel; the

*Reprinted from *Studies in Short Fiction* 9, no. 1 (Winter 1972):101–3. Reprinted by permission of the journal.

senile priest; the proud, psychotic widow; the tough, young gigolo; the head-strong dentist — these are only a few of the characters who inhabit the South American province about which García Márquez writes. The stories themselves constitute a remarkable and brilliant kaleidoscopic vision of life in an isolated Colombian town.

In "Tuesday Siesta," a twelve-year-old girl and her mother travel to a neighboring town to visit the grave of a petty thief, the old woman's son and the girl's brother. As the story progresses, García Márquez reveals that the dead man had once been a boxer, taking beatings every Saturday night so that his family could eat. Later he became a petty thief, but he promised his mother never to steal anything that someone else might need to survive. This struggle against unrelenting, impossible economic and social obstacles characterizes perfectly the life of those miserable wretches caught in that very special South American brand of poverty. The petty thief is a criminal in the eyes of the priest. Can there ever be any justification for petty thievery? The old woman, however, sees the situation differently. Her boy has not done anything wrong. She knows what it is to be hungry and to be exploited. She knows that if one must elect between stealing or dying of hunger, one must always choose the lesser evil. The woman, like a modern Antigone, is undaunted by the hostility of the people in the town where her son lies in an anonymous grave. Reaffirming the right of the poor to dignity, she pays her respects to her son and continues, undefeated, her difficult journey through life.

"Artifical Roses" is one of the most subtle stories in this collection. Superficially, it is about a young girl, Mina, who misses Mass on a particular first Friday. But her anguish seems too pronounced to be caused by what appears to be merely a stroke of bad luck. The author does not explain fully, but he does point out that the young girl has been writing love letters to someone. And the fact that Mina throws away a bundle of letters that she has tied with a pink ribbon seems to indicate that the real crisis is about a boy friend who has left town. The whole drama is contained in a cryptic conversation between Mina and her friend Trinidad:

> "He went away," she said.
> Trinidad looked at her without blinking. A vertical wrinkle divided her knit brows.
> "And now?" she asked.
> Mina replied in a steady voice.
> "Now nothing."

Although Mina pretends that her frustration and pain have been caused by missing Mass, her blind grandmother has intuitively guessed her secret.

The story about Baltazar, the carpenter who makes the most beautiful bird cage in the world, opposes the artist to the philistine, the modest craftsman to the miserly rich man. Baltazar had built the cage for the rich man's son, but when the cage is taken to the boy's house, his father refuses to pay for it. Baltazar, moved by the boy's cries of anguish, gives him the cage. And then the carpenter goes to the pool hall, says he has sold the cage and buys drinks for everyone. Immune to the harsh realities of life, Baltazar ends up drunk in the street, dreaming the sweet dream of artistic triumph.

Perhaps the story that may seem most enigmatic is the one entitled "One of These Days." The mayor of the town goes to the office of its only dentist and insists on having a tooth pulled. The dentist prepares his instruments, but he demands that the extraction be without anesthesia. The tooth is pulled; the mayor leaves. And there the story ends. The short narrative makes more sense if one relates it to *La mala hora*, García Márquez's second novel. There one can find the same situation and the same dénouement. One observes that the mayor's tyranny — his fanatical abuse of authority — elicits not only the righteous indignation of the dentist, but also it is evident that his tyranny will soon provoke a much stronger reaction. Obviously, the situation of the mayor and dentist cannot remain as it is: violence will surely break out one of these days.

García Márquez's curious manner of telling a story makes a few of his narratives appear somewhat obscure. Most of them, however, are accessible to all readers; they are subtle, sometimes even funny, always beautiful, undoubtedly some of the best short stories ever written in Latin America. *No One Writes to the Colonel* must not be mistaken for just another collection of short stories. It is an excellent first volume of short fiction by a major writer.

The Gossip on the Wall

Robert Coover*

Late in 1955, recently arrived in Paris, penniless and jobless and in more or less self-imposed exile (he was unpopular with the dictatorial regime back home in Colombia, which had just closed down the newspaper he'd been working for), Gabriel García Márquez announced to a friend that he'd decided to write "the story of the lampoons," based on a real event that had taken place in a remote riverside village he'd visited occasionally as a boy: someone there had once started pasting up anonymous, scandal-mongering broadsides, which in turn had provoked fights, feuds, even killings, and had eventually caused a lot of people to pack up and abandon the town altogether, without anyone ever finding out who'd put the wall posters up.

*Reprinted from *New York Times Book Review*, 11 November 1979, 3, 30. Copyright © 1979 by The New York Times Company. Reprinted by permission.

The story grew into a novel — in fact, more than one: a piece of it broke away to become *No One Writes to the Colonel*, and others formed the bases for at least a half-dozen other stories. After languishing for years at the bottom of a world-traveling suitcase, the story-turned-novel eventually surfaced in Colombia under its present title to win the Esso Literary Prize of 1961. It was published in Madrid in 1962, arrogantly corrected into "Proper Castillian," and then again in Mexico, its true text restored, in 1966, about the time its author was completing there the first draft of his soon-to-be world-famous masterpiece, *One Hundred Years of Solitude*.

Now in 1979, nearly a quarter of a century after its conception, *In Evil Hour* appears at last in English, thereby filling in the last significant gap in the García Márquez opus. Given its wit, perception, imaginative richness and easy accessibility, it is astonishing that we have had to wait so long.

Colombia in the mid-1950's was enmeshed in that seemingly endless epoch of civil wars and bloody repressions known as "la Violencia," which is said to have claimed at least 250,000 lives between 1948 and 1962. The young García Márquez, moving away from the experimental fantasy and lyricism of his early stories toward his own sense of "social realism," chose to transpose his tale of the lampoons into the contemporary Colombian reality, in this way interlacing a comic craziness with a terrible one.

When the novel opens, the unnamed "village" — which, in spite of some superficial similarities and even a contradiction or two, is *not* the famous Macondo — has been experiencing a period of enforced and artificial "peace," this peace being useful to the authorities in the consolidation of their wealth and power. The first immediate effect of the mysterious lampoons (though an accurate enough translation of *pasquines* or "pasquinades," the word is somewhat misleading, for the wall posters are merely gossipy, not satirical) is to instigate a seemingly apolitical crime of passion. Indeed, this is how the "mayor" of the town perceives it, and it inspires him to dust off the old forgotten lawbooks and prosecute the case in a "proper" manner, thereby throwing into relief the essential lawlessness, even barbarity, of his own regime.

As the slanderous broadsides proliferate, the villagers — especially those of the dominant middle class — grow increasingly restless and fearful, and finally the Catholic Dames, led by the redoubtable Widow Asís, prevail upon the local priest, Father Angel, to take a public stand against them. The priest in turn, needing the support of authority, persuades a reluctant, preoccupied (he is busy getting rich) mayor to take the lampoons seriously — "It's a question, if one might say so," he says, "of a case of terrorism in the moral order" — and ultimately a curfew is imposed, with citizens deputized to stay up all night to try to catch the person or persons responsible.

With the return of the curfew, the political opposition seems also to be revived, subversive pamphlets reappear, and eventually a boy is caught distributing them at the cockfights (but *not* putting up lampoons). The boy is murdered during his interrogation by the police, and "la Violencia" returns, unmitigated and undisguised: "The little jokes are over," the mayor says, his carbine trained on the priest and doctor. "We're at war, Doctor." To which the doctor, laughing and pulling the stupefied priest away, replies: "I like it this way, General. . . . Now we are beginning to understand each other."

The mystery of the authorship of the lampoons is never solved; indeed, by the end of the novel, with its brutal political realities and in spite of its final teasing ellipsis, it no longer seems important. "Never, since the world has been the world," one of the characters has warned us, "has anyone found out who puts up the lampoons" — which is more like a statement of underlying principle than an insinuation of enigma. The one who seems to get closest to some kind of answer is a visiting circus fortuneteller called Casandra, Mirror of the Future: "It's the whole town and it's nobody."

This air of unfathomable mystery, intensified by García Márquez's love of exotic dreams, mad seers' ghosts and circuses, legends, marvels and comic exaggeration, has caused the Peruvian critic and novelist Mario Vargas Llosa to declare in his *History of a Deicide* (an exhaustive and seminal but as yet untranslated study of García Márquez's work) that although "the victory of the imaginary . . . is here so subtle, so disguised, that to many critics *In Evil Hour* seems like the most 'realistic' of all García Márquez's books," it is, excluding the earliest stories, "the first 'fantastic' text that he has written."

The truth is, though, that the conflict in this book between the "realistic" and the "fantastic" is never adequately worked out. The mysterious, almost magical, lampoons are at the very heart of the plot, yet the final state of affairs, brought on by the clandestine political fliers and the boy's murder, has almost nothing to do with them. It's like two stories overlaid on each other but not yet interlaced. The author himself concedes as much: "Nobody talked about the lampoons. In the hubbub of the latest happenings they were nothing but a picturesque anecdote of the past."

A resolution of sorts (reasonable, but never quite satisfying) is achieved by taking the whole tale to be a kind of parable — or "fairytale," as the author suggests — on the disturbing, truth-provoking power of art. The book itself, then, becomes a kind of mysterious lampoon, telling the people "what they already know" and making itself irrelevant in the end with its own success. Not that the artist ever entirely disappears: There will always be a need for his disruptions, so he remains, ready to return at any moment, hovering in the ellipses just beyond the book.

The translator from the original Spanish on this occasion is the gifted Gregory Rabassa, who has been spoken of in these pages as "one of the best translators who ever drew breath." True, but alas, *In Evil Hour* is not the best testimonial to that reputation. It remains lively and readable, but there are too many careless mistranslations, wooden metaphrasings and unimaginative options taken for a professional translator of such indisputable talent. There is the Colombian's love of the idiomatic *vaina*, for example, which might be translated as anything from "predicament" or "difficulty" to "nonsense," "trouble" or "fiasco," but which Mr. Rabassa obstinately renders over and over as, "mess," until he gets in an awful one. Fortunately, he and we are extricated by García Márquez's natural humor, energy and love of story, for which we can all, in whatever evil hour, be grateful.

[Review of *One Hundred Years of Solitude*]

Michael Wood*

> And now I had in my hands a vast methodical fragment of the total history of an unknown planet, with its architectures and its playing cards, with the terror of its mythologies and the murmur of its idioms, with its emperors and its seas, with its minerals and its birds and its fishes, with its algebra and its fire, with its theological and metaphysical polemics. All of it articulated, coherent, without any apparent doctrinal intention or tone of parody. . . .

The echo of Conan Doyle is as characteristic as the pale, swaying prose and the willful, ironic precision of the list. Architectures in the plural, playing cards, emperors, minerals, algebra. The voice is that of Jorge Luis Borges, decadent poet of the twenties turned delicate joker of the forties and fifties, author of brief, insubstantial fictions that seem to have changed the whole course of Latin American literature.

In one sense, they have. Almost single-handed, and almost overnight, Borges rescued his continent from naturalism, from a desperate, and as it now seems wrongheaded, devotion to the methods of Zola and Blasco Ibáñez. Borges' inventions, his rival planets, his abolitions of space and mortality combined to suggest that naturalism was a doubly false direction, twice removed from the truth, like poetry for Plato, since it could copy only things, and things, perhaps, were features of our imagination, creations of a Cartesian mind trapped in the circle of its own perceptions. Reality itself, perhaps, was a fiction. The world then would no longer be a problem or a potential document, but a game, a form of assembly kit from which we, or our culture, would piece together our lives. The very titles of many books since Borges reflect this movement: *Fictions* (1944), Borges' own most important work; *Hopscotch* (1963), Julio Cortázar's immense puzzle novel; *Three Trapped Tigers* (1965), a Joycean language romp by

*Reprinted from the *Colombia Forum* 13, no. 2 (Summer 1970):160–65.

Guillermo Cabrera Infante (the title is taken from a familiar tongue-twister, *Tres tristes tigres tragaban trigo en un trigal*).

Yet my concern here is not with this striking inheritance, this redirection of a literature, but with a longer tradition, which Borges exemplifies brilliantly but does not invent, and which finds its most recent and most vivid expression in Gabriel García Márquez' *One Hundred Years of Solitude* (published in Spanish in 1967 and in English this year), to which I will return shortly.

For there is a sense in which Borges changed nothing. He simply gave a tantalizing form to a haunting theme, to a familiar and lasting concern of Latin Americans: their fear that they are not quite real people, that their world is not entirely a real world. This is not a metaphysical or epistemological problem, it is not the European anguish of Kafka or Beckett, and it is not the uneasiness of North Americans faced with a fast-changing social and physical landscape. It is an old and intimate feeling, an actor's weariness with a never-ending career, a feeling that what is happening cannot really be happening, that it is all too fantastic or too cruel to be true, that history cannot be the farce it appears to be, that a daily life cannot be merely this losing battle with dust or insects, that this round of diseases, drink, ceremonies, sadness, and sudden death cannot be all there is. Tlön, then, the planet evoked above by Borges, a place without proper nouns, a place where a belief in the existence of material objects becomes a scandalous and virtually incomprehensible heresy, is not simply an evasion, an escape from the world and time and the self. It is also a description, a plain statement of what it is like to be alive, or almost alive, in Latin America.

Historically, as Octavio Paz says, Latin America is a European invention, "a chapter in the history of European utopias," the last chance of a dying Spanish or Portuguese kingdom. Geographically, it is a beautiful but hostile landscape, which earlier fiction always represented as a killer. "The jungle swallowed them." Carlos Fuentes, quoting this description of the disappearance of the heroes in a famous old story, remarks that the words might serve as a commentary on almost a century of Latin American novels: "the mountain, the pampas, the mine, the river swallowed them." What is missing then is a whole middle zone, a bridge between a false culture and a harsh countryside. *That* reality remains to be invented, and the enterprise becomes a major theme in works that show very little trace of Borges' influence—independent proof of the depth and the extent of the preoccupation.

There is Juan Rulfo's *Pedro Páramo* (1955), for example, where a man in search of his father finds only a place full of echoes, tired laughter, dogs howling, leaves falling—although there have been no trees in the village for a long time. He finds ghosts, voices of ghosts, and, in the sense that they tell him the story of his father's life and death, he finds his father.

Or there is Alejo Carpentier's remarkable *Lost Footsteps* (1953). The novel opens with a description of a house and garden, and a suggestion that time has changed nothing here. Then, oddly, a tap on a stone bench makes it sound like wood; the narrator's footsteps create hollow echoes beneath him. Slaves and wounded soldiers go by, and the language finally gives the game away: this is a stage set for a play about the American Civil War. Time has changed nothing here because this place is the same every night, the same words are spoken here once a day, and twice a day on holidays and weekends. The play has been running for 1,500 performances, and, far from liberating the leading actress, the narrator's wife, it has become a prison for her: Devil's Island, as Carpentier says. The escape from time is an escape into illusion, and the illusion closes behind you. At the end of the book, the narrator has found an alternative retreat, an authentic refuge from time and unreality, a kind of moral El Dorado on the upper reaches of the Orinoco. But he can't get back to it, and in any case he is a musician, and musicians, like all artists, are condemned to live in history, even if history itself is a mirage. The vacations of Sisyphus, he tells himself, are over.

Perhaps Latin Americans *enjoy* their sense of unreality, perhaps history and geography are ultimately less to blame than they seem to be. Borges has suggested as much: "And yet, and yet. . . . To deny temporal succession, to deny the self, to deny the astronomical universe, is an ostensible despair and a secret solace. Our destiny . . . is not fearful because it is unreal; it is fearful because it is irreversible and iron-clad. . . . The world, unfortunately is real; I, unfortunately, am Borges." Is there collaboration, then, complicity, a taste for the privileged status of specters? This is the proposition that emerges from Gabriel García Márquez' *One Hundred Years of Solitude.* For the first time, I think, a writer has caught not only the color and shape of Latin American despair but also its tone: elegant, ironic, slightly complacent, the sound of ghosts laughing sadly; disciplined, self-conscious smiles on too many pleasant faces. Surely a large part of this spectacular novel's immense success in Latin America is the shock of recognition it provides for its readers: this is how they talk to themselves.

The hundred years of the title are those of Macondo, a jungle hamlet that becomes a thriving town before its final decay and death; of Ursula, matriarch and memory of the place; of her family; of Pilar Ternera, kind witch, fortune-teller, initiatress, great-aunt to everyone, buried at last beneath the dance floor of her zoological brothel. The solitude is that of most people in the book, but especially that of Colonel Aureliano Buendía, Ursula's sad revolutionary son, fighting vague lost battles, and ultimately betraying his dimly understood cause to return to the loneliness of Macondo.

Macondo has a charm against death, or against some deaths. Aureliano is given poison, faces a firing squad, tries to put a bullet through his own chest after giving up the revolution, but he dies at home one day when a circus passes, his shoulders hunched up, his head pressed against the old chestnut tree where his father's ghost, which he has never been able to see, is still tied up. The language of *One Hundred Years of Solitude* reflects this magical delay, or destiny. A kind of retrospective future tense runs through it like a refrain:

> Many years later, facing the firing squad, Colonel Aureliano Buendía was to remember that distant afternoon. . . .

> She was the last person Arcadio thought of, a few years later, as he faced the firing squad. . . .

There is a suggestion of a teleology here, of a work moving toward its resolution. But the suggestion is a trick. Aureliano is rescued from the firing squad and does not die until much later, so his memory then is just a memory, what he thinks of at a high point in his life. Nothing is finished. On the other hand, Arcadio, Aureliano's nephew, *is* shot by the firing squad, but then so what? Nothing ends with Arcadio except Aureliano's life.

And yet things do end — even within death, as one character learns, there is a dying; even ghosts disappear one day. Even the Buendía family, with its supernatural energy, patience, and longevity, fades out at last. Macondo is a country of myth, metaphor, hyperbole, a place where life has the purity of a proverb, where lovers die of love, where people who withdraw into silence really never speak again, where the evil banana company can conjure up a four-year flood to erase the traces of its massacre of 3,000 striking workers. But the myth is not an escape, time is not to be deceived by poetry or folklore, the improbable flood really wipes out the town. A hundred years is a good tenure, almost a miracle of duration, but even a hundred years is not forever.

The teleological refrain then ("he was to remember") is not false but simply deceptive, a recurring red herring that is also a clue. The work *is* written out of an awareness of its end, the expiration of the Buendía family fate. Before they founded Macondo, Ursula had refused to sleep with her husband, who was also her cousin, because she was afraid that the closeness of their blood would breed a monster, a child with a pig's tail, like the child of one of her aunts. Her fears turn out to be unwarranted, but incest looms over the family throughout the hundred years, aunts exercising an awful attraction over their nephews. Finally, the last Buendías give in, and fulfill the portent: their child has a pig's tail. The mother dies, the child itself, left alone for a moment, is eaten by ants, and the last Aureliano, an illegitimate great-nephew of the colonel, returns to the Sanskrit documents he has been deciphering. Like a character in Borges, he realizes belatedly that the documents are the history of his house, and that when he finishes reading, the history will end, that his death is what is described on the last Sanskrit page.

Ursula's fears, in fact, like the refrain, are both false and true, for the last literal freak of the family is merely a mocking epilogue to the lineage: a dynasty of monsters, inhuman incarnations of pride, loneliness, inbreeding, introspection, and despair. I need to insist here, perhaps: this is a rich, funny, powerful, and appealing book, but it is all but silenced by the sound of the echoing word, solitude. Loneliness in Macondo and among the Buendías is not an accidental condition, something that could be alleviated by better communications or more friends, and it is not the metaphysical loneliness of existentialists, a stage shared by all men. It is a particular vocation, a shape of character that is inherited, certainly, but also *chosen*, a doom that looks inevitable but is freely endorsed. The Buendías seek out their solitude, enclose themselves in it as if it were their shroud. As a result they become yet another emblem of the unreality I tried to describe earlier, living ghosts less real than the ghosts around them.

In this perspective, the popularity of *One Hundred Years of Solitude* in Latin America looks almost sinister. If this is a portrait, then the fact that so many people have found it attractive starts a vicious circle, with readers recognizing and liking themselves, their own isolation, and tenderly nurtured gloom. Well, the writer must be critical anyway. I think he must. In fact, I am not quite convinced that García Márquez himself does not in the end enjoy all this proud distress as much as anyone else. Where does that leave us? "And now I had in my hands a vast methodical fragment of the total history of an unknown planet, with its architectures and its playing cards, with the terror of its mythologies and the murmur of its idioms, with its emperors and its seas, with its minerals and its birds and its fishes. . . ." Tlön. Macondo. Another illusion, a place of mirrors, a city of fiction, the same old mirage.

Myth Is Alive in Latin America   John Leonard*

You emerge from this marvelous novel as if from a dream, the mind on fire. A dark, ageless figure at the hearth, part historian, part haruspex, in a voice by turns angelic and maniacal, first lulls to sleep your grip on a manageable reality, then locks you into legend and myth. *One Hundred Years of Solitude* is not only the story of the Buendía family and the Colombian town of Macondo. It is also a recapitulation of our evolutionary and intellectual experience. Macondo is Latin America in microcosm: local autonomy yielding to state authority; anticlericalism; party politics; the coming of the United Fruit Company; aborted revolutions; the rape of

*Reprinted from *New York Times*, 3 March 1970, 39. Copyright © 1970 by The New York Times Company. Reprinted by permission.

innocence by history. And the Buendías (inventors, artisans, soldiers, lovers, mystics) seem doomed to ride a biological tragi-cycle in circles from solitude to magic to poetry to science to politics to violence back again to solitude.

A GALLEON, A PLAGUE, A BLOOD BATH

Which isn't to say that the book is grimly programmatic. It is often wildly funny, and superbly translated by Gregory Rabassa. Nor does the specific get buried under the symbolic. Macondo with its rains, ghosts, priests, Indians, Arabs and gypsies, is splendidly evoked. So richly realized are the Buendías that they invite comparison with the Karamazovs and Sartorises. Indeed, specificity overwhelms incredulity, setting up the reader for imagist explosions more convincing than mere data can ever be: Anything goes, and everything comes back.

Would you believe, for instance, men with machetes in search of the sea hacking their way through "bloody lilies and golden salamanders" to find in a swamp a Spanish galleon? A plague of insomnia? A stream of blood feeling its path across a city from a dying son to a grieving mother? A mule that eats sheets, rugs, bedspreads, drapes and "the canopy embroidered with gold thread and silk tassels on the episcopal bed"? A Sanskrit manuscript predicting the 100 years of Macondo, down to the very deciphering of the prediction by the last Buendía? A paterfamilias chained to a tree in the garden, muttering in Latin? Or, when that paterfamilias finally dies, this consequence:

> A short time later, when the carpenter was taking measurements for the coffin, through the window they saw a light rain of tiny yellow flowers falling. They fell on the town all through the night in a silent storm, and they covered the roofs and blocked the doors and smothered the animals who slept outside. So many flowers fell from the sky that in the morning the streets were carpeted with a compact cushion and they had to clear them away with shovels and rakes so that the funeral procession could pass by.

DEAD STRIKERS AND A MIRACLE

I believe — in the last Buendía infant born as prophesized with the tail of a pig, and eaten alive by ants. In the brothel with alligators. In the 3,000 dead strikers against the banana plantation, hauled away by silent train; and Remedios the Beauty, plucked up by the wind and flown to God as she hung up bedsheets to dry; and Melquíades, who introduces Macondo to the miracle of ice. I believe in all the Buendías, from the original José Arcadio and the original Ursula (cousins who marry and by mythic mitosis divide into generations of Arcadios and Aurelianos and Amarantas) down through "the most intricate labyrinths of blood" to the end of the family line in a room full of chamber pots in "the city of mirrors (or mirages)" as the wind comes to sweep away all memory.

Family chronicle, then, and political tour de force, and metaphysical speculation, and, intentionally, a cathedral of words, perceptions and legends that amounts to the declaration of a state of mind: solitude being one's admission of one's own mortality and one's discovery that that terrible apprehension is itself mortal, dies with you, must be rediscovered and forgotten again, endlessly. With a single bound Gabriel García Márquez leaps onto the stage with Günter Grass and Vladimir Nabokov, his appetite as enormous as his imagination, his fatalism greater than either. Dazzling.

[Review of *One Hundred Years of Solitude*]

Robert Kiely*

To speak of a land of enchantment, even in reference to a contemporary novel, is to conjure up images of elves, moonbeams and slippery mountains. Along with the midgets and fairies, one can expect marvelous feats and moral portents, but not much humor and almost certainly no sex. The idea, it would seem, is to forget the earth. At least that is one idea of enchantment.

It is obviously not shared by the Colombian novelist Gabriel García Márquez, who has created in *One Hundred Years of Solitude* an enchanted place that does everything but cloy. Macondo oozes, reeks and burns even when it is most tantalizing and entertaining. It is a place flooded with lies and liars and yet it spills over with reality. Lovers in this novel can idealize each other into bodiless spirits, howl with pleasure in their hammocks or, as in one case, smear themselves with peach jam and roll naked on the front porch. The hero can lead a Quixotic expedition across the jungle, but although his goal is never reached, the language describing his quest is pungent with life: "The men on the expedition felt overwhelmed by their most ancient memories in that paradise of dampness and silence, going back to before original sin, as their boots sank into pools of steaming oil and their machetes destroyed bloody lilies and golden salamanders. For a week, almost without speaking, they went ahead like sleepwalkers through a universe of grief, lighted only by the tenuous reflection of luminous insects, and their lungs were overwhelmed by a suffocating smell of blood." This is the language of a poet who knows the earth and does not fear it as the enemy of the dreamer.

*Reprinted from *New York Times Book Review*, 8 March 1970, 5, 24. Copyright © 1970 by The New York Times Company. Reprinted by permission.

Near the end of *One Hundred Years of Solitude* a character finds a parchment manuscript in which the history of his family had been recorded "one hundred years ahead of time" by an old gypsy. The writer "had not put events in the order of man's conventional time, but had concentrated a century of daily episodes in such a way that they coexisted in one instant." The narrative is a magician's trick in which memory and prophecy, illusion and reality are mixed and often made to look the same. It is, in short, very much like Márquez's astonishing novel.

It is not easy to describe the techniques and themes of the book without making it sound absurdly complicated, labored and almost impossible to read. In fact, it is none of these things. Though concocted of quirks, ancient mysteries, family secrets and peculiar contradictions, it makes sense and gives pleasure in dozens of immediate ways.

The family chronicle centers on five generations of descendants of José Arcadio Buendía and his wife Ursula, who sometime early in the 19th century founded the village of Macondo on a river of clear water somewhere in South America. The uncertainties about time and place, like other factual puzzles in the book, are not fashionable evasions on the part of the author but genuine reflections of the minds of the people about whom he is writing. From the beginning we are told that Buendía knew nothing about the geography of the region. He comes to love maps and compasses, but his sense of where he is remains very much his own. He plays with an astrolabe and sextant, but, with characteristic excess, almost contracts sunstroke "from trying to establish an exact method to ascertain noon."

The book is a history, not of governments or of formal institutions of the sort which keeps public records, but of a people who, like the earliest descendants of Abraham, are best understood in terms of their relationship to a single family. In a sense, José and Ursula are the only two characters in the story, and all their children, grandchildren and great-grandchildren are variations on their strengths and weaknesses. José, forever fascinated by the unknown, takes up project after project, invention after invention, in order, among other things, to make gold, discover the ocean and photograph God. He eventually goes mad, smashes things, refuses to speak except in Latin and is tied to a giant chestnut tree in the middle of the family garden.

Ursula is the personification of practical endurance and sheer will. It is she who mends the pieces and sweeps the house clean after disaster; it is she who continues to raise various offspring long after her own children have grown to adulthood; and it is she who remains strong and clear-headed until the age of 114 or 122—as usual, no one is quite sure.

A mixture of obsessive idealism and durable practicality informs the lives of the Buendía descendants. The males, all named Arcadio or Aureliano, go off to sea, lead revolutions, follow gypsies, fall disastrously in love with their sisters and aunts (except one who develops a passion for a

12-year-old-girl), but most of them add to the family's stature and wealth and all contribute generously to its number. The women are not overshadowed by the men, One eats dirt when she is depressed; another burns her hand in the oven and wears a black cloth over it for life when her lover commits suicide; another, named Remedios the Beauty, is so innocent that one day when folding linen in the backyard she ascends into heaven with the family sheets.

But to isolate details, even good ones, from this novel is to do it peculiar injustice. Márquez creates a continuum, a web of connections and relationships. However bizarre or grotesque some particulars may be, the larger effect is one of great gusto and good humor and, even more, of sanity and compassion. The author seems to be letting his people half-dream and half-remember their own story and, what is best, he is wise enough not to offer excuses for the way they do it. No excuse is really necessary. For Macondo is no never-never land. Its inhabitants do suffer, grow old and die, but in their own way.

Various hard and familiar aspects of reality intrude on their world all the time. What seems unreal or at least unconventional to an outsider is the manner in which the Buendías respond to and explain facts like birth, death, war, sickness and even weather. When it gets hot in Macondo, it gets so hot that men and beasts go mad and birds attack houses. A long spell of rain is remembered to have lasted, not weeks, but four years, eleven months and two days. When a plague hits the region, it is no ordinary killer but an "insomnia plague," which gradually causes people to forget everything including the names and uses of the most commonplace objects. In order to combat the memory loss, the villagers label chairs and clocks, and even hang a sign on the cow: *This is the cow. She must be milked every morning so that she will produce milk, and the milk must be boiled in order to be mixed with coffee to make coffee and milk.*

More serious than bad weather or plague are the intrusions from outside, the mysterious gypsies, the corrupt government officials, the brutal soldiers (both Conservative and Liberal), the foppish Italian piano tuner, the ingenious French prostitutes and, finally, with the railroad, the sweating gringos "planning to plant banana trees in the enchanted region that José Arcadio Buendía and his men had crossed in search of the route" to the sea. At first it looks as though the North Americans will be absorbed into the dream life of Macondo, but they do mean to change things, including the terrain and the weather, and they do eventually build their own sensible counterpart to Macondo, a village of houses in neat rows with tennis courts and swimming pools.

It might have been just another phase in the incestuous life of Macondo, like the 32 revolutions or the insomnia plague, but enchantment and solitude cannot survive the gringos any more than they can avoid the 20th century. Like so much else in this strange and moving narrative, the end seems to have been inevitable. And yet the North American reader—in thinking of this narrative filled with haunting creatures and events—can hardly help being particularly haunted by the spectacle of his country-men, "the perspiring guests—who did not even know who their hosts were—[trooping] in to occupy the best places at the table." Márquez has shown us, with extraordinary art, who some of the hosts were or, what is more important, who they thought they were. He has also written a novel so filled with humor, rich detail and startling distortion that it brings to mind the best of Faulkner and Günter Grass. It is a South American Genesis, an earthy piece of enchantment, more, as the narrator says of Macondo, "an intricate stew of truth and mirages."

Stew is too modest an image with which to describe the wit and power of this lusty fantasia, but if the strong savor banishes visions of twinkletoes, it has served a purpose.

Orchids and Bloodlines   Anonymous*

Gabriel García Márquez spent the first eight years of his life in Aracataca, a steamy banana town not far from the Colombian coast. "Nothing interesting has happened to me since," he has said. His experi-ences there were eventually transformed into a tenderly comic novel, just published in the U.S. after three years of enormous success in Latin America. It has survived export triumphantly. In a beautiful translation, surrealism and innocence blend to form a wholly individual style. Like rum *calentano*, the story goes down easily, leaving a rich, sweet burning flavor behind.

FLYING CARPETS

Outwardly the book is a picaresque saga of the extraordinary Buendía family in Macondo, the town they helped to found more than a century ago in the dense Colombian lowlands. Pioneer settlers from a foothills town, José Arcadio Buendía and Ursula, his wife-cousin, start with nothing but the vehemence of their blood. They soon make Macondo into a strange oasis in the orchid-filled jungle, a primitive, otherworldly place resonant with songbirds, where there is no death, no crime, no law, no judges. The only outside visitors are gypsies, who astound the residents with magnets, false teeth, telescopes, ice and a flying carpet.

First civil war, then a railroad and a huge, U.S.-owned banana plantation gradually penetrate the town's isolation and open it to dissen-sion and prosperity. Six generations of Buendías, all touched with fantasy

*Reprinted from *Time*, 16 March 1970, 96. Copyright 1970 Time Inc. All rights re-served. Reprinted by permission from *Time*.

and fatalism, all condemned to fundamental solitude, are born and die, often violently. Just before the family line ends in disaster, Macondo is almost abandoned, the banana farms destroyed by nearly five years of rain. Only the red-light district remains active. Finally, an inexplicable cyclone erases the town and the family.

The Buendía men are introverted, impulsive, richly eccentric. José Arcadio, the founding father, all common sense when it comes to law or town design, is lured into alchemy and other esoteric sciences: he tries to use a daguerreotype machine to find the invisible player of his pianola. One of his sons, Colonel Aureliano Buendía, becomes a revolutionary leader who organizes 32 armed uprisings against a distant and corrupt "government." He loses them all, but wins the war — only to lose the peace. Aureliano II is a roistering spendthrift who takes on all comers in eating contests. He falls only once, comatose with turkey, in a four-day duel with a fastidious lady known as "the Elephant."

García Márquez's women are magnificent. Stern, stoic, preserved by duty and the dynastic urge, they struggle to keep their men sane. The primal mother Ursula, even at the age of 100, is so sure of her ways that no one realizes she is blind.

Reduced to essences, the exotic Buendías become immediate — yet mythically compelling like Tolstoy's Rostóv family, or the doomed scions of Faulkner's *Sartoris*. But *One Hundred Years* is more than a family chronicle. The author is really at work on an imaginative spiritual history of any or all Latin American communities. In the process, he fondly reveals more about the Latin soul than all Oscar Lewis' selective eaves-dropping does.

Indeed, the whole enchanted continent, originally colonized by white men in pursuit of El Dorado and the Fountain of Youth, is encapsulated in Macondo. The only trace of the Protestant ethic in the town is the operation of the U.S. banana company — and the "gringos" are plainly mean, greedy, and probably crazy too. The Buendías, on the other hand, are inspired mainly by the magic in life. They see no limit of human potential, mostly because natural miracles abound — a plague of insomnia, showers of dead birds or yellow flowers, the arrival of death as a lady in blue. When Remedios Buendía (whose beauty and musky odor drive men mad) suddenly ascends to heaven while folding sheets, her sister-in-law merely grumbles that the sheets, which also rose, are lost forever.

For all its range and length, the book is satisfyingly cohesive where it might be sprawling. The key to this unity is García Márquez's treatment of time. Consider the superb opening sentence: "Many years later, as he faced the firing squad, Colonel Aureliano Buendía was to remember that distant afternoon when his father took him to discover ice." Such compression of time makes the novel taut with a sense of fate. Atavistic dictates of blood must be followed. Premonitions invariably come true. A series of coded predictions, written when Macondo was still young, are deciphered only when every prediction has been fulfilled, including the final, devastating wind that takes apart Macondo. The future, is thus history, the end is the beginning, and the reader is tempted to start again.

[Review of *La increíble y triste historia de la cándida Eréndira y de su abuela desalmada*]

Howard Fraser*

Gabriel García Márquez's new collection of short fiction is not entirely new. Most of the stories have already appeared in such varied publications as the *Revista mexicana de literatura, Cuadernos hispanoamericanos, Revista de la Universidad de Mexico, Esquire, New American Review*, and *Playboy*. In addition, all but three of these stories appeared alongside Gregory Rabassa's translation of *La hojarasca* in *Leaf Storm and Other Stories* (New York: Harper and Row, 1972). Thus, as a result of the wide acclaim accorded García Márquez in English, a good portion of this volume has received ample comment in the many published reviews of *Leaf Storm*. (See Earl Shorris, *Harper's*, February, 1972, Alfred Kazin, New York *Times Book Review*, February 20, 1972, Martha Duffy, *Time*, March 11, 1972, Richard Locke, New York *Times*, March 17, 1972, Michael Wood, New York *Review of Books*, April 6, 1972.)

Although Macondo has disappeared as a background, most of the tales are set in the isolation of the desert in an atmosphere of solitude. Other stories develop the theme of loneliness in coastal settings where García Márquez's characters contemplate the endless ocean of their barren lives. As in the author's earlier novels and stories, these short pieces portray man's fundamental dignity and stoical determination to survive despite the forces of degradation which threaten his existence.

Faithful readers of this Columbian author will recognize the multiple dimensions of his fantasy which characterizes his former works. In "El mar del tiempo perdido," Sr. Herbert swims to the bottom of the ocean in search of food. Beyond the reaches of sunlight, he observes a sunken village, illuminated by bioluminescent organisms with the inhabitants of the town riding a merry-go-round. In the title story, Ulises, lover of the beautiful Eréndira, touches glass objects and they change color as a magical index of his love. Here, too, is the author's characteristic description of the world from a simple, child-like point of view. Eréndira claims, ["I've never seen the sea,"] and Ulises replies, ["It's like the desert, but with water."]

*Reprinted from *Chasqui* 2, no. 3 (May 1973):68–70, by permission of the journal.

Through the simplicity and magic of the tangible world there emerges the parable of Spanish American decadence and decay, a process of degeneration which is unaffected by the promise of material progress. "El mar del tiempo perdido," the oldest of the works in this collection (originally published in 1962 and not included in *Leaf Storm*), describes a dying coastal village. Señor Herbert, the richest man in the world, arrives to help humanity lift itself out of despair and poverty. He distributes cash in exchange for a demonstration of each recipient's talent. For example, Patricio receives forty-eight dollars for imitating the call of forty-eight different birds. Despite the promise of unbounded wealth, this method of improving the villagers' financial situation has its drawbacks as the unfortunate Jacob discovers. He challenges Sr. Herbert to several games of checkers in hopes of winning twenty dollars. In so doing he fails as a hustler just as Sr. Herbert fails as a philanthropist. Jacob loses a total of $5,742.23, and pays this debt by giving his house to Sr. Herbert who sleeps for centuries while the town continues unchanged.

The longest and most recent story in the collection, "La increíble y triste historia de la cándida Eréndira y de su abuela desalmada," appears here in its complete form for the first time. The epic style of its title indicates the far-reaching implications of the narrative's content. It is a combination of fairy tale, odyssey, novel of chivalry, and historical allegory. As a *cuento de hadas* [fairy tale], it portrays an imprisoned damsel who awaits deliverance by her lover. In a curious, modern way, however, García Márquez reverses the ending of the stereotyped model and thus puts to rest the myth of the heroic male and the passive, mindless heroine. "La increíble y triste historia" traces Eréndira's escape from bondage. Her grandmother holds her captive because she accidentally set afire their viceregal mansion. Eréndira pays off her debt with fees obtained from several years of prostitution. Finally, she motivates Ulises, who has fallen in love with her, to release her from debt and servitude by murdering her grandmother.

The resourceful protagonist, Eréndira, is the product of careful development throughout García Márquez's fiction. In "El mar del tiempo perdido," she is foreshadowed by a village prostitute who accepts one hundred lovers financed by Sr. Herbert. In his masterpiece *Cien años de soledad*, García Márquez creates the precise prototype of Eréndira in a mulatta who must erase a monumental debt to her grandmother for burning down their home:

[Since then her grandmother carried her from town to town, putting her to bed for twenty cents in order to make up the value of the burned house. According to the girl's calculations, she still had ten years of seventy men per night, because she also had to pay the expenses of the trip and food for both of them as well as the wages of the Indians who carried the rocking chair.]

Although prostitution is of minor importance in "El mar del tiempo perdido" and *Cien años de soledad*, it is central to "La increíble y triste historia." In the metaphor of prostitution the author describes the vast proportions of the exploitation of human liberty. As Eréndira serves her monopolistic grandmother, she embodies the frustration of individual and continental freedom. Exemplifying the theme of independence, Eréndira, once released from slavery by Ulises, runs into the desert and is never heard from again.

Despite the fact that García Márquez draws inspiration for his stories from the historical and political realities of his native land, nonetheless, in his work there are traces of the rich heritage of Spanish American fiction. Eréndira's tent of love recalls Vargas Llosa's *casa verde*. It is not mere coincidence that the hapless Ulises is called *cara de angel*, recalling Asturias' tragic protagonist of *El Señor Presidente*. Of course, García Márquez is the author of his own fictional tradition as his earlier works leave their resonance in this new collection.

In conclusion, while it is true that much of García Márquez's recent short fiction recapitulates themes and values of former works, *La increíble y triste historia* reflects the always fascinating world of extraordinary events which emanate from the familiar and everyday. Moreover, destroying the myth of material progress, the stereotype of individual heroism, and the convention of the subservient and ever-waiting woman, García Márquez's characters achieve a highly human significance. They reaffirm a vital impulse and undermine the myths that stifle human growth.

[Review of *Innocent Eréndira and Other Stories*]

Martin Kaplan*

García Márquez's fictional universe has the same staggeringly gratifying density and texture as Proust's Faubourg Saint-Germain and Joyce's Dublin. As his friend Mario Vargas Llosa said of *One Hundred Years of Solitude*, García Márquez's work is "in the tradition of those insanely ambitious creations which aspire to compete with reality on an equal basis, confronting it with an image and qualitatively matching it in vitality, vastness, and complexity." It is now just over a decade that García Márquez has been received as a world-class novelist. Since the death of Neruda he is arguably the best of the Latin Americans; as testimony from both the United States and Europe accumulates, his early reception as a great regional writer is giving way to a climate in which Proust and Joyce

*Reprinted from *New Republic* 179 (26 August 1978):44–46 by permission of the journal.

can be invoked by enthusiasts without worried sidelong glances at the critical pack.

The landmark, of course, is *One Hundred Years of Solitude*. The epic of the Buendía dynasty of Macondo, it is an utterly accessible novel that manages to combine irresistible anecdotal charm with breathtaking structural inventiveness — this, in a post-modernist jungle where perhaps the only quality admired by artists more tenaciously than "difficulty" is a knack for offending the audience. Since *One Hundred Years of Solitude*, only one major new work has appeared: *The Autumn of the Patriarch*. The book caught some Macondo cultists off guard. Its narrative mazes, its one-paragraph and one-sentence chapters, its absence of virtually any punctuation at all: these hurdles suggested to some disappointed readers that García Márquez was bucking for fashionable *nouveau roman* spurs.

But *The Autumn of the Patriarch* has also been welcomed as the necessary *Wake* of the Buendía Bloomsday. The book is really an ancient song, an oral myth about the toppling of a centuries-old Caribbean despot. Its story and structure giddily enact the eternal carnival of history; it dances the dialectic of *change and no change* without lapsing into the ideological self-righteousness of the one or the reactionary pucker of the other.

The remaining García Márquez fiction which Gregory Rabassa's exquisite translations have sent our way can be characterized by an embarrassingly simple rule of thumb: the later, the better. This is much the case for the new collection, *Innocent Eréndira and Other Stories*. The first half of the book — a novella and two stories — is superb, a new chance to enter the tent of the best conjurer in modern letters. The remaining nine stories in the collection, all dated between 1947 and 1953, are interesting archaeology, compelling mainly because they pander to the glimmers-of-greatness triumphs of literary hindsight.

The very first lines of "The Incredible and Sad Tale of Innocent Eréndira and Her Heartless Grandmother" are enough to signal our presence in Márquez-land: "Eréndira was bathing her grandmother when the wind of her misfortune began to blow. The enormous mansion of moonlike concrete lost in the solitude of the desert trembled down to its foundation with the first attack. But Eréndira and her grandmother were used to the risks of the wild nature there, and in the bathroom decorated with a series of peacocks and childish mosaics of Roman baths they scarcely paid any attention to the caliber of the wind." His writing — heady, secure, outrageous — is unmistakable. As always, when he is at his best, García Márquez blithely asks us to take as ordinary realism a story in which the touch of a lovesick boy turns glass objects blue, diamonds grow in oranges, and a glowing manta ray floats through the storm-heavy air.

Dated 1972, the novella tells of a 14-year-old whose grandmother sentences her to a life of prosperous nomadic prostitution as payment for accidentally fire-gutting the mansion. All the dazzling tricks that left readers of *One Hundred Years of Solitude* and *The Autumn of the Patriarch* saucer-eyed are also on display here: the false journalism that deploys precise detail to win belief in the most outlandish fictions; the perfect and economical set-dressing, from the childish Roman mosaics to "a convoy of slow covered trucks" whose only lights "were wreaths of colored bulbs which gave them the ghostly size of sleepwalking altars"; the great obsessions that permeate his sagas—solitude, destiny, repetition, illusion.

It is the same with "The Sea of Lost Time" (1961) and "Death Constant Beyond Love" (1970). García Márquez is fond of quoting Chesterton's claim that he could explain Catholicism starting from a pumpkin or a tramway. Whether García Márquez is telling of the time the sea smelled like roses and the gringo philanthropist came to town, or of a stunning black girl whose father fertilized his cauliflower patch with his first wife's quartered corpse, the same, seemingly inexhaustible devices and daimons are at work.

García Márquez is singing the same tale over and over, each time with extraordinary new characters. "Death Constant Beyond Love" is a perfect miniature of García Márquez's obsessions. "We are here for the purpose of defeating nature," says Senator Onésimo Sánchez in his reelection campaign. As he extends the politician's immemorial promises of manna and Mammon, his retinue plants prop trees with felt leaves in the saltpeter soil and covers the miserable real-life shacks with cardboard facades of brick and glass.

> When he saw that his fictional world was all set up, he pointed to it. "That's the way it will be for us, ladies and gentlemen," he shouted. "Look! That's the way it will be for us."
> The audience turned around. An ocean liner made of painted paper was passing behind the houses. . . .

The same senator recently learned that he would be dead before next Christmas. Happy and untouched by his sentence to mortality, he falls hopelessly and irrevocably in love.

Politics—like religion, art, and work—is a machine for denying the realities of time and death. Revolutions and routines are ideal ways to evade our fundamental isolation and wormy dénouements. But occasionally something pierces through the terribly important projects that consume and narcotize us, and we are touched at once by ecstasy and death. For Senator Onésimo Sánchez, it is the beauty of Laura Farina, daughter of the cauliflower murderer, that rescues him from the torpor of paper moons—and also condemns him to "Remember, he remembered, that whether it's you or someone else, it won't be long before you'll be dead and it won't be long before your name won't even be left."

The pumpkins and tramways of the rest of this collection also lead to solitude, the Catholicism of Márquez-land, but the journey is more contrived, more self-conscious, more obvious and earnest about courting our complicity in the shell-game of fiction. García Márquez's best work cares not at all about our complicity; it assumes it and plunges onward. "For me, literature is a very simple game, all the rules of which have to be accepted," he has said, and for the 20 years that he's stuck to that conviction he has beggared Houdini. The early stories, with their O. Henry punch lines, purple atmosphere, and "experimental" ambitions, are simply less fun — and less haunting — than the later work.

Gabriel García Márquez has discovered that the funniest thing about us is how we spend our lives figuring out ways to forget that we die. For García Márquez — who has worked both for J. Walter Thompson and Fidel Castro, and who recently devoured the memoirs of Jackie Onassis's chauffeur with evident pleasure — the comedy of this endlessly inventive self-blindness is more worth capturing than the tragic residue of our delusions. "Just imagine the disorder there'd be in the world if people found out about these things," the gringo philanthropist warns young Tobías after showing him the village with little white houses at the bottom of the sea.

The Posthumous Present

Paul West*

One way of setting the stage for comments on this engrossing new novel by García Márquez is to reaffirm that, in the English-speaking countries at any rate, the anti-style rabble is still with us, waiting to pounce, in its crypto-puritan fashion, on any piece of writing it thinks flashy, flamboyant, exhibitionistic, exaggerative, or voluptuous. The same goes for any writing that seems to draw attention to itself as distinct from its "content" (as if that rancid old dichotomy made any sense in the first place) or ventures, heaven forbid, into areas not "traditional" to the novel, such as science, instead of the ups and downs of little people with mortgages and fireplaces that leak smoke. Anyone who, as I have, has been called "pretentious" for involving his or her narrative with something as outrageous as the genetic code, will understand what's meant.

It's this. The novel has certainly come of age, but its readers by and large have not. I have written at length elsewhere[1] about the preposterous situation in which, through some unwritten agreement between pip-squeak readers and the pundits who pronounce *thou shalt nots* to them, thinking has nothing to do with art, certainly not with fiction, and the novelist is somehow duty-bound not to trespass into areas that form the domain of any intelligent mind. "The Milky Way!" exclaimed one novelist

*Reprinted from *Review* 18 (Fall 1976):76–78 with permission of the journal and the Center for Inter-American Relations.

of my acquaintance, upon being told I had written a novel making structural and thematic use of it, "I could only write about such a thing if a piece of it fell on my characters while they were in bed." Rather than try to argue with such hebetude, I content myself with the thought that whatever fell on them would be part of the Milky Way anyway and couldn't be anything else. Deep down, this attitude (if it has any depth at all) is homocentric or homo-chauvinist, quite failing to see that *homo sapiens* is special because he has occurred in a context that's unthinkably bigger than he is, or ever will be. Even in the third third of the twentieth century, with our robots working capably on Mars and at MIT a gene synthesized that is able to function inside a living cell, the parochialists insist that we do no more than rewrite The Forsyte Saga or *The Mill on the Floss* (I speak as one who writes in English, but I imagine Latin American novelists hear an equivalent litany). I can only say that such lack of a sense of wonder increases my own sense of wonder still further and makes me thankful for the novelists I do read (hardly any of them, any more, English or American), such as Claude Simon and Maurice Blanchot, and of course those I think of as composing the Latin American star team of ecumenical fiction: Cortázar, Carpentier, Donoso, and García Márquez himself.

Numerous reviewers will ferret out and paraphrase the so-called plot or story-line of *The Autumn of the Patriarch*, no doubt with the relief of those who sight a clean-shaven chin among a crowd of beards. I need only, for my purposes here, say that once upon a time (as well as under it, and through it, and beyond it, such is García Márquez's elastication of the arbitrary category called "event"), a dictator had a double who was assassinated. . . . What is supremely interesting here, and more so than anything in *One Hundred Years of Solitude*, is García Márquez's *modus operandi*, which a merely cursory description would have to call a voluptuous, thick, garish, centripetal weaving and re-weaving of quasi-narrative motifs that figure now as emblems, now as salient samples of all the stuff from which the world is made (at least the Caribbean one), now as earnests of a dominant presence who might be the dictator's wife Leticia, the dictator aping his double, the double aping the dictator's aping the double or the dead head of either or schoolgirls, or even an indeterminate chorus of voices all of whom have something to contribute to the burgeoning mythos of one distended career in honor of which, posthumously, someone created for him the rank of "general of the universe," with ten pips on the epaulette.

Hyperbole is the keynote, of course; even when it isn't on stage it is hovering, off, ready to be exploited. But what lodges in the mind after finishing the book is a technique I'd call horn-of-plenty bravura, not so much hyperboles amassed as Caribbean phenomena keenly registered non-stop, so that what you read is a flood, a crop, a spate, all the more poignant because, as often as not, it's the general's vision of "life without him," by and large going on as if he had never been. It's the copious version of Abram Tertz's austere one in *The Trial Begins*, when the character looks at the chair by his bed and sees that it will survive him, so he begins to loathe it. A great deal of García Márquez's book, therefore, is construable as posthumous present, with the constant implication that, insatiable as it is, the observing eye takes in the merest fraction of available phenomena and has to make do with, in fact, next to nothing.

Such is my own reading of this technique, at any rate. Crammed with data, the book is a bulging elegy for the unseen, the not-experienced. On the one hand, as we're told, he has seen the perfumed volcano of Martinique, the tuberculosis hospital, the gigantic black in lace blouse who sells bouquets of gardenias to governors' wives on the church steps, the "infernal market" of Paramaribo, the crabs that came from the sea into the toilets and onto the tables of the ice cream parlors, "the solid gold cows on Tanaguarena beach," the rebirth of Dutch tulips in the gasoline drums of Curaçao," the ocean liner that passed through the hotel kitchens of the city center, and much, unthinkably much, more. Isn't, someone asks him, the world large? And not just large but insidious as well? And "the whole universe of the Antilles" is a mere speck, although unassimilable. The evoked theme is ancient, a fusion of *carpe diem* and Husserl's "More than anything else the being of the world is obvious." Not that García Márquez lists things; he does, but he assembles them in such a pell-mell fashion that the movement from one item to the next becomes almost a narrative kinesis in its own right, while the items themselves, far from being mere entries in a stock-book, are epitomes of action: people, animals, plants, waves, clouds, captured in moments of characteristic and definitive doing. The effect is extraordinary, creating a textural narrative to counterpoint (even abolish) the story line that involves an air force, a league of nations, an assassination, and ambassadors Kipling, Palmerston, Maryland and Wilson to a tyrant aged between 107 and 232. Try to figure out what is happening and you end up with a better knowledge of event's context than of event itself. It just isn't that kind of novel. Its point is its precision-studded vagueness. Its content is a mentality, a sensibility. Its power is that of what I think radio technicians call side-band splash, when to receive one thing you must receive another. And that means the novel is all accretions, almost like a language being spoken century after century until, at some point, one asks: *What was Indo-European like? When?* What follows those questions is the work of sheerest hypothesis; such a proto-language must have been there spoken by such and such a people, maybe the Kurgan people around 3,000 B.C. Much the same applies to the plot of this novel: you have to move toward it through what it has generated, and when you get there it has gone, and you are encountering an hypothesis of your own.

So, then, this volcano of Proustian saliences is a demanding book to read, yet only as harvests are hard to swallow down. García Márquez's forte is that he always provides enough material in the next twenty syllables, and always in greater detail than most novelists can muster. Something Keatsian is going on here, in that he not only loads every rift with ore, he also evokes an obsolescent Hyperion trying to figure out why one set of gods has to give way to another. The book is an ode to "the uncountable time of eternity" that always comes to an end, whether we call it autumn or the general's reign. For example, we see this:

> Leticia Nazareno moved aside the herniated testicle to clean him up from the last love-making's dinky-poo, she submerged him in the lustral waters of the pewter bathtub with lion's paws and lathered him with *reuter* soap, scrubbed him with washcloths, and rinsed him off with the water of boiled herbs as they sang in duet ginger gibber and gentleman are all spelled with a gee, she would daub the joints of his legs with cocoa butter to alleviate the rash from his truss, she would put boric acid powder on the moldy star of his asshole and whack his behind like a tender mother for your bad manners with the minister from Holland,

Wrenched thus out of context and flow, it's not as effective as its reinstated version, but notice how the general, at once baby and sexually deformed adult meets the world's substances on a primitive level. In fact he is learning how to read and write at the same time as, in the world outside, the black vomit is thinning out the rural population, except that no one dares tell him. At almost any juncture in the book there are as many different things going on; the compound ghost of the narrator speaks with mouth full. An effect of marmoreal amplitude is what you end with, not least because this is a book of no paragraphs, few sentences, and many, many commas, all toward a cumulative surge of the whole, Beckettian in rhythm yet full of all the stuff that Beckett leaves out, Nabokovian in its appetizing abundance yet quite without his mincing, dandyistic sheen.

It is such a book as, at the lowest level, would teach a fiction student how to write, what to keep on doing; every sentence, every phrase, *has enough* in it. At a much higher level, it's a book which raises the ghost of something truly unnerving: the chance that, after all is said and done, literature has nothing to say, no message, no interpretation, no answer, but only a chance to catalogue what the senses find and cannot do without.

Note

1. "Sheer Fiction: Mind and the Fabulist's Mirage," *New Literary History*, Spring 1976.

Death among the Ruins

Stephen Koch*

In 1970 a long novel called *One Hundred Years of Solitude*, written by a previously admired, but ignored, Latin American short-story writer named Gabriel García Márquez, appeared in English translation. Though grounded in characteristic sources of Latin American fiction — most noticeably an intensely self-conscious awareness of modernist aesthetics (surrealism above all) in union with a marvelously vivid tradition of folkloristic storytelling — the book seemed to be in a class by itself. Page after page was so bizarre, so amazingly well written (even through the almost invisible veil of translation), so brilliantly conceived, that it was impossible to think of the book in routine terms. I remember my own introduction to it. An editor, over drinks, shoved the book my way and said: "Read the first sentence. Just the first sentence." I did, and I remember it still: "Many years later, as he faced the firing squad, Colonel Aureliano Buendía was to remember that distant afternoon when his father took him to discover ice."

Everything to come sustains the promise of that first sentence. The book is a masterpiece. Passing through the generations of a mythic family in the hot isolation of the semitropics, it is a saga possessed throughout by an elegant, baroque conception of narrative time and of the passage of the years; a conception adumbrated by the stunning narrative trigonometry of that first sentence's three-point location in the unnamed event to which the firing squad comes "later"; the moment before death; and the childhood memory of the little boy from the semitropics discovering ice, to him a wonder.

And now the much-awaited *Autumn of the Patriarch*, the book on which García Márquez has been working since *One Hundred Years of Solitude*, has appeared. In fairness to García Márquez and the reader, this book ought to be discussed outside the context of its predecessor. It seems a bore, not to say unjust, to keep turning the pages with the thought: This is not *One Hundred Years of Solitude*.

It is not. It is quite different — not quite as exciting but nonetheless a creditable and remarkable performance in its own terms. Yet for all its obvious difference *Autumn of the Patriarch* is artistically, formally, a companion volume to *One Hundred Years of Solitude*, a companion in contrast, an alternative in a rich artistic vision and dilemma.

In contrast to the first book's elegant elaboration on time's passage, *Autumn of the Patriarch* obliterates the sense of time in a series of verbal whirlwinds moving around a set of obsessional images. These are images of brutal power and of the fear of death expressed variously by and about a Latin American dictator who is found dead in his presidential palace. No

*Reprinted from *Saturday Review*, 11 December 1976, 68–69. © 1976 *Saturday Review* magazine. Reprinted by permission.

one knows how long he has been dead; vultures are picking at his corpse; the palace is in ruins; pigs and chickens wander in the collapsing corridors. He has been a kind of Collier brother of autocracy. For years — centuries, it seems — he has ruled, his story lost in myth. He has lived among dogs and guards and dodges and plots. He has been glimpsed only through the windows of carriages and limousines, a brute surrounded by tawdry magnificence. In a Joycean delirium of language and associations, the novel proceeds to swirl around and through the megalomania of power, the strategies, the brutalities, the myths, and the hysteria of his endless, his timeless, reign of gloom. In the process García Márquez creates an intensely suggestive structure of meanings that radiate outward from the mythic general's struggle to let absolutely *nothing* change in his war against death.

The Joycean manner has shipwrecked more than one first-rate practitioner, but García Márquez never loses mastery for a moment, and one is easily swept into his torrential invocations of autocracy and folklore and history and superstition. In the Joycean manner (it is here that Gregory Rabassa's seamless translation is, to my ear at least, most remarkable), his prose moves easily back and forth from gutter talk to the highest high style, and the political and spiritual ironies and passions resonate continuously. García Márquez himself seems almost delirious with his own incantatory prowess, and the cornucopia of his talent seems never to fail. Yet it is possible for the manner to pall. The pace and rhythm of *One Hundred Years of Solitude* were astonishingly varied. In the new book, the Joycean sentence assumes a slow, unchanging single beat and frequently rolls on for twenty pages at a time. Because the prose lacks the energy of the full stop, a certain slack monotony can and does sometimes set in. The sentence becomes a kind of vacuum cleaner of vividness, endlessly sucking one along.

Yet all of that is part of García Márquez's entire vision, and even if it is a weakness, one should not complain too much. In a typical late-modernist manner, he is obsessed with the problem of real life in the real world of real time, and of the solitude (that solitude mentioned in his great title) of the isolated imagination, intoxicated by itself. In contrast to the lush absorption in time's texture presented in his first novel, *Autumn of the Patriarch* finds its form in a brilliant delirium of language and finds its content in a crazed, comic megalomania of power that tries to hold off forever the natural processes of life, history, time itself. The ripples from that crackbrained static center spread everywhere: to politics and to what García Márquez seems to see as Latin America's war against history; to sex, with the general's mad notions about love and manhood; to the spiritual and emotional life; and to the obsession with control. Moving slowly through 100 years of solitude, García Márquez delivered himself over, paradoxically enough, to this solipsistic ecstasy, and if his new novel is in many ways a lesser achievement, it nonetheless would seem to have kept him true to himself, for it reads like a brilliant exorcism of that dilemma. When the corpse of that self-infatuated old man is finally cleared away, García Márquez speaks, on his final page, about the "crowds who took to the streets singing hymns of joy at the jubilant news of his death and . . . the rockets of jubilation . . . that announced to the world the good news that the uncountable time of eternity had come to an end."

The Solitude of Power   Ronald De Feo*

Though he is one of the wittiest and most exhilarating of contemporary Latin American writers, García Márquez has repeatedly created characters who live, to varying degrees, in a state of solitude. From the earliest work, *Leaf Storm*, to the wonderful novella *No One Writes to the Colonel*, to the masterwork *One Hundred Years of Solitude*, we find people existing not only in spiritual isolation but in physical isolation as well: Macondo, the author's miraculous mythical town—the setting of much of his work—has been "condemned" to solitude, and indeed is so remote from the rest of the world that it possesses its very own laws of nature and logic.

The Autumn of the Patriarch (which has been superbly translated by Gregory Rabassa) is García Márquez' most intense and extreme vision of isolation. In this fabulous, dream-like account of the reign of a nameless dictator of a fantastic Caribbean realm, solitude is linked with the possession of absolute power. The author has worked with this theme before—notably when tracing the career and increasing loneliness of Colonel Aureliano Buendía in *One Hundred Years of Solitude*—but here it receives the grand treatment.

Yet the book is in no way a case history or a psychological portrait of a dictator. It is, rather, a rendering in fantastic and exaggerated terms of a particular condition of might and isolation. As such, it is essentially plotless, though it is stuffed with enough anecdotes and incidents for several novels. When, at the beginning of the book, an unidentified party breaks into the decaying presidential palace and discovers the lichen-covered body of the patriarchal general who has governed the country for well over two centuries, a flood of memories of his incredible reign is released, and it is these memories, both collective and individual, flowing in free-associative, temporally jumbled repetition, that form the entire novel.

*Reprinted from *National Review* 29, no. 20 (27 May 1977):620–22. Copyright National Review, Inc., 150 E. 35th St., New York, N.Y. 10016. Reprinted with permission.

As the holder of absolute power, García Márquez' patriarch is the dictator to end all dictators. He continues in his role year after year, decade after decade, surviving betrayals by aides, plots against him, assassination attempts. His personal make-up is such that he is still able to rule, to cultivate "the solitary vice of power," while fully aware of the deceivers all around him and after learning of the brutal murder of his family. He controls his world so completely that he can easily transform a slum into a suburban paradise (simply to gratify a special woman), rig the national lottery so that he will always win, alter television soap operas so that they will reflect happiness instead of gloom, even sell the Caribbean Sea to North American buyers.

And yet the stronger the general grows, the more removed from humanity and truth he becomes. The novel is studded with images of him securing his door at night (lowering three cross-bars, locking three locks, throwing three bolts). He often seems to be in limbo, marking time as he waits for an end that refuses to come. We are told at one point that he would spend time with his double (who served as a target for potential assassins) "watching it rain, counting swallows on languid September afternoons like two aged lovers, so far removed from the world that he himself did not realize that his fierce struggle to exist twice was feeding the contrary suspicion that he was existing less and less."

No summary or description of this book can really do it justice, for it is not only the author's surrealistic flights of imagination that make it such an exceptional work, but also his brilliant use of language, his gift for phrasing and description. As with *One Hundred Years of Solitude*, the reader is repeatedly surprised by the grace and ease with which an image is recorded, a phrase is turned.

And yet one must note, regretfully, that for all its brilliance *The Autumn of the Patriarch* is a difficult book to stay with for an extended length of time, difficult not because of the sentences that run on for pages or the absence of paragraphs, but because of an overabundance of riches. At times, the marvelous details accumulate so rapidly that the reader is simply overwhelmed by them. He seeks relief, a subdued passage in which to rest, but the author does not accord him that opportunity. At times, García Márquez' passion for inflation causes him to create a tale that is, even in a fantastic context, a shade too strained and whimsical — such as the account of the two thousand children kidnapped by the government to prevent them from revealing their role in the general's crooked lottery.

Still, of course, it is that very same passion for the absurd and the exaggerated that is responsible for the innumerable grand, witty passages we find — for example, the general discovering the hidden sentiments of his staff through the graffitti in the palace bathroom, or the account of a traitor who is served as a main course to the general's staff ("Major General Rodrigo de Aguilar entered on a silver tray stretched out on a garnish of cauliflower and laurel leaves . . . embellished with the uniform of five golden almonds for solemn occasions"). Here and elsewhere throughout this unique, remarkable novel, the tall tale is transformed into a true work of art.

Truth Is Stranger Than Fact   Edith Grossman*

Thirty years ago, the town of Sucre, Colombia, was rocked by a crime that touched many of the people García Márquez had known in his youth: a newly-wed husband returned his bride to her parents because he discovered on their wedding night that she was not a virgin. The girl was forced to name her lover, who was then hunted down and murdered by her brother. The people involved—bride, brother, groom, lover, their families and the witnesses to the murder—were long-time friends, neighbors or kin of García Márquez who, after a lapse of three decades, finally wrote the unbelievable novel that the incredible crime demanded, saying that the death of his friend, the presumptive lover, had hurt him more than his teeth do now. The novelist claims he has extirpated the pain with his latest book, *Crónica de una muerte anunciada* (Chronicle of an Announced Death, Bogotá: La Oveja Negra, 1981).

One of the effects of its widely publicized first printing was an avalanche of reporters who poured into Sucre to interview the surviving protagonists in this bloody provincial drama. Numerous articles appeared in Latin American newspapers documenting the memories, the feelings, the thoughts of the people left behind in the wake of a sensational murder and scandal.

Some readers have expressed disappointment in *Crónica*. . . . They complain that García Márquez has used the techniques of yellow journalism to create suspense, that the novel's phenomenal success (over a million copies in the first printing) is the direct result of an easily renewed interest in the notorious thirty-year-old crime that is its subject, and that the public's expectations have been unduly heightened by García Márquez's past successes as well as by his six year silence. But the question of the relationship between history and the imagination in literature has noble antecedents that go back to Aristotle's mimetic theory—his notion that literature could express a more ideal image of experience, one that is shaped by the author's creative ordering of parts so that the whole is made to seem necessary, probable, coherent. Once this connection between fact and fiction had been suggested, and despite the mysteries of its dynamic, it was only a matter of time and the translation of the *Poetics* into Latin:

*Reprinted from *Review* 30 (September–December 1981):71–73, by permission of the journal, and the Center for Inter-American Relations.

the novel, the "new genre" that emerged during the European Renaissance, would bond those apparent polarities into a union that has on occasion been frayed but has never been completely torn asunder.

Cervantes saw the possibilities of that ambiguous union, and his comic vision gave birth to the modern novel. He forged his ingenious mimetic verisimilitude out of the novelistic documentation of an environment localized in time and space and teeming with a historical specificity of events, places and people. These he mingled (no hard demarcations or differentiations here) with the brilliant characters and actions of his fictive imagination. Don Quixote and Sancho may be universal and fictional, but the world they travel through is eminently particular and actual.

From that time on novelists have succumbed to the siren call luring them to the treatment of history as if it were fiction and fiction as if it were history — to the ideal ordering of reality and the creation of an apparent reality within the fictional. At the heart of the Western realistic tradition, and perhaps at the very heart of the novel itself, is an image of a history and a fiction that occupy the same planes in a literary diorama. Over and over again writers have made real places, historical events and actual people the very stuff of their novels. They have dipped into the pool of our common experience, perhaps to confound the reader, to convince us that imagined events, places and people are (or could be) real, perhaps to novelize and order the factual in order to understand its apparent chaos. Tolstoy first read of Anna Karenina's suicide in the newspapers, Dos Passos and Doctorow have known the charms of the chronicle-*cum*-novel, Capote and Mailer have intentionally blurred the distinction between journalism and the novel with so much success that neologisms have been created to generically describe their works.

Oriana Fallaci, who wrote of her relationship with Alekos Panagulis in *A Man*, has insisted that her book is a novel, not a memoir: "The novel is a story pulled away from the chronicle and rebuilt in an enlarged truth . . . . a construction where reality is re-invented; the memoir is an account where every particular must be given as it really happened. . . . A novel doesn't need to tell all; the memoir must. . . ."[1]

In *Crónica de una muerte anunciada*, García Márquez has also reinvented a reality that was part of his own lived experience, using as the basis for his book events so real and so historically specific that current photographs of the people involved, their present-day reactions to the crime, and their explanation of motives thirty years after the fact have actually appeared in newspapers published in 1981. Ambiguous as always, García Márquez has written a mystery turned inside out (from the beginning, the reader knows the identity of the victim and the murderers; the names of the real-life protagonists have been changed to protect the innocent, but we know who the innocent — and the guilty — are). Ambiguous as always, he has called his work a chronicle and published it as a novel, but beware: he has also called the history of Latin America as recorded in the chronicles of the Spanish conquerors an unbelievable, imaginative, almost legendary tale. Ambiguous as always, he stresses the deep relationship between the reporter's copy and the novelist's manuscript, between journalism (the modern chronicle) and fiction: "For the first time I have managed a perfect integration of journalism and literature . . . journalism helps maintain contact with reality, which is essential to literature. And vice versa: literature teaches you how to write. . . . I learned how to be a journalist by reading good literature."[2]

With all the sensational trappings of the latest tabloid scandal (a crime of passion, pruriently vivid details of bloody violence, men and women living by the wrathful dictates of machista moralism, furtive sexuality looming in the background, and even a good-hearted prostitute) García Márquez toys with the historicity of the events he narrates. In a time game that would seem almost Cervantine if it were not actually true, García Márquez does in this novel what journalists actually did after the publication of *Crónica* . . . : with a point of view that is far from omniscient, the narrator / author plays the role of investigative reporter, interviewing those who knew the victim and the murderers and who saw the crime, for significantly, and as if to throw further doubt on the reliability of history and its historians, the narrator is not an eye-witness to the crime. He even indicates that there is more than one version of how things "really" were on that bloody day in Sucre some thirty years ago. The Cervantine resonances are in no way fortuitous: remember that the "real" author of *Don Quixote* is in fact the Arab Cidi Hamete Benengeli, and everyone knows, Cervantes reminds us, what liars the Arabs are.

Not quite reliable history, the distortion of misremembered events, communal moralism, sex and death — these are the raw material of legend in the Latin America ironically chronicled by García Márquez: history is unreal, chroniclers cannot distinguish between the actual and the mythical, anachronism is a fundamental truth, and the marvelous and the sordid reign in a bitterly comic partnership. In this semi-legendary place that the author invents rather than documents, journalism is as ambivalent as the oral tradition or the conquerors' histories: it creates legendary figures who emerge to play a scene on the stage of history and then return to the shadows of myth. In this novel / chronicle García Márquez has imposed an Aristotelian ordering of events that presupposes the existence of an ineluctable fate of mythic proportions. In contrast to the gratuitousness of the actual murder of Cayetano Gentile Chimento, the Santiago Nasar of the novel, in *Crónica* . . . there is a chorus of onlookers who know that the Vicario brothers will disembowel the alleged lover of their sister Ángela. They know, but they do nothing to prevent the murder, to stop the brothers, to warn the victim, for how can they interfere with what has already been determined by Fate and the demanding Furies of honor and machismo? Not even Zeus had the power to deny destiny.

To my mind, the important question is not whether García Márquez has engaged in a facile confusion of genres, but rather how he has reshaped the reality of historical events and people and altered them with his uniquely comic and mythic touch. How is the fiction different from the fact?

Consider the figure of the bridegroom, whose wounded sexual pride and machista ethic are the catalyst for a drama of honor avenged that would have astounded even Calderón de la Barca. In the novel his name is Bayardo San Román. He is romantic and exotic. He has golden eyes and private reasons for coming to town. He is the prototypical mysterious stranger who is wealthy and wildly attractive, whose origins and destination are unknown. When someone finally asks him the purpose of his visit, he answers: "I've been going from town to town looking for someone to marry!" The narrator comments: "It might have been the truth, but he could just as easily have said something else, since he had a way of speaking that hid more than it told."[3] San Román claims to be an engineer, but he is an expert telegraph operator, has wide medical knowledge, is a champion swimmer, and even takes communion (a fact that the narrator's mother notes with satisfaction, although she also says he reminds her of the devil). He drinks but never brawls, and the townspeople guess that he is a soldier of fortune, a bear tamer, a diver for buried treasure. The "truth" is always unbelievable in the world of García Márquez: he is the son of General Petronio San Román, the hero of the conservative forces who defeated Colonel Aureliano Buendía at the battle of Tucurinca; his mother is Alberta Simonds, a mulatto who had once been declared the most beautiful woman in the Antilles. The wedding is an expensive, extravagant, boozy feast that turns into a public celebration. Finally, when San Román returns his bride to her mother, his only words are a quiet, "Thank you for everything, Mother . . . You are a saint,"[4] followed by an astonishing kiss on his mother-in-law's cheek.

Bayardo San Román is a princely figure—a cowboy hero, a knight, an adventurer. His real-life counterpart, Miguel Reyes Palencia, is an insurance agent with twelve children. Born in Sucre, he was, according to a newspaper interview, the victim's friend, classmate and drinking companion. His action caused the death of Cayetano Gentile, but Reyes Palencia has no regrets. All the justification he needs for what he did is the statement that he thought he was marrying a "decent woman." He drank so much at his own wedding that he passed out, and the couple could not begin their sexual encounter until dawn; when he discovered that his bride was not a virgin, he abused her verbally and physically, hitting her and throwing her against the wall. After he returned Margarita (in the novel Ángela Vicario) to her parents, he went to the house of friends, to whom he told the entire story with no redeeming reticence. They gave him a knife so that he could kill her. To his credit he refused, saying he was not a murderer, but later he offered her the knife with the recommendation that she do the job herself. He was able to pardon her, he explains today, because Cayetano had already been killed, even though Margarita was the one who should have died. He was, he thinks, "as good a catch" as Cayetano. Thirty years after his indirect involvement in the murder of his life-long friend, this comment and the statement that he has always been sorry that Cayetano had to die are the only indications of doubt, his only responses that are not self-congratulatory, not imbued with the monolithic moralism of machismo.[5]

The Miguel Reyes Palencia of the newspaper interview is a small-town bourgeois with the soul and the pride of a bantam rooster. The Bayardo San Román of *Crónica . . .* is the Demon Lover whose arrogance is almost acceptable. Only he could have received a letter each month for twenty-three years from his bride—letters that he never answered and never opened—and then finally have appeared on her patio saying: "All right. Here I am," and carrying a suitcase full of thousands of her unopened love letters.[6] This is the stuff of comic legend. But Miguel Reyes Palencia only saw Margarita, the bride, to have her sign the annulment papers and then, many years later, to discuss her financial problems (he does not explain why she came to him for advice).

The provincial suitor expected to marry a girl as faithful to the double standard as he was. García Márquez has transformed the substance and the spirit of Reyes Palencia's character and has retained only the skeletal outline of his place in the drama and the significance of his actions: the absolute arrogance and hard insensitivity required to return a bride to the place of purchase as if she were defective merchandise. Beyond that lies the undeniable glamor of the fictional San Román, the laconic mystery that surrounds him, the suggestion that he, like the Flying Dutchman, has wandered endlessly looking for the faithful woman, only to be deceived, only to return more than two decades later in a parody of eternal romance.

Comparable alterations have been made in other characters and other events: the number of avenging brothers, the fictional visit of the bishop, the splendor and duration of the wedding, the house where the couple spent their ill-fated wedding night. In each case the fictional version expands, heightens and enlarges the panorama of figures and events so that potential legend seems to hover in the background. Still the action is familiar, the mad humor recognizable, the plot and its denouement known from the beginning. García Márquez holds onto the journalistic details, the minutiae of the factual, that constitute the great novelistic inheritance of Western realism, and at the same time throws doubt on their reliability through his narrative technique and by means of the subtle introduction of mythic elements. Once again García Márquez is an ironic chronicler who dazzles the reader with uncommon blendings of fantasy, fable and fact.

Notes

1. "A Conversation with Oriana Fallaci," PEN American Center Newsletter, no. 47, September 1981, pp. 4–5.

2. Francisco Fajardo, "El último opus de García Márquez," *La Mañana* (Montevideo) May 10, 1981, no page numbers (translation mine).

3. Gabriel García Márquez, *Crónica de una muerte anunciada* (Bogotá: La Oveja Negra, 1981), p. 37 (translation mine).

4. *Crónica* . . ., p. 64 (translation mine).

5. Graciela Romero, "García Márquez. Fui testigo del crimen," *Hoy* (Chile), August 12–18, 1981, pp. 37–38 (translation mine).

6. *Crónica* . . ., p. 125 (translation mine).

Articles and Essays

William Faulkner and Gabriel García Márquez: Two Nobel Laureates

Harley D. Oberhelman*

William Faulkner and Gabriel García Márquez are two of the most important seminal novelists to appear on the literary horizon of North and South America respectively in the twentieth century. Both have been translated into the major languages of Europe, thereby achieving broad international respect and acclaim from many corners of the globe. Numerous literary prizes have been bestowed on both writers, with the Nobel Prize for Literature awarded to Faulkner in 1950 and to García Márquez in 1982 certainly the most significant.

At about the time Faulkner was preparing to make the journey to Stockholm to receive the Nobel award, Gabriel García Márquez was beginning an uncertain career in journalism and creative writing on the Caribbean coast of his native Colombia. Forced to abandon his law studies in Bogotá due to the violence which followed the assassination on 9 April 1948 of the Liberal leader Jorge Eliécer Gaitán, García Márquez moved to Cartagena, where he was first introduced to the mysterious land of Yoknapatawpha County. There, and later in Barranquilla, he was to begin an assiduous and at times frustrating study of the lion of North American letters. Friends and mentors in Cartagena and Barranquilla were to guide him in this pursuit, and his novels and short stories of this early period are imbued with the presence of Faulkner.

Beneath the flow of thirty years of writing fiction, the evidence of Faulkner's presence is apparent in varying degrees. It is most evident in certain early short stories, in *La hojarasca*, to a degree in *Cien años de soledad*, and — at least stylistically — in *El otoño del patriarca*. Faithful to the roots of their native soil, both Faulkner and García Márquez are dedicated to the revelation of the struggle of human beings against social and material decadence, the common lot dealt to all in Yoknapatawpha County and Macondo. Both writers show a hostility to "intellectuals" and critics and prefer to allow their writings to speak for them. Although both

*This essay was written specifically for this volume and appears here for the first time by permission of the author.

have granted interviews and engaged in public discussions of their works, these remarks are at times misleading and contradictory.

Donald McGrady's 1972 study was the first to point out the Faulknerian techniques used in García Márquez's early short stories. These works are frequently discounted by critics as short stories of minor importance that deal primarily with death and irrational states of mind. McGrady, however, points out definite relationships between such stories as "Nabo, el negro que hizo esperar a los ángeles" (1951) and *The Sound and the Fury*. Both employ multiple points of view and chronologically move from a point in time near the end of the action backward and forward without any discernible temporal pattern. Various stories are carried on simultaneously, and only at the end do all the pieces fit together into a unified tale. Nabo, one of García Márquez's few black protagonists, is in charge of an idiot girl; Versh, and later Luster, have identical roles in relation to the idiot Benjy, the stream-of-consciousness narrator of the first section of *The Sound and the Fury*. Benjy's sense of smell is related to his older sister Caddy, who "smells like trees" as a child but who upsets Benjy as she grows up and begins to use perfume. Nabo has a similar acute sense of smell for the odors of the stable that he tends.

"La otra costilla de la muerte," published in 1948 shortly after García Márquez arrived in Cartagena, gives further evidence of Faulkner's early presence in his fiction. Here García Márquez inserts fragments of past recollections within the framework of interior monologues written in the present tense. Although James Joyce may be ultimately responsible for this approach to writing, Faulkner made almost constant use of the same technique in most of his major works. In the short stories published by García Márquez before 1955, the vague silhouette of Macondo and of its inhabitants begins to take shape. Although Antonio Olier traces the first pages of *La hojarasca* to an obscure corner of the *El Universal* newspaper office where García Márquez worked from 1948 to 1949,[1] McGrady points out four short stories called the La Sierpe series, which appeared in *El Espectador* in 1954 as a preview of Macondo as it was to appear in later fiction.[2] The dates of original publication of all of these first stories have been established, but it must be remembered that many of them were written during earlier years. The central figure of the La Sierpe series is La Marquesita, in many ways the prototype of Mamá Grande and Úrsula Buendía, Macondo's greatest matriarchs. Immensely wealthy, La Marquesita de la Sierpe ruled with an iron hand and with the help of the devil over ["a legendary country inland from the Atlantic coast of Colombia"].[3] The costumbristic details of magic spells and ageless despots in the tropical coastal region clearly prefigure *La hojarasca, Los funerales de la Mamá Grande, Cien años de soledad*, and *El otoño del patriarca*. In 1955, with the publication of *La hojarasca*, García Márquez's own Yoknapatawpha County was ready to emerge as a vehicle for some of his most significant statements regarding the human comedy.

With good reason, *La hojarasca* is considered by most critics to be García Márquez's most Faulknerian novel. Written during the years he spent on the Caribbean coast, it shows the plot pattern and style of the author of *As I Lay Dying*. In its creation of a fictional setting based on the realities of the Aracataca region, one can see the presence of *The Hamlet*, the first novel to be read by the Grupo de Barranquilla. The three long, intercalated monologues recall the narrators of *The Sound and the Fury*, and the moral and economic pillage of Macondo by the North American banana company is reminiscent of the carpetbaggers who invaded Jefferson and Yoknapatawpha County in *The Unvanquished* and *Absalom, Absalom!* The axis around which the memories of the past swirl in *La hojarasca* is the body of a mysterious French doctor whose strange and defiant actions caused great hostility in Macondo. The vicissitudes of burying the body of a prominent or controversial figure were to appear frequently in García Márquez's later fiction, but the archetypal burial sequence in Faulkner is the struggle to overcome the forces of fire and flood in *As I Lay Dying* so that Addie Bundren's family can transport her remains to Jefferson for interment according to her wishes. There is a pervasive feeling of solitude that dominates all of the action of *La hojarasca*, and the title itself suggests the idea of decadence and decay. This mood is frequently present in Faulkner as he describes the disintegration of the South which later generations attempt to expiate. Both Yoknapatawpha County and Macondo bear the scars of prior civil strife, and both contain enigmas that are insoluble.

La hojarasca is developed through a series of twenty-eight monologues by three characters attending a wake for the doctor, an unnamed recluse who appeared in Macondo twenty-five years earlier. The three narrators are Isabel, an abandoned mother; her father, a retired colonel who is highly respected in Macondo; and Isabel's ten-year-old son. The action of the novel is centered on the colonel's determination to carry out a promise made three years earlier to give the doctor a decent burial. There is great opposition on the part of the inhabitants—especially the mayor and the new priest—inasmuch as the doctor had refused to care for the wounded men brought to his door years ago during a local political confrontation. The promise of a decent burial informs the novel in much the same manner that Anse Bundren's promise to his wife that he would take her body to Jefferson to be buried with her kin creates the framework of Faulkner's novel.

As I Lay Dying is made up of the thoughts and feelings of fifteen characters, whereas only three relate their stories and memories in *La hojarasca*. In both bodies, the process of physical deterioration is parallel to exterior natural and emotional forces that react against the "decent" burial. Natural disasters confronting the Bundrens are accentuated by Darl, the second son, who feels broken and rejected and suffers mental disintegration following his mother's death. His anguish leads him to attempt to burn the barn where Addie's body is temporarily resting, but Jewel, Addie's illegitimate son, rescues the body. The colonel "rescues" the doctor's body from those in Macondo who still hold revenge in their hearts. The novel closes as the doors of the doctor's house open, and the casket emerges into the afternoon light. The novel ends here, and the reaction of the town's inhabitants is never related. The suggestion that violence may follow is present, and it is violence that dominates the atmosphere of many subsequent short stories and novels published by García Márquez after 1955. This atmosphere is described by José Stevenson in the following fashion: ["We see the assimilated influence of Faulkner, but already in a mature stylistic personality that aspires to dominate form and harvest new directions. In those languid, parsimonious monologues which spring from within subjects rooted in a pueblo where nothing happens, where time and progress have stopped, we hear the angry echo of the shipwreck of certain values: love, loyalty, fidelity; fear and, finally, hate are sentiments that seem to continue after death"].[4]

The dramatic tension apparent in both works is derived from a social conflict between one's ethical sense of responsibility (the burial promise) and societal pressures to allow emotional reactions to intervene. The end result is what J. G. Cobo Borda calls ["the fatal curse destined to be inherited until it is absorbed in some way"].[5] This condemnation of the South and of Macondo continues throughout the fiction of both authors. Regional history is the backdrop for both writers, but after *La hojarasca*, García Márquez gradually places historical events in a mythical perspective. Macondo becomes more ahistorical and offers its creator greater freedom of development. Yoknapatawpha County, on the other hand, remains firmly within an historical (although fictional) context. García Márquez ultimately destroyed Macondo, but death denied Faulkner the opportunity to describe Yoknapatawpha County's doomsday.

Only from the vantage point of his later novels is a retrospective assessment of Faulkner's impact on *La hojarasca* possible. Macondo existed in embryonic form before the appearance of García Márquez's first novel. While still in Barranquilla, he frequently made reference to a work called "La casa," which was never published with that title. "La casa" was an ambitious attempt that was later to produce *La hojarasca* and ultimately *Cien años de soledad*. García Márquez developed this relationship in dialogue with Mario Vargas Llosa when he stated: ["*Leaf Storm* was the first book that I published when I saw that I couldn't write *One Hundred Years of Solitude*. And now I realize that the real precursor of *One Hundred Years of Solitude* is *Leaf Storm*, and in between are *No One Writes to the Colonel*, the stories of *Big Mama's Funeral*, and *In Evil Hour*"].[6] He continues with the statement that as the Colombian political situation began to deteriorate, his level of political consciousness began to identify him more closely with the national drama.

El coronel no tiene quien le escriba, *La mala hora*, and certain short stories in *Los funerales de la Mamá Grande* corroborate this statement. Neither of the novels is set in Macondo, but the title story and two others in *Los funerales* do continue the development of Macondo. The novels take place in an unnamed town called "el pueblo" and recall geographical details of the river port of Sucre where García Márquez's parents lived for a time after leaving Aracataca. The creation of a new milieu for these works may correspond to an effort on the part of the novelist to free himself from the Faulknerian tag which was so often given to *La hojarasca*. Many critics felt that the first novel fell into a Faulknerian trap and that García Márquez failed to demonstrate the profound human vision Faulkner accomplished in the Yoknapatawpha cycle. In any case, the second and third novels are quite different from *La hojarasca* and do not represent a continuation of the chaos and lack of discipline sometimes associated with the Faulknerian influences in the first novel.

Los funerales de la Mamá Grande is a traditional work, yet Agustín Rodríguez Garavito sees in it ["the always present influence of . . . (and) the literary model of Faulkner"].[7] It is not the style or the use of multiple narrators that occasioned this observation, but rather the emergence of reappearing characters, family clans, and recurring episodes that show a continuing presence of Faulkner's method. Colonel Aureliano Buendía, certainly García Márquez's most fully developed character, is mentioned in many of these novels and short stories, and the Montiel, Asís, and Buendía families emerge to parallel the Sartoris, Compson, and Snopes families of Yoknapatawpha County. Emir Rodríguez Monegal asserts that "A Rose for Emily," translated into Spanish in Cartagena in 1949, is most certainly a model for many of the stories in the Mamá Grande series.[8] There are close parallels between this story and many of the stories in *Los funerales de la Mamá Grande*. Miss Emily Grierson's death and the subsequent discovery in her decaying house of the decomposed body of her lover, Homer Barron, are analogous to "La viuda de Montiel" and "Un día después del sábado," both of which describe widows living in solitude, isolation, and spiritual poverty. Resistance to the will of authority, as demonstrated by Miss Emily's refusal to pay local taxes, recalls the dignity and inner strength of the mother and her daughter who arrive in Macondo to lay flowers on the grave of her son, accused and subsequently shot for attempted robbery. "La siesta del martes," which relates this event, is one of the best stories in the collection. "Un día después del sábado," also set in Macondo, introduces two other motifs—a plague of dying birds, which suggests to the village priest the approach of the apocalypse, and the vision of the Wandering Jew—that recur in *Cien años de soledad*.[9]

These short stories are valuable in that they form links with *La hojarasca* as well as with future novels to be published by García Márquez. The doctor in the first novel, who commits suicide in the same house in which he lived with the Indian servant Meme, and the colonel, who is determined to bury him properly, recall the details of "A Rose for Emily" and "La siesta del martes." The five short stories set in "el pueblo" suggest incidents and delineate characters later to appear in *La mala hora*, a novel steeped in "la violencia" that swept over Colombia after the 1948 assassination of Jorge Eliécer Gaitán. "Un día de estos," the second story in the collection, appears in altered form in *La mala hora*, as do the incidents described in "La viuda de Montiel" and "Rosas artificiales."

"Los funerales de la Mamá Grande" is the longest and most significant work in the collection. It is a pivotal story, precursory of the future form of García Márquez's novels, *Cien años de soledad* and *El otoño del patriarca*. Mamá Grande, the matriarch of Macondo, is a legendary figure whose power reaches even the Vatican and whose illness and death shake the very foundations of the nation and of the ecclesiastical world. Satire and gross hyperbole accompany the rhetorical style used to describe in mythical terms the demise of a social and economic order. Macondo moves from a historical realm as seen in *La hojarasca* into a timeless myth in "Los funerales de la Mamá Grande." This process will reach its climax in *Cien años de soledad*, where the apocalypse, vaguely perceptible in "Un día después del sábado," is finally realized. The matriarchal Mamá Grande is a prototype of the strong female characters who inhabit Macondo and who are the "glue" that holds together the pieces of Faulkner's Yoknapatawpha County. The reverse side of the coin is apparent in the title of *El otoño del patriarca*, but here the patriarch is a straw demon, feared by those who rarely see him, and ultimately a victim of the very reign of terror he so carefully designed.

With *Los funerales de la Mamá Grande*, the stage is set for *Cien años de soledad*, García Márquez's most successful novel. Here the maturity of the Colombian novelist is most evident, and Macondo achieves its broadest mythical dimensions before its final destruction. The magical realism through which its characters move is very different from Yoknapatawpha County. Yet at this stage it is possible to compare two writers at their prime who use similar techniques and motifs, different literary styles, and their own unique versions of particular myths.

With the 1967 publication of *Cien años de soledad* and its unprecedented popularity in Spanish America, Europe, and the United States, García Márquez passed from the ranks of obscure secondary writers of contemporary Spanish American fiction to the spotlight of critical attention and furor of public interest. Following the initial success of *Cien años*, critics began to evaluate such earlier works as *La hojarasca*, *Los funerales de la Mamá Grande*, *La mala hora*, and *El coronel no tiene quien le escriba* in terms of his most popular novel. Various collections of his earlier short stories and newspaper articles were published, but his readers were forced to wait until 1975 for the appearance of his next novel, *El otoño del patriarca*. At almost every turn, a Faulknerian tag was pinned to *Cien años*, and at times to *El otoño del patriarca*, in much the same way that critical opinion had correctly viewed *La hojarasca*.

In a conversation with Rita Guibert, García Márquez accepted Faulkner as a mentor, especially in his early works, but he rejected the notion that he consciously or unconsciously sought to imitate Faulkner.[10] As he read Faulkner in Cartagena and later in Barranquilla, he found that the American South was very much like the Caribbean coast of Colombia. Later, travel through the South had convinced him of these similarities and cultural affinities. *Cien años* and *El otoño del patriarca* are mature works that stand alone and merit a comparison with Faulkner's Yoknapatawpha saga. Such a comparison of both writers' understanding of Macondo and Yoknapatawpha on a parallel mythical and conceptual level reveals the common factors that shape their view of human destiny.

Ronald Christ's perspective of the two writers is that the Colombian novelist is explicitly inspired by Faulkner and his evocation of life through his imaginary county.[11] Christ goes on to state that *Cien años* has single-handedly mythologized a whole continent in telling the multiple story of guilt and innocence in a prototypical endeavor to establish a society. The founders of Macondo, José Arcadio Buendía and his wife Úrsula Iguarán, establish the village with others who have accompanied them on a long journey through mountains and dense forest. In the first half of the novel, the village and the family move forward on an ascendant path. Decadence begins in the second half of the novel as civil wars degenerate into senseless conflicts, and the banana company, first viewed as the savior of Macondo, abandons it to the wiles of man and nature. The destruction of the village is parallel to the disintegration of the Buendía family. In the development of the narrative there are some fifteen primary figures, most of them members of the Buendía clan, but the principal figure is, without a doubt, Colonel Aureliano Buendía. His father, José Arcadio, and his mother, Úrsula Iguarán, are also important characters. Úrsula is the strength of the family. She lives to be one hundred fifteen years old, and with her dedication to hard work and common sense, she serves as a counterpoint to the caprices of her husband and sons, who, for the most part, dedicate themselves to counterproductive experiments in a household laboratory, to internecine warfare, and to sexual exploits.

Subsequent generations sink deeper into the morass of solitude and despair in their confrontation with forces from the outside world and with deterioration from within. José Arcadio, the founder of the dynasty, dies tied to a tree in the central patio of the house where he has been left to spend the last years of his life. Years later, his son, Colonel Aureliano Buendía, totally disillusioned with the futility of the endless wars between liberals and conservatives, watches the annual parade of an itinerant circus and then leans against the same tree and dies. Near the end of the novel, the last Aureliano and his aunt, Amaranta Úrsula, are the only Buendías remaining. Aureliano has never left Macondo, but he has taught himself to read Sanskrit, the language of the mysterious manuscripts in the family laboratory. Amaranta Úrsula has been educated in Europe, and on her return to her decaying family home she fails to realize the exact blood relationship between herself and Aureliano. A torrid love affair between these last Buendías produces the child with a pig's tail. Amaranta Úrsula dies in childbirth. As the red ants devour the forgotten child in the patio, Aureliano reads the last sheets of the manuscript that describe recent events. Meanwhile, the inevitable hurricane approaches and obliterates Macondo from the face of the earth.

García Márquez's use of Macondo as a microcosm for the study of a whole society was also the technique used by Faulkner when he created his own locale in which to reexamine the South, its great tragedy, and its system of traditional values. Jefferson and Yoknapatawpha County were first delineated in 1929 in *Sartoris* and *The Sound and the Fury*, and ultimately this region was to be the home of his families and their subsequent generations. In *Cien años*, the development of the Buendía family through five generations parallels Faulkner's creations. Both novelists offer a panoramic view of the vicious circle of civil war and incestuous societal decadence. The primeval paradise of Yoknapatawpha as undeveloped Indian territory and of Macondo in its earliest years is lost when human exploiters come to violate the innocence of nature. Later intruders—carpetbaggers and the banana company—arrive to accentuate the decline through the exploitation of the "fruit" of the land. The history of Macondo, written by the ubiquitous gypsy Melquíades, who, like Virginia Woolf's Orlando, lives from century to century, is a tale that ends in an apocalyptic whirlwind of dust and rubble, spun by the wrath of the hurricane. Faulkner's creation did not suffer destruction, but he had planned as a grand finale a "Doomsday Book," after which he would break his pen and quit. *The Reivers*, Faulkner's last novel, certainly is not his "Doomsday Book," and shortly after its appearance, he died of a heart attack on 6 July 1962.

One of the most extensive and accurate comparative studies of Faulkner and García Márquez is to be found in the work by Florence Delay and Jacqueline de Labriolle.[12] These French critics find much in common between the two novelists. A sense of fatal decadence, they believe, informs the writings of both novelists, and whereas the male protagonists are those primarily responsible for the fatal chain of events, strong female figures attempt and ultimately fail to hold the fabric of society intact. Úrsula Buendía and the other cofounder of Macondo, the prostitute Pilar Ternera, are among the last to die as the inevitable hurricane nears Macondo. Miss Jenny of *Sartoris*, Rosa Coldfield and Clytie Sutpen in *Absalom, Absalom!*, and the black maid Dilsey in *The Sound and the Fury* furnish a sense of stability and continuity as the postwar South crumbles about them.

A counterpoint to the theme of decadence is Faulkner's obsession with incest in many of his most important novels and the Buendías' fear of incest itself—or the appearance of incest—as certain to cause the birth of a child with a pig's tail. The rational obsession in Faulkner and the folkloric, irrational fear in García Márquez are nevertheless equal in their power of control over the various protagonists. Faulkner's characters react against this taboo as an aberration, and, as in the murder of Charles Bon by his half-brother Henry Sutpen in *Absalom, Absalom!*, as a means of preventing the double tragedy of incest and miscegenation. Úrsula Buendía's fear is based on family tradition and augmented by the prediction of Melquíades that the last Buendía would fulfill the prophecy and would be devoured by a horde of red ants. On a second level, both Macondo and Yoknapatawpha County suffer a type of societal incest that is only exacerbated by isolation and spiritual solitude. New blood to rejuvenate both societies is never accepted, and decay from within continues its inexorable advance.

Both novelists employ the repetition of names, suggesting thereby that the many protagonists are interchangeable pieces in the puzzle of life. These protagonists face a struggle against time which assumes a circular form. Events, names, and sequences seem to swirl about both created locales without any regard for chronological order. This duplication of circular time is the frame of reference in *El otoño del patriarca*. Time makes futile circles that result in a chronological and spatial fragmentation. The six circular divisions of the novel all begin at a point near the time of death of an unnamed patriarch who governs an unnamed Caribbean nation for an indeterminate time and who lives to an age of between one hundred and seven and two hundred and thirty-two years. This hyperbolic study of a Latin American dictator opens as vultures are circling the palace; cows munching velvet curtains are wandering through the vast rooms; the patriarch is dead. As his timid subjects enter the decrepit palace, there is an air of uncertainty, inasmuch as a previous "death" of the patriarch had turned out to be that of his perfect double. Because no one has really seen the man for many years, his identification is at first only provisional.

Within the circular divisions of the novel, the details of the patriarch's rise to power are offered in fragmentary reminiscences by the patriarch himself and by a series of unnamed witnesses. Some of these witnesses only retell bits and pieces of legendary materials passed down from generation to generation since none could have been witness in the true sense of the word to events that took place over a hundred years ago. His birth as the bastard son of a bird woman; his rise to power with the support of the British and later the Americans; the disappearance of his favorite mistress, Manuela Sánchez, during an eclipse of the sun; and the death of his wife and son, Leticia Nazareno and Emanuel, who are torn to bits in a public market by trained dogs, are events that gradually fall into narrative sequence as the past is recalled in fragmentary pieces. An additional technique is the interpolation of hyperbolic elements that give the work a tone of magical realism.

At first blush, it is apparent that *El otoño del patriarca* is quite different from *Cien años de soledad*. It is a meditation on the solitude of absolute power, a theme suggested in the presentation of the figure of Colonel Aureliano Buendía in García Márquez's earlier writings. Instead of a fictional town such as Macondo or Jefferson, García Márquez has created an entire fictional nation with a Caribbean setting, a nation the capital of which is reminiscent of Havana or Caracas. There is no lack of models for his prototype of a dictator. William Kennedy traces the genesis of the novel in the following manner: "In 1968 when he began to write this majestic novel, Gabriel García Márquez told an interviewer that the only image he had of it for years was that of an incredibly old man walking through the huge, abandoned rooms of a palace full of animals."[13] Kennedy goes on to say that García Márquez, as he witnessed the downfall of Marcos Pérez Jiménez in Venezuela, mentioned to friends that he would one day write such a book. An earlier Venezuelan dictator, Juan Vicente Gómez, is the principal model used for the novel's dictator. The timeless, nameless, and imprecise qualities of the patriarch elevate him from the realm of the specific to the world of myth. There are antecedents to *El otoño del patriarca* in García Márquez's earlier fiction. The use of various narrators who recall the life of a person now dead is the method used in *La hojarasca* and in Faulkner's *As I Lay Dying*. The gross exaggerations of García Márquez's short story, "Los funerales de la Mamá Grande," prefigure this more recent novel as do the fantastic, imaginative tales of the short-story collection, *La increíble y triste historia de la cándida Eréndira y de su abuela desalmada* (1972). And, of course, the style of *El otoño del patriarca* recalls what Kennedy describes as "a densely rich and fluid pudding that makes Faulknerian leaps forward and backward in time . . . making the novel a puzzle of pronouns, consistently changing narrative points of view in mid-sentence."[14] It is precisely this change of style that is the most Faulknerian aspect of this novel. With the publication of *El otoño del patriarca*, it is necessary to reconsider the matter of style and Faulkner's possible presence.

Faulkner's better known novels are often described as "difficult" for the average reader. The presence of some fifteen narrators in *As I Lay Dying* demands constant shifts on the part of the reader to organize the sequence of events that describe the journey of Addie Bundren's body to Jefferson. *The Sound and the Fury*, although it uses only four different points of view, is even more fragmented and complicated. These novels retell the past, combining the traditional narrative with a stream-of-consciousness technique. The scope of *Absalom, Absalom!* is much greater in that it covers an historical period from 1817 to an ambiguous present. García Márquez was especially interested in this latter novel, and its structure and technique are evident as models for *Cien años de soledad* and *El otoño del patriarca*. In 1929, when *The Sound and the Fury* appeared, Faulkner seemed to invite the reader to share with him in a search for order, truth, and significance. Much the same was in store for the readers of later Faulknerian novels. García Márquez first used this method in *La hojarasca*. In *Cien años*, there is a false sense of linear progression in story development, but many flashbacks are required to complete the picture of Macondo and its final destruction. *El otoño del patriarca* breaks what was a deceptively facile narrative style for chronological, narrative, and stylistic complexity. The repetition of the verb *vimos* allows constant shifts in point of view, but first, second, and third-person verb shifts make the task of the reader much greater as he sorts out chronology from such a large volume of material.

In many of Faulkner's writings and in *El otoño del patriarca*, the work begins at or near the end of the action, and flashbacks related by different narrators fill out the picture. Each point of view is incomplete; often it is the memory of the past as recalled in a nebulous present. Often there is an incompleteness at the end of the work, and the reader is called upon to "finish" the novel. The Civil War in Faulkner, the thirty-two revolutions that Aureliano Buendía lost, and the long dictatorship in *El otoño del patriarca* are the antecedents of a present sense of fatality. Time makes futile circles that result in chronological and spatial fragmentation. Clarity is achieved only after events pass into a distant historical perspective, only after the reader has had time to decipher their meaning. *Absalom, Absalom!* ends with Quentin Compson and his Harvard roommate, Shreve McCannon, attempting to decipher the meaning of events and motives that Quentin has related about his family in Jefferson. *Cien años* ends as the last Aureliano rapidly translates the manuscripts written much earlier by Melquíades; as he finishes the translation, the hurricane wipes the last vestiges of the Buendía family from Macondo. The timelessness of these novels permits the characters and events to achieve universal meaning on a mythical level. In this way, the regional characters of both novelists become protagonists with universal problems and concerns.

Magical realism, the introduction by a novelist of the improbable and the fantastic within a realistic world, is far more evident in García Márquez than in Faulkner. This element would seem, at first glance, to set *Cien años de soledad*, the short stories of the *Eréndira* collection, and *El otoño del patriarca* apart from the world of Faulkner, but it is only in the degree that García Márquez employs magical realism that the difference is marked. Faulkner found a sense of the marvelous and wondrous in nature; it is the central theme of *The Bear*. Kulin observes that in *Old Man* it is the elusive body of a deer that is the representative of the soul of the convict as the two desperately seek salvation in the swirling waters of the flood.[15] An even greater sense of irreality informs *A Fable*, and there are moments of the magical in *As I Lay Dying* and *Light in August*. García Márquez takes the marvelous to much greater extremes: gypsies with flying carpets, yellow flowers falling on Macondo like rain, the exaggerated sexual prowess of the Buendía males, and the apparent immortality of Melquíades and the ancient patriarch.

A final comparison is necessary. Although it is easy to see the presence of Faulkner in García Márquez's first novel, *La hojarasca*, and in his early short stories, it is less evident as the Colombian reaches artistic maturity. Both deal with similar societies at a time when they are attempting to survive the jolting effects of civil strife and exploitation. The labyrinthine prose so common in Faulkner does not appear in García Márquez until *El otoño del patriarca*. Yet in the final analysis, García Márquez's debt to Faulkner is undeniable. Faulkner left as part of his legacy a moral tone and standard by which human beings could judge his characters and ultimately themselves. His faith in man was evident in his Nobel address when he insisted that man would not merely endure but would prevail. The last sentence of *The Wild Palms*, "between grief and nothing I will take grief," reasserts his dedication to the struggle of humanity for survival. Whereas García Márquez ends *Cien años de soledad* with the unmitigated statement that races condemned to a hundred years of solitude do not have a second opportunity on earth, he concludes *El otoño del patriarca* with the ringing of bells announcing that the time of seemingly eternal dictatorship has come at last to a close. Both Faulkner and García Márquez seek a world of justice for a new generation. Macondo exists no longer, and death brought the end of the saga of Yoknapatawpha County, but a message of hope lingers propitiously above the ruin and ashes of destruction.

Notes

1. Personal communication with Antonio Olier, 12 March 1977.

2. Donald McGrady, "Acerca de una colección desconocida de relatos de Gabriel García Márquez," *Thesaurus* 27 (1972):293–320. The La Sierpe stories are more readily available in *Crónicas y reportajes* (Bogotá: Instituto Colombiano de Cultura, 1976), 11–50.

3. Gabriel García Márquez, "La Marquesita de La Sierpe," *Crónicas y reportajes*, 11.

4. José Stevenson, "García Márquez, un novelista en conflicto," *Letras Nacionales* 2 (1965):60.

5. J. G. Cobo Borda, "*La hojarasca*. 1955," *Boletín Cultural y Bibliográfico* 11 (1968):65.

6. Gabriel García Márquez and Mario Vargas Llosa, *La novela en América Latina* (Lima: Carlos Milla Batres / Ediciones Universidad Nacional de Ingeniería, 1968), 47.

7. Agustín Rodríguez Garavito, "Los funerales de la Mamá Grande," *Boletín Cultural y Bibliográfico* 12 (1969):108–9.

8. Emir Rodríguez Monegal, "Novedad y anacronismos de *Cien años de soledad*," *Revista Nacional de Cultura* 29 (1968):5.

9. Alfonso Fuenmayor (personal communication, 22 March 1977) stated that the plague of dying birds was suggested to García Márquez by a sentence in Virginia Woolf's *Orlando*: "Birds froze in mid-air and fell like stones to the ground." Reference is made to the

underground in *No One Writes to the Colonel* is obviously fighting for a more liberal and just form of government, no direct references are made to party affiliations.

García Márquez purposely shuns the direct description of brutality so typical of much fiction dealing with war and civil strife. Instead he relies on the art of allusion to activate his reader's imagination and in this way heighten the impact of the political drama. Thus, Agustín's murder is merely referred to obliquely in connection with the colonel's desire to keep the fighting cock left to him. Forbidden propaganda is distributed surreptitiously among members of the underground, including the colonel, while they go about their everyday business. One of the characters refers to the musician's demise as "the first death from natural causes we've had in many years." Sabas's exclamation, "I almost forgot we are under martial law," is provoked when the tyrannical mayor reminds the mourners that no procession, not even that of a funeral, is allowed to pass by the police barracks. The colonel sets his clock by the eleven o'clock curfew. Press censorship and the unlikely possibility of elections in the near future are fleeting topics of conversation when the doctor scans the newspapers he receives in the mail. The colonel's visit to the pool hall in search of Alvaro results in his almost being caught red-handed during a police raid with underground communications in his pocket. Father Angel's role as movie censor, though unrelated to politics, is but another example of the oppressive measures imposed on the citizenry.

The colonel bears a certain resemblance to the absurd hero, i.e., the protagonist whose passion for life enables him to struggle unceasingly against overwhelming odds. The absurd hero emerges triumphant from his confrontation with the world because, although he is tormented by the certainty of ultimate defeat in the form of death and nothingness, he comes to realize that his total responsibility and the commitment to the struggle constitute his grandeur. The writers of the absurd frequently mock rational man's obsessive efforts to impose order on chaos by depicting ridiculous situations that negate reason and illuminate the absurdity of the human condition. An example of such a situation in *No One Writes to the Colonel* is the episode depicting the colonel's visit to his lawyer to inform him that he will seek legal advice elsewhere. He finds the lawyer "stretched out lazily in a hammock . . . a monumental black man with nothing but two canines in his upper jaw." His desk is a keyless player piano "with papers stuffed into the compartments where the rolls used to go." Fanning himself in the sweltering heat, the lawyer sits down in a chair "too narrow for his sagging buttocks" while explaining in a pompous, meaningless jargon the ins and outs of administrative procedures. Moments later the colonel adopts "a transcendental attitude" to announce the purpose of his visit, but the solemn moment is interrupted by the abrupt entrance into the office of a mother duck followed by several ducklings. The lawyer then begins to turn his office upside down, getting "down on all fours, huffing and puffing," to locate the mislaid power of attorney authorizing him to act in behalf of the colonel. As for the colonel's proof of claim for his pension, which documented his monumental and laudable task of delivering two trunks of funds to the appropriate revolutionary leaders almost sixty years before, the lawyer believes it has all but disappeared in the "thousands of offices" of a government headed by seven presidents in the past fifteen years, each of which "has changed his cabinet at least ten times, and each minister his staff at least a hundred times."[3]

The colonel's principal weapons against this absurd chaos are a seemingly inexhaustible supply of good humor and hope. For example, when Sabas complains about his diabetes, distastefully displaying a pill he will use to sweeten his coffee ("It's sugar, but without sugar"), the colonel's analogy softens the sting of his friend's bitterness by injecting a note of irony into the conversation ("It's something like ringing but without bells"). When the colonel's wife, "dressed very strangely, in her husband's old shoes and oil cloth apron and a rag tied around her head," chides him for his utter lack of business sense, he interrupts her, saying, "Stay just the way you are. You're identical to the little Quaker Oats man." When she hesitates to plant roses because of her fear the pigs will eat them, he replies, "All the better. Pigs fattened on roses ought to taste very good." And when she examines his emaciated body and exclaims in horror, "You're nothing but skin and bones," he attempts to belittle her concern by declaring, "I'm taking care of myself so I can sell myself. I've already been hired by a clarinet factory."

The colonel's long-awaited letter concerning his pension emerges as a symbol of ritualistically renewed hope reflecting his human condition and justifying his platitude, "Life is the best thing that's ever been invented." This fundamental optimism is reaffirmed metaphorically when he comes across an old, moth-eaten umbrella won by his wife in a raffle many years before. In contrast to her grumbling remark—"Everything's that way. We're rotting alive"—he opens the umbrella, and, gazing upward through its network of metal rods, observes, "The only thing it's good for now is counting the stars."

The fighting cock is the novel's most complex symbol, perhaps because its meaning evolves, illuminating the existential dilemmas of both the protagonist and his community. At first the bird embodies hope, leading the colonel to comment, "He's worth his weight in gold. He'll feed us for three years." And even when his wife reminds him that one cannot eat hope, he adamantly clings to his optimistic expectations. "You can't eat it but it sustains you. It's something like my friend Sabas's miraculous pills."

Because the rooster is a legacy of Agustín—who died a rebel—and because the whole town plans to bet on it in the forthcoming contest, the colonel feels an obligation to resist his wife's pleas to sell it to Don Sabas. Moreover, the longer he keeps it, the more closely its fate becomes identified with his own. One Friday the colonel is on his way to meet the mail boat when he is suddenly reminded that the trials for the cockfights are to take place that very day. Hastening to the cockpit just in time to witness his rooster's successful trial bout, he picks up the bird whose "warm deep throbbing" makes him realize "he had never had such an alive thing in his hands before." As he leaves the arena with it tucked under his arm, he is greeted by cheers and applause from the enthusiastic spectators. Though stunned and embarrassed by the ovation, the colonel feels a certain pride at the thought that the town has suddenly come to life after having lain "in a kind of stupor, ravaged by ten years of history." When he arrives home, his wife tearfully informs him of how "they" came for the cock during his absence, saying it "didn't belong to us but to the whole town." The colonel's reply—" 'They' did the right thing"—and his firm decision not to sell the rooster, express his solidarity with the community, which he believes has at last been inspired to unite against the forces of oppression. The cock, then, not only symbolizes hope, but ultimately emerges as a symbol of the absurd hero's (the colonel's) fight against fate. And because of the bird's beneficial effect on the townspeople, they too acquire characteristics of the absurd hero.

Immediately after this episode the colonel's cantankerous wife fires a volley of questions at him regarding their desperate economic straits, eliciting his statement that on January 20, the day of the cockfights, they will have no more worries. Her continued nagging brings the novel to its climactic ending.

> "If the rooster wins," the woman said. "But if he loses. It hasn't occurred to you that the rooster might lose."
>
> "He's one rooster that can't lose."
>
> "But suppose he loses."
>
> "There are still forty-four days left to begin to think about that," the colonel said.
>
> The woman lost her patience.
>
> "And meanwhile what do we eat?" she asked, and seized the colonel by the collar of his flannel nightshirt. She shook him hard.
>
> It had taken the colonel seventy-five years—the seventy-five years of his life, minute by minute—to reach this moment. He felt pure, explicit, invincible at the moment when he replied:
>
> "Shit."

Critics are divided on the implications of the colonel's last word, some viewing it as an indication of complete surrender to despair. The word itself unquestionably expresses frustration and anguish. The fact, however, that upon uttering it he feels "pure," "explicit," and "invincible," implies an attitude of defiance. It also suggests that he realizes confrontation with the absurd has given his life new meaning and if victory in this life can be achieved, it will come through commitment to action and revolt, not through passive hope. And inasmuch as he has cast his lot with that of the recently awakened town, his exclamation could be construed as an invitation to collective political and moral action.[4]

The colonel's final reply is also highly ironic because it explodes all previous patterns of his behavior, i.e., his gentle humor, stoic sense of dignity, naïveté, and, above all, his puritanical objection to the use of profanity, as demonstrated by a scene in the tailor shop quoted below:

> "Goddamn it, Colonel."
> He was startled. "No need to swear," he said.
> Alfonso adjusted his eyeglasses on his nose to examine the colonel's shoes.
> "It's because of your shoes," he said. "You've got on some goddamn new shoes."
> "But you can say that without swearing," the colonel said, and showed the soles of his patent-leather shoes. "These monstrosities are forty years old, and it's the first time they've ever heard anyone swear."

A book of little action and limited plot development, *No One Writes to the Colonel* is saved from monotony by its technical perfection and keen psychological insights. The emphasis on mimetic scene rather than resumé, the rapid, spare dialogues, and the concise descriptions consisting of unique details to suggest a total reality, create dynamic movement and enhance dramatic effect. Reader interest is also sustained by the frequent use of the third-person-reflector technique, which filters the fictional material through the minds of the characters, sharpening the narrative focus and increasing credibility by temporarily eliminating the distant and less convincing omniscient author. Thus in the following example the colonel is seen through the shrewd, morbidly piercing eyes of his wife as he is combing his unruly hair:

> "I must look like a parrot," he said.
> His wife examined him. She thought he didn't. He didn't look like a parrot. He was a dry man, with solid bones articulated as if with nuts and bolts. Because of the vitality in his eyes, he didn't seem to be preserved in formaldehyde.

Movement is also accelerated and events highlighted by the occasional use of cinemagraphic techniques including the close-up, the speed-up, and the fade-out, as illustrated by the following impressionistic description of the colonel's visit at the home of the dead musician's mother to offer his condolences.[5] Upon entering the house, the colonel is abruptly confronted with death when he is "pushed through a gallery of perplexed faces to the spot where — deep and wide open — the nostrils of the dead man were found." After having spoken with the grief-stricken mother, he almost loses his balance as he finds himself once again

> being pushed against the corpse by a shapeless crowd which broke out in a quavering outcry . . . He spun his head around and was face to face with the dead man. But he didn't recognize him because he was stiff and

dynamic and seemed as disconcerted as he, wrapped in white cloths and with his trumpet in his hands. When the colonel raised his head over the shouts, in search of air, he saw the closed box bouncing toward the door down a slope of flowers that disintegrated against the walls. He perspired. His joints ached. A moment later he knew he was in the street because the drizzle hurt his eyelids, and someone seized him by the arm and said:

"Hurry up, friend, I was waiting for you."

The novel's artistic balance is enhanced by its many contrasts (the colonel's naïveté — his wife's skepticism; the colonel's strong sense of honor — Don Sabas's dishonesty; the colonel's idealism — his wretched material existence; the colonel's dry wit — the constant menace of tragedy), which create dramatic tension and compositional balance, and its numerous leitmotifs (the October rains, the tropical heat, the colonel's gastritis, his wife's asthmatic wheezing, and the references to death), which generate a lugubrious tonal quality.

No One Writes to the Colonel emerges as a minor masterpiece for a variety of reasons: its aesthetic perfection, ironic ambiguity, and, perhaps most important of all, the endearing personality of its protagonist, one of the most memorable in Latin-American letters. The book's intuitive quality and masterful execution can perhaps be explained by the fact that the protagonist was inspired, at least in part, by García Márquez's dearly-loved grandfather, and also by the fact that the manuscript was rewritten as many as ten times while García Márquez himself was living in Paris on a shoestring budget. Still, in spite of the unfavorable conditions under which the novel was written and the dismal lives it depicts, it is far less pessimistic than *Leaf Storm*, primarily because its overall vision is directed toward an uncertain future rather than toward a decadent past. The protagonist's emergence as an absurd hero, moreover, conveys the conviction that man's definition and grandeur lie in the struggle he wages against his adverse reality.

Notes

1. According to García Márquez, the principal defect of the Colombian novelists of *la violencia* is their propensity to describe the brutalities of the conflict directly instead of the ambiance of terror it produced. He greatly admires Albert Camus's novel, *The Plague*, because Camus concentrates on the reactions of the healthy to the epidemic rather than on the ravages of the disease.

2. Generally speaking, *la violencia* was felt less in the coastal region, where Aracataca is located, than in the interior. Sucre is much further inland.

3. This description of political instability is an example of the hyperbole so characteristic of García Márquez's later works. In reality Colombia had five presidents between 1941 and 1956.

4. The colonel does not express his acute metaphysical anguish as do many absurd heroes of French existentialism, perhaps because García Márquez, like so many contemporary

novelists, makes no effort to define the absurd but instead merely depicts its effects. The negative portrait of the priest in *No One Writes to the Colonel* implies a rejection of traditional religion. Moreover, the depressing allusions to poverty, illness, and death combined with the colonel's final expression of revolt agains his sordid reality could be viewed as a revolt against God. As Albert Camus has written, "In absurd terms . . . revolt against men is also directed against God: great revolutions are always metaphysical." (*The Myth of Sisyphus*, New York, 1955, p. 94.)

5. García Márquez has always been fascinated by the cinema. In 1955 he took a course in film directing at the Experimental Movie Center in Rome. The influence of this medium is most evident on his works prior to *One Hundred Years of Solitude* because of their highly visual quality.

Time and Futility in the Novel *El coronel no tiene quien le escriba*   Richard D. Woods*

Gabriel García Márquez, for the success of his six works of prose, is today one of the better known of the Spanish American novelists. In *Cien años de soledad*,[1] his most recent novel, themes, characters, and landscape, somewhat embryonic in form in earlier works, seem to mature. Like William Faulkner, who finds his geographical and human landscape in Yoknapatawpha County, Mississippi, García Márquez exploits imaginary Macondo, Colombia, for his material.[2]

La hojarasca, 1955, initiated the series on Macondo with a multiple first-person narration of the funeral of a mysterious doctor whose life is developed through sporadic flashbacks suggesting the economic formation of the city and the interrelations of the various characters. Six years later García M. published one of his best works, *El coronel no tiene quien le escriba* [*No One Writes to the Colonel*],[3] the object of this study. Focusing mainly on one figure, a veteran of an anonymous civil war in Colombia and now a resident of Macondo, the author hints at "la violencia." However, this theme remains subdued until *La mala hora*[4] [*In Evil Hour*][4] completed in 1962, the same year in which the public saw his first collection of short stories, *Los funerales de la Mamá Grande* [*Big Mama's Funeral*].[5] Each story unfolds the personality of one of the regional picturesque inhabitants such as Father Antonio Isabel del Santísimo Sacramento del Altar or Mamá Grande. Finally, *Cien años de soledad*, [*One Hundred Years of Solitude*], exhausting themes and characters peripheral in his other fiction, consequently is as large as his combined previous works and gives an in depth view of Macondo.

Through his technique of straight linear narration with references to the past, García M. seems almost antipodal to some of the modern Spanish

*Reprinted from *Kentucky Romance Quarterly* 17, no. 4 (1970):287–95. Reprinted by permission of the journal. Copyright 1970 University Press of Kentucky.

American novelists—Julio Cortázar, Carlos Fuentes, and José Lezama Lima who fragment reality.[6] Within his rather traditional narrative technique, García M.'s exploitation of time appears deceptively simple. For example, though he may include a paragraph of reverie or non-chronologically present episodes as in *Cien años*, he never juxtaposes time. In other words, this author does not utilize a cubistic account of one incident achieved through the multiple narration of different characters, a technique which leaves to the reader the task of completing the entire scene.

Within his traditional approach, the trajectory of his literary creation reveals a unique pattern or a formula for time—the frequent indication of the exact hour and minute, a recurrent mentioning of the day or the month, a suggestion that time is static, and finally an occasional reference to clocks. Yet only one work, *El coronel*, both epitomizes and exemplifies García M.'s employment of time within the novel. This Colombian author, through the intense view of one character who dominates each scene, proves how effective "time" may be used in its traditional sense for the development of both personality and theme.

In this short novel he utilizes time as the scaffolding on which to construct the theme of futility—the empty life of a Colombian colonel who waits 56 years for a military pension. Patterned to elaborate this motif, time can be considered as a descending spiral. The outer circle represents the greatest quantitative unit of time or the past, the second circle, the present, in which most of the story occurs can be refined to recurring months, to weeks with Friday as their axis, and finally to hours and minutes. Regardless of its moment on the temporal continuum, from the recollected past to the observed present, an incident almost invariably emphasizes futility. Only the future which can be thought of as the core of the spiral, seems to lighten the somber present.

Unity is given to these cumulative moments of time through the personality of the colonel and the theme of death which permeates all periods of his existence. Implying that life should have accomplishment before it ends, the presence of death continually rebukes the colonel for his inertia and simultaneously magnifies his stagnation.

Present time, interrupted by scattered recollections of the past or by projections into the future by his thoughts on destiny, is the frame which encloses the main action of the story. In the now-moment the colonel, expecting the pension from Bogotá, suffers from illness and struggles to keep up appearances in spite of increasing poverty. Notice how the first pages of the text telescope the life of this veteran of one of Colombia's civil wars and set the tone for the next three months of monotony:

["A difficult morning to get through, even for a man like himself who had survived so many mornings like that one. For fifty-six years—since the end of the last civil war—the colonel had done nothing else but wait."][7]

The fragmented past is reconstructed through reminiscences. In the first chapter an old umbrella, which his wife had won at a fund-raising drive for his political party, unlocks the memories of happier, earlier days:

["That same night they had attended an outdoor show which was not interrupted in spite of the rain. The colonel, his wife and their son Agustín — who was then eight years old — watched the show until the end, seated under the umbrella."][8]

[" 'Who are you talking with,' his wife asked. 'With the Englishman disguised as a tiger who appeared in Colonel Aureliano Buendía's camp,' the colonel replied." (Ed. Note: How abruptly the intrusive past appears!)][9]

Recorded in the aborted steps taken by the protagonist to gain his pension, the preceding half century is also noted by his parasitical lawyer, who elaborates on the reason for delay:

[" 'But in the last fifteen years the officials have changed many times,' the lawyer pointed out. 'Just think about the fact that there have been seven presidents and that each minister changed his staff at least a hundred times.' "][10]

What could aggravate the present desperation even more by robbing the past of its only value than the death of their son Agustín through political violence? In reference to the son's premature end, his wife becomes resentful. ["Those cursed cocks were his ruin . . . If on the third of January he had stayed at home, his evil hour would not have come."][11] Yet on other occasions her bitterness is fed by the useless wait of twenty years ["waiting for the little colored birds they promised you after each election and all we have to show for it is a dead son. Nothing except a dead son."][12]

Through the technique of resuscitating the past the author creates an unbroken line of uselessness which fuses with the present. Recurring Friday and October, both empty and disappointing, are the latest moments of this futility. A symbol of the paralysis in the colonel's life, October in the first chapter not only sets the time of the story but also accentuates an uninspired existence. ["October was one of the few things that arrived"][13] confronts the reader with the aimlessness of the life of the protagonist.

["It must be terrible to be buried in October."][14] characterizes October as a more traditional symbol. The autumn month accords with the thoughts the colonel's wife has about death and the wake that her husband is about to attend. Then November finally arrives and the colonel's attitude toward the previous month is described. ["More difficult than the four weeks of October the colonel didn't think he would survive."][15] Monotonously returning and evoking thoughts of death, the month reinforces the image of a hollow life. ["October had moved in on the patio."][16] seems more than an original way to note the inevitability of time and suggests that it is an enemy to be endured as a siege. ["It's October,"][17] he murmurs, equating the thought with death as his wife has just done. At the suggestion that he see a doctor, the officer replies, ["I'm not sick," he said. What happens is that in October I feel as if I had animals in my gut."][18] October, a somber rhythm repeated frequently, represents death, the desperation of waiting, and the necessity of withstanding time.

Yet of greater significance is Friday, the intensification of futility and the epitome of the exhausted pulsation of this military man's life. For more than half a century he has followed a ritual that begins with the anticipation of the arrival of the letter, climaxes with disappointment, and evolves into the expectation of another Friday.

[The postmaster handed him his mail. He put the rest in the bag and closed it again. The doctor got ready to read two personal letters. But before opening the envelopes he looked at the colonel. Then he looked at the postmaster.

"Nothing for the colonel?"

The colonel felt terrified. The postmaster tossed the bag onto his shoulder, got off the platform and answered without turning his head:

"No one writes to the colonel."

Contrary to his habit, he didn't go right home. He drank a cup of coffee in the tailor shop while Agustín's companions leafed through the newspapers. He felt cheated. He would have preferred to stay there until the next Friday to keep from having to face his wife that night with empty hands. But when they closed the tailor shop, he had to face up to reality. His wife was waiting for him.]

["Nothing?" she asked.

"Nothing," the colonel replied.

The next Friday he went back to meet the boat. And like every Friday he returned home without the letter he had expected.][19]

Regardless of his disillusionment, the colonel returns each Friday to fulfill the compulsive ritual of asking for the mail. ["He went out to the street stimulated by the thought that that afternoon the letter would come."][20] Inspiring hope but bringing frustration, the tantalizing letter synthesizes a life; in another sense it typifies the town of Macondo. ["He wasn't sorry. For a long time the town had been in a sort of stupor, ravaged by ten years of history. That afternoon — another Friday without a letter — the people had awakened."][21]

The main character here resurrects another era in a flashback, but the quote applies both to him and Macondo. ["She had spent the morning mentally organizing the budget for the next three years without their Friday agony"][22] proves that the repetition of the rites of Friday affects not only the non-hero but also his spouse.

Through the technique of packaging time, the colonel's life is neatly marked out in measured units of emptiness. Time, like a frame around a blank sheet of paper, encloses hours, days, and months in which nothing happens. We are aware of the precise hour which only underscores another static moment for the officer as when he hears the bells, the aural censorship on movies exercised by the local priest. ["A little after seven the bells in the tower rang out the censor's movie classifications."][23] On the following page, four and one half hours pass as the colonel reads the news.

> [He read them in chronological order from the first page to the last, including the advertisements. At eleven o'clock the trumpet blew curfew. The colonel finished his reading a half hour later, opened the door of the patio onto the impenetrable night, and urinated, besieged by mosquitoes, against the wall studs.][24]

In still another scene only the monotony of life is noted. ["For half an hour he heard the rain against the palm leaves of the roof. The town sank into the deluge. After the curfew sounded, a leak began somewhere in the house."][25] Itemized time may incorporate larger moments. ["I was thinking that the man has been dead for almost two months and I still haven't expressed my condolences."][26]

In the contemporary setting more than in any other the theme of death accelerates. Having occurred in the distant or immediate past, the deaths yet deal their full force on the present. For its constant reminder of the termination of life, death profoundly accents the theme of futility in the present. An excerpt from Hans Meyerhoff's *Time in Literature* best summarizes the plight of the colonel.

> . . . looking back upon a lifetime spent as a succession of fragmented, isolated moments of experience and judged by the social standards of one's "time" — man may well envision death as the most ominous symbol of a "wasted life," a painful, bitter reminder of the lack of unity, purpose, continuity, satisfaction, significance, and worth of human existence; a betrayal of the "real" life the individual meant to live but did not live because he was a victim of "time and circumstances," as these are defined by the "realities" of the world in which he did live.[27]

Immediately death impinges now in the wife's thoughts about her son. [" 'He was born in 1922,' she said, 'exactly one month after our son.' "][28] Soon after, the theme of death is almost a mental dialogue as she broods about their lost son and the father thinks of the wake he will attend shortly. From here death concretizes when the colonel at the wake faces the corpse in a moment of macabre humor which generalizes man's reaction to eternity. ["He felt himself being shoved against the corpse by a shapeless mass which broke into a quavering outcry. He looked for a firm support for his hands but couldn't find the wall."][29]

More subtly in the following chapter the death motif interjects itself in the daily routine. Reading the newspaper, the colonel's eyes move from international affairs to a public invitation to a burial.[30] ["The patients have died."][31] is the greeting the doctor gives when he arrives to examine his patients. Though relieved by humor, the idea of death is still insistent when in a later passage after a haircut the colonel brags: ["When I feel well I'm capable of reviving a dead man."][32] ["The umbrella has something to do with death"][33] opens a scene in which death incarnates itself as the wife of don Sabas.

> ["Everybody says that death is a woman," the woman continued. She was fat, taller than her husband, and with a hairy wart on her upper lip. Her manner of speaking resembled the buzzing of the electric fan.
>
> Don Sabas couldn't stand any more . . .
>
> "You've been bothering my friend with your foolishness for half an hour."][34]

The characteristics of femininity, ugliness, and monotony fuse the woman and the idea of death which obsesses the major figure of this book. When the desperation in their lives has become acute, death intrudes for the last time at the end of the novel. ["I don't want to die in the dark," she said.][35] Like a dull chorus lingering in the present and underlining the nothingness of the existence of the colonel and his wife, the death theme relates to the now and its futility.

Nothingness is conveyed also by the clock, a symbol of the lifetime of waiting. First mentioned in the initial chapter when it is wound, as yet the clock is still only one of the props of setting which later achieves the value of a symbol. ["The colonel calculated that it would soon be time for the curfew, but the clock had stopped."][36] Here the stopped machine encompasses almost the entire life of the colonel. In the same scene, upon hearing the church bell he resets the timepiece, an action symmetrical with the weekly ritual of Friday and the pilgrimage to the post office. A comment by the colonel's spouse points to the worthlessness of time and its expiration. ["That we can sell the clock."][37] However, defending himself and his mode of life, the man is horrified. ["It's like going around with the Holy Sepulcher," he protested."][38] Even though the metaphor of "santo sepulcro" again evokes the idea of death and the end of time for the colonel, the clock and, naturally, time still have meaning for him as is seen later as he inevitably awaits the coming month. Not sold but repaired, the timepiece here suggests that the married couple yet has some life remaining to them. When the novel closes, nevertheless, the officer again refers to it after his wife urges that he sell the rooster.[39] Symbolizing the life of the colonel, the clock here is an image of a static life relieved only by thoughts of the future, the sole motive for living.

Myopically he can see only as far as the next December and January, the fortunate months in which his rooster might win. [" 'By then it will be the twentieth of January,' the colonel said, perfectly conscious. 'They pay twenty percent that same evening.' "][40] Each approaching Friday provokes the excitement of the expected letter from the capital, inevitable frustration, and the hope that next Friday must bring better news. To wait more than fifty years for an army pension and to abstain from any activity in the present indicates the dominant role of tomorrow for the colonel.

Hence through the technique of the division of time from the fractionalized past to the present the theme of futility is developed. The stasis of now-time intensifies with the realization that the present is just a rerun of the past. By reverse alchemy the chimerical gold of the future, money from Bogotá and victory of the rooster, is converted into the same worthless lead of the present. The entire spectrum of the protagonist's life is futility. Pervasive and unremitting at any moment in his existence, the theme of death makes the idea of uselessness more emphatic through its inherent reminder of the end of time. Never with direct description does the author detail the plight of the colonel, but through the implication of futility derived from his special use of time. This is one of García Márquez' major and most innovative contributions and is borne out mainly in *El coronel no tiene quien le escriba*.

Notes

1. Gabriel García Márquez, *Cien años de soledad* (Buenos Aires: Editorial Sudamericana, 1969.)

2. Luis Harss and Barbara Dohmann, *Into the Mainstream: Conversations with Latin-American Writers* (New York: Harper and Row, Publishers, 1967), p. 310–341.

3. Gabriel García Márquez, *El coronel no tiene quien le escriba* (Buenos Aires: Editorial Sudamericana, 1968).

4. Gabriel García Márquez, *La mala hora* (México: Ediciones ERA, S. A., 1966).

5. Gabriel García Márquez, *Los funerales de la Mamá Grande* (Buenos Aires: Editorial Sudamericana, 1968).

6. Emir Rodríguez Monegal, "La hazaña de un escritor," *Visión*, 18 julio de 1969, p. 27–31.

7. García Márquez, *El coronel no tiene quien le escriba*, op. cit., p. 7.

8. *Ibid.*, p. 10.

9. *Ibid.*, p. 23.

10. *Ibid.*, pp. 40–41.

11. *Ibid.*, p. 47.

12. *Ibid.*, p. 65.

13. *Ibid.*, p. 7.

14. *Ibid.*, p. 8.

15. *Ibid.*, p. 45.

16. *Ibid.*, p. 8.

17. *Ibid.*, p. 9.

18. *Ibid.*, p. 16.

19. *Ibid.*, pp. 34–35.

20. *Ibid.*, p. 81.

21. *Ibid.*, p. 84.

22. *Ibid.*, p. 71.

23. *Ibid.*, p. 21.

24. *Ibid.*, p. 22.

25. *Ibid.*, p. 44.

26. *Ibid.*, p. 62.

27. Hans Meyerhoff, *Time in Literature* (Berkeley: University of California Press, 1955) pp. 117–118.

28. García Márquez, *El coronel*, op. cit., p. 8.

29. *Ibid.*, p. 13.

30. *Ibid.*, p. 21.

31. *Ibid.*, p. 24.

32. *Ibid.*, p. 32.

33. *Ibid.*, p. 57.

34. *Ibid.*, pp. 57–58.

35. *Ibid.*, p. 89.

36. *Ibid.*, p. 63.

37. *Ibid.*, p. 49.

38. *Ibid.*, p. 49.

39. *Ibid.*, p. 91.

40. *Ibid.*, p. 92.

Lampooning Literature:
La mala hora
Wolfgang A. Luchting*

[It is difficult for the state to allow itself to be represented by its writers.]

[Poetry is more and more in the street, in certain forms of renovating action, in the anonymous discovery.]

[The hero of the novel is the novel itself.][1]

As Mario Vargas Llosa has pointed out, in *One Hundred Years of Solitude*, the time and space of the narrator's world and the time and space of the world he narrates merge during the final destruction of Macondo:[2] writing, literature and creation are annihilated both as an activity and as the product of an activity.

An act of creation, whether literary or not, is ultimately a part of reality, whereas the product of the creative act is an addition to it and thus a change, a critique, of reality *quo ante*. The destruction of the product of the creative act in *One Hundred Years of Solitude* should evoke surprise and wonder in the reader, for he holds in his hands a book whose last pages attempt to convince him that, in *its* reality, he cannot possibly be holding

*Reprinted from *Books Abroad* 47, no. 3 (Summer 1973):471–78. Copyright 1973 by the University of Oklahoma Press. Reprinted by permission.

it for it is being destroyed in Macondo. The reader, *idealiter*, begins to doubt and thus to criticize reality. Reading itself becomes an act of creation, and as such it changes reality. The reader becomes, in Cortázar's words, "a reader-participant."

If with *One Hundred Years of Solitude* the destruction of that part of reality the author has created leads the reader to a creative critique of reality, or of his own vision of reality, in *La mala hora* (The Evil Hour [published in English as *In Evil Hour*]) writing and reading at one point actually destroy the readers: "a village . . . was destroyed in seven days by the lampoons. Its inhabitants ended up killing each other" (p. 33). Writing, or literature, both creates reality and destroys it.

Carlos Fuentes has pointed out (*La nueva novela hispanoamericana*, Mexico City, Mortiz, 1969, pp. 60–61) that in *One Hundred Years of Solitude* writing is used on one occasion to preserve rather than destroy. José Arcadio combats the disease of forgetfulness (the effects of time) by putting little notes on animate and inanimate objects surrounding him and his family, giving their names and the way to use them: "This is a cow. It must be milked daily, the milk boiled so that it can be used for *cafe con leche*." The lampoons in "The Evil Hour" have a similar function. Writing, then, or literature, can both create reality and preserve it.

If literature has increasingly turned inward upon itself, how have its practitioners come to regard it? How do they understand themselves as writers? Above all, how are writers and their work understood in Hispanoamerica? Some of the best-known statements are Vargas Llosa's. For example, he asserts that literature is the "manifestation of a permanent insurrection," or that "the more truly good novelists there are in a country, the worse off it is."[3] Cortázar's opinion reaches into epistemology: "Hopscotch is a kind of plea for the total authenticity of man, urging him to shake off, through a process of self-review and ruthless scrutiny, all preconceived notions, all cultural traditions, not necessarily in order to reject them out of hand but rather to examine them, to try to discover the vulnerable spots which allowed breaks in something that might otherwise have been much more beautiful than it is" (*Cosas*, p. 100). Sábato has said that "the artist is in general a dissident [*disconforme*] and antagonistic being, and . . . in good measure it is precisely his hostility toward the reality which it is his lot to live that leads him to create another reality in his art" (*El escritor y sus fantasmas*, Aguilar, 2nd ed., 1964, p. 163). Carpentier maintains that to write about the world "is to fulfill a revolutionary function" (*Siempre!*, Mexico City, 25 December 1963). And Gabriel García Márquez?

> I think that surely literature, and above all the novel, has a function. Now, I don't know whether fortunately or unfortunately, I believe it is a subversive function — right? — in the sense that I know of no good literature that would lend itself to exalting established values. In good literature I always find the tendency to destroy that which is established,

that which is already imposed, and to contribute to the creation of new forms of living, new societies; in one word, to better the life of man. (*Diálogo*, p. 8)

Literature seen as an activity subversive to the status (or the State) quo is neither new nor particularly Hispanoamerican, unless in its *tercermundismo* [thirdworldism] and deep conviction, assertiveness, almost aggressiveness, and of course in its invariably leftist orientation: "The writer *in a capitalist society* is by nature in the opposition; creativity is against power, and it's great that this is so" (Cortázar; *Cosas*, p. 122).

The caveats come to mind immediately. The Hispanoamerican writers are aware of this. Thus, Vargas Llosa asked García Márquez, "Can this subversive power . . . be foreseen or planned in any way" and can the writer "foresee the seditious, subversive consequences his book will have" (*Dialogo*, p. 8)? In other words, will he tend to write lampoons? García Márquez's answer is unequivocal:

> if this is foreseen, . . . if the subversive power or intent of the book one is writing is premeditated, deliberate, from this very moment on the book becomes a bad one. . . . Every writer brings with him an ideological formation, and if it is firm and if the writer is sincere . . . this ideological position will be visible in his story, and it is from this moment on that the story may show that subversive power. . . . I don't think it is deliberate, but it definitely is inevitable. (pp. 8–9).

"The Evil Hour" tells the following story: "After the political wars that have laid waste to Macondo, and when days of peace and tranquility were proclaimed publicly, there begin to appear on the walls lampoons that reveal the secrets and shameful deeds, true or false, of the townspeople . . . the mayor decides to pick a scapegoat" (transl. from the back cover. Note: the village in this novel is *not* Macondo: it is the *pueblo*. "The only books of mine that take place in Macondo are *Leaf Storm* and *One Hundred Years of Solitude*" (García Márquez in *Cosas*, p. 18). The mayor represents governmental power and ruthlessness: "The principal drama is the solitude of the mayor; he came to conquer the village but instead gradually sinks into it and feels conquered by it" (*Cosas*, p. 19). In other words, the novel ultimately is eminently political. Recognized by many analysts, this fact has been studied specifically by Jacques Gilard in his "Gabriel García Márquez's 'The Evil Hour': The Writer and the Politician" (*Cahiers du monde hispanique et luso-brésilien*, No. 17, 1971, pp. 57–85). At one point he states, "One might then ask himself if García Márquez is a politically committed novelist" (p. 78). Toward the end of his study he writes, "The political nature of García Márquez's novels on contemporary subjects is indisputable, especially his *Leaf Storm*, because it concerns a difficult liberation, a political act par excellence" (p. 84). Is "The Evil Hour," then, what García Márquez has called a "bad book," a pamphlet? No. Gilard is careful to note that García Márquez "does not pretend to offer actual facts: he makes facts enter into the experience of his characters. The writer does not become involved" (p. 79), i.e., he has his characters invoke the political facts as hearsay or as their own experience.

Vargas Llosa calls his chapter on this novel "la revolución *silenciosa*" (p. 421), meaning an indirect revolution. Was García Márquez's purpose in writing "The Evil Hour" political in any way at all? Obviously. To E. González Bermejo he said that after *Leaf Storm* he was thinking about *One Hundred Years of Solitude* (yet to be written at that time) but asked himself, " 'How can I continue working on this mythical terrain . . . in the circumstances in which we are living. Seems like an evasion.' *It was a political decision*, a wrong one, I think today." "I decided to get closer to the reality of the Colombian moment and wrote *No One Writes to the Colonel* and "The Evil Hour' " (pp. 21–22).

How was he to avoid writing a "libro malo" if the intention *ab initio* was so imbued with political impulses? The best way was to make the "[real facts] enter into the experience of his characters."

Pursuing this line of thought further, I would suggest that the lampoons are a metaphor of literature; better yet: the lampoons are a metaphor of the novel itself.

To be sure, "literature" and "novel" as defined above. At one point in the book the lampoons are described as "a symptom of social decomposition" (p. 122). It is by now common knowledge that Vargas Llosa and Sábato, among many others, consider the flourishing of the novel to be a product of periods of decay and degeneration in a society's history. The Colombia of "The Evil Hour" is surely in such a phase. Or think of Balzac who wrote (Vargas Llosa uses the sentence as a motto for his *Conversación en la catedral*) ". . . the novel is the private history of nations." What, if not chapters, fragments, paragraphs from the private history of Colombia (or of the *pueblo*, symbol of the country), are the lampoons? One may object: "of *nations?*" Why not? García Márquez has said the principal drama of the mayor was "*evidently*, a reflection of the situation of the whole country."

We have, then, once again, a novel about the novel (or at any rate about literature, or if one prefers, about writing and reading), only in this case it is a novel about the protest novel. What is more, we detect in this use of literature within literature a structural similarity to *One Hundred Years of Solitude*. Vargas Llosa has pointed out that "The Evil Hour" shows the final battle (before *One Hundred Years of Solitude*) between "objective reality" and "imaginary reality" (within the "fictional reality" of the novel, of course), a battle in which the latter wins ("but this defeat of the objectively real is not evident, because the imaginary here, as in Kafka, wears the clothes of the quotidian" [p. 466]). The transformation from one mode to the other he calls "the secret change [muda secreta]" (p. 447), which "takes place at the very instant the fiction ends" (Ibid.), just as in *One Hundred Years of Solitude*. Vargas Llosa then goes on to trace in detail the phases of the battle (pp. 447–56). I believe that any reading of Vargas Llosa's detailed analysis in the light of the interpretation that I suggest of the lampoons will confirm that interpretation.

II

I remember how I worked on the other books [before *One Hundred Years of Solitude*]: *they were all subject to planning, a rigid organization perfectly laid out before beginning to write the book.* (*Cosas*, p. 17)

Thanks to [the artists], *the powerful can never affirm that everyone agrees with their acts.* (L. Buñuel to C. Fuentes, *New York Times Magazine,* 11 March 1973)

If the first quotation is true,[4] then there can be little doubt that García Márquez was quite aware — to the extent, of course, that a novelist is ever aware ("Never trust the writer, trust the tale," says D. H. Lawrence) — of what he was doing in "The Evil Hour," particularly with respect to a detail of such a strong narrative valence as the lampoons possess. Besides, García Márquez is known — see any interview with him — to be quite a literary prankster. It should not surprise us to find him disguising the political and denunciatory, the "lampooning" intent of his novel, as lampoons! In "The Evil Hour," as often happens in fictions conscious of their narrative techniques, there is at least one incident that reflects the structure of the whole novel, mirrors the manner of telling it and is like a seed that grows into a plant. On page 99, Dr. Giraldo receives a telegram requesting instructions about the delivery of a shipment (*despacho*). We do not know of what. He writes "*an* answer," explaining "*without any great scientific conviction*," that "It's the hydrochloric acid." Circumstantially — as an "explanation" to the *telegrafista* (who has asked for none) — this might pass; but why should Giraldo do any explaining at all? Unless, of course, he is putting up a smoke-screen, a possibility that becomes probable if we remember the startling, irrelevant comment about the "scientific conviction" he felt lacking in his explanation. Obviously, there is another level on which to interpret the incident, especially since we do not get the text of the telegram sent. The shipment probably concerns subversive material, perhaps the "clandestine sheets" that a few pages later, and for the very first time in the entire novel, appear in the dentist's office. Note that it is *reading* (the telegram received) and *writing* (the one sent) which raise the subversion to a politically more active level than the lampoons. Similarly, the "llamado [call]" for "demonstrations of force" and "authoritative measures" (p. 128) which Padre Angel *writes* to the mayor intensifies the repression, the "terrorism within the moral order," as the priest calls it (surely one of the most devastating formulations ever found — and in the mouth of a priest! — to justify a bloody, inhuman and cruel repression): the mayor decrees a curfew. Just as the physician disguises the real nature of the shipment as acid, so García Márquez hides protest literature, literature as permanent insurrection, and, finally, his own declared political purpose in writing "The Evil Hour," in the disguise of the lampoons (which soon have as offspring accompanying them the "clandestine leaflets"). One might even say that García Márquez himself in this novel is also engaging in moral "terrorism." It is true that morals and literature today appear to live in a strained relationship; but they only "appear" to, for what is a "permanent insurrection" — ultimately always political — if not in the end moral? Especially in Colombia, in Hispanoamerica, where García Márquez (with so many others) wants to change, or at least criticize, the morals and mores of politics. The lampoons pop up one day on the very walls of those found to be morally wanting as politicians or as oligarchs, of those in "social decomposition," and begin the "silent" rebellion against the status quo; they turn into clandestine opposition propaganda, force the powers that reign and maintain the status quo (oligarchs, church, government, bureaucracy, police) to show their repressive hand and arms, and thus drive the oppressed, once more, "out into the wilderness [al monte] to join the guerrillas" (p. 202). And that is where literature, reading and writing, stops: "In such times justice is not achieved by paper: it is won by guns [a tiros]" (p. 129), says the most correct and open figure in the novel, Señor Benjamín, expert in the writing of petitions. It is not gratuitous that after the proclamation of the curfew there reigned in the pueblo a "sense of collective victory" (p. 141): official literature (radio, films or film-censorship, reports, even drum-rolls and decrees) had shown that "insurgent" literature was right all along.

But do the lampoons tell the truth? Who writes them? To the first question, the answer is twofold and has to do with the "irremediable duplicity" (Vargas Llosa; cf., especially Cosas, p. 76) of writers and of literature. The former write at one and the same time "lies" (literature as fiction) and the "truth" (fiction as a metaphor of reality). Artaud has said that art is "never real and always true." José Donoso speaks of "the metaphor, hidden or open, that is necessarily the substance of literature" (Historia personal del "boom," Anagrama, Barcelona, 1972, p. 103). A revealing example of this relationship between art and life is given, again within the novel and analogous to the structural function of the disguise I pointed out above, during the visit Giraldo makes at Don Sabas's, a recent victim of lampoons. Told of the accusation they lampooned Sabas for, the physician comments: "That story has all the appearance of being the truth" (pp. 101–102), just as a good novel would!

Note, in this context, that the method of killing cattle Don Sabas is accused of in the lampoons is later used to kill Pepe Amador, distributor of the clandestine sheets and alleged author of the lampoons: literature prefigures, within the novel, events in the novel's reality. Cocteau said artists were the antennae of society. Vargas Llosa speaks of a "defeat of objective reality"—here, the power-constellation of oligarchy-church-government—"by an object that, slowly, implacably, reveals its imaginary nature in the course of the story: the lampoons" (p. 445). In *One Hundred Years of Solitude*, José Arcadio's notes preserved the social utility of things by naming them; in "The Evil Hour," the lampoons name the social inutility, i.e., the more or less immoral or criminal or at any rate socially unjust conduct and acts of those in power. Thus, the mayor's repressive "authoritative measures" too are useless " 'Don't waste powder on vultures, lieutenant,' " reads a lampoon hung on his bedroom door. Several times in the book the lampoons contain what everybody knew about anyway: "that's what everybody says" (p. 29); "they only say what people already say; even though one may not know it" (p. 37); "That has always been a characteristic of the lampoons. . . . They say what everybody knows, which certainly is *almost* always the truth" (p. 102). In other words, the lampoons tell the truth just like protest, denunciatory literature does "even though one [i.e., the reader] may not know it"; or although one does know it, as it reads on the next page. True, César Montero's wife may not have had an affair with Pastor, whom César kills at the beginning of the novel upon reading about the alleged infidelity in a lampoon on his door. But precisely by killing him he creates the impression ("*almost . . .* the truth") that the accusation may have been true. Or it may not have been true. The readers of and in the novel do not know; but the account has "all the appearance of being the truth." Besides, for the political effect aimed at it is only of relative importance whether everything in the lampoons is true. Among other things, their purpose is to get the oppressor or the "ricos" to react and show their true character, and above all to prove that they can get away with a lot (as does Montero, who is, in a certain way, in cahoots with the mayor). The point is to expose corruption in the administration of justice in a thoroughly corrupt government. This is the "truth" aimed at by the lampoons. The "decent people" get away with things the "poor people" would never get away with, not even if they did *not* do them (Pepe Amador; possibly, Pastor).

The pen is mightier than the sword then? Certainly its effects can be. Thus, as the dentist, arch-opponent of the regime and therefore severely persecuted by it for many years, reflects, "It would be funny if, after the mayor and his henchmen haven't been able to drive us away with bullets, they were now to drive us out with a sheet of paper on the door" (p. 124). Of course he will *not* be exposed to a lampoon, for he is in the opposition (and therefore moral? García Márquez never goes into this problem). The lampoons' function is social criticism, just as literature's is—in the eyes of Hispanoamerian writers, anyway. It is the on-going critique of a given political reality (cf., Vargas Llosa's long statements about this in *Cosas*). And as such, literature will survive. The lampoons do: the book closes, as it opened, with the priest's servant girl stating—after a repression is again in full swing and the somehow unreal "days of peace and tranquility" proclaimed by the government are over—that "despite the curfew and despite the bullets . . . ," the lampoons are back! They are like *samizdat* literature. But what about literature if social justice, happiness or utopia is ever achieved? "La literatura desaparecerá cuando la humanidad sea feliz, dijo Vargas Llosa [Literature will disappear once humanity is happy, says Vargas Llosa]" (Headline of an EFE news dispatch from Madrid).

Who writes the lampoons? The novel provides several answers, all of them vague or given in what I suspect to be a half-joking manner by García Márquez. Some of them clearly (tongue-in-cheek?) establish the connection between the lampoons and literature, or the novel. Thus Judge Arcadio states "Este es un caso sencillísimo de *novela policíaca* [detective novel]" (p. 33), a term that here takes on an ironical ambiguity. Then he tells of having belonged to an "organization devoted to deciphering enigmas confronting detectives": "Of course, my knowledge of the classics helped me" (Ibid.). Such as *Oedipus* (the plague and the lampoons)? At the *center* of the book, Don Sabas and the physician converse: " 'Be very careful, doctor, I don't want to die without knowing how this novel ends. . . .' 'What novel?'—'The pasquines.' " (pp. 101–102). On page 117, García Márquez makes Arcadio say again that reading the lampoons "is like reading detective novels." The fun (for García Márquez) lies of course in the fact that "The Evil Hour" never reveals who did it. It has been pointed out that *Leaf Storm* is similar to Greek tragedy (*Antigone*); the lampoons too have the ominous tone of a chorus calling out more or less terrible crimes. The name Casandra for the circus-clairvoyante is surely no accident, nor are the allusions to legends and superstitions, the blind grandmother of Mina who insists that everything "is written down" (p. 165). *One Hundred Years of Solitude*, too, we remember, turns out in the end "to have been written down." Delphically, the judge's secretary maintains, "Never, since the world has begun to exist, has it been known who puts up the lampoons" (p. 34), a sentence which itself indicates that the lampoons are meant to be more than mere lampoons. Virtually the same formula describes the official (government) "literature": after the curfew-decree has been read, with drum-roll and a town-crier no less, the widow Montiel exclaims, "since the world exists, the decree has never brought anything good" (p. 131). Each time such "official" literature appears—circulars, instructions, "levantamientos" [uprisings], autopsy-findings—it brings or confirms some repression, i.e., it is conservative; whenever non-official "literature" is mentioned—the lampoons, caricatures, films, "clandestine leaflets"—it represents an incitement to or confirmation of rebellion, i.e., it is subversive. And note that among the ranks of "official literature" we also find comic strips:[5] the mayor's soldiers read *Terry y los pirates* (pp. 39–40); i.e., a kind of "reading"-matter that on the repressive side (the soldiers are ex-convicts, murderers et cetera commissioned by the government) corresponds to the "dibujos" (lampoons-caricature). The writer(s) of the lampoons, although these may have a childish, artless appearance (another disguise? cf., pp. 13, 75 and 93), must be pretty sophisticated and above all aware of the effects achieved by writing.

The question of the origins of the lampoons is actually two: who composes them and who distributes them? But since García Márquez himself does not make this distinction, I believe it does not particularly matter; all the more so if this lack of a distinction heightens the anonymity of the subversive authorship, an anonymity aimed at by García Márquez: Padre Ángel says that "this is an observant village" (p. 46), i.e., the "pueblo" writes the lampoons (through its antennae, the writers); and they tell about what people do "with the lights turned off" (p. 81) — "the *private* history of nations." Thus, Arcadio's "wife," who does "all [her] things in broad daylight," as does Señor Benjamín (with the difference that he does not copulate at all for fear of what others might say, whereas Arcadio and his "wife" habitually do so with the door open), has no fear of lampoons, nor does Benjamín, for "nobody wastes his time putting up a lampoon on my door, whereas the doors of all the oligarchs of the village are covered with them" (p. 81). This "class-consciousness" of the lampoon-ers would explain why Padre Ángel attributes the "papeluchos" [ugly messages] to "the envy in an exemplary village," to which Dr. Grimaldo says, "We doctors didn't diagnose people that way even in the Middle Ages" (p. 104). In other words, the priest's terminology and the ideology it reveals are no longer relevant: social unrest and rebellion against social injustice can no longer be waved aside as "sin"; they have become a right. Therefore, "in the homes of the poor, too, people talked about the lampoons but in a different way and even with a healthy joy [*alegría*]" (Ibid.). Are the lampoons a sort of vox populi, then? At any rate, they are *vox pauperi*. Judge Arcadio points to their anonymous origin explicitly: "the lampoons were not the work of one single person. They don't seem to be part of a concerted plan. . . . Perhaps it is not one man or one woman. Perhaps they are different men and different women, each one acting by him- or herself" (pp. 141–42). Like novelists. Finally, so as to leave no more doubt—or no more certainty—at all, no less than Casandra, consulted by the mayor, reads her cards and states: "Es todo el pueblo y no es nadie" (It is the whole village and it is nobody; p. 149). Remember "Fuenteovejuna": "todos a una"?

Who then *does* write the lampoons?

Gabriel García Márquez does. And "The Evil Hour" is the most detailed and the best disguised, the most complex and the most sophisti-cated lampoon of them all.

I think it is just to conclude this article with a quotation from page 327 of *One Hundred Years of Solitude* that I consider singularly appropri-ate: "La literatura era el mejor juguete que se había inventado para burlarse de la gente" (Literature was the best toy that had been invented to make fun of people).

Notes

1. H. N. Fügen, "Literaturkonsum und Sozialprestige," in *Der Leser als Teil des literarischen Lebens*, Bonn, Bouvier Verlag, 1971, p. 35: ". . . it is difficult for the State to have itself represented by its literati" (translation by W.A.L.) Julio Cortázar, *Pameos y meopas*, p. 9. Claude Lévi-Strauss, "Du mythe au roman," in *L'origine des manières de table*, Paris, Plon, 1968, p. 106.

Italics in quotations are always mine, unless otherwise stated. Passages quoted that originally were not in English represent my own translations. Where Spanish texts are easily understood through cognates, no translation was made. I used the eighth edition (Colección Indice) of *La mala hora*. Editorial Sudamericana, Buenos Aires, 1972.

2. Mario Vargas Llosa, *García Márquez: Historia de un deicidio*, Barcelona-Caracas, Monte Avila Editores, 1971, p. 541. The chapter on *La mala hora* comprises pages 421–56. Cf., also the introductory chapter.

3. *Cosas de escritores* (interviews by Ernesto González Bermejo with García Márquez, M. Vargas Llosa, J. Cortázar), Montevideo, Biblioteca de *Marcha*, 1971, p. 89. See also *La novela en América Latina: Diálogo* (García Márquez — Vargas Llosa), Lima, C. Milla Batres / Ediciones Universidad Nacional de Ingeniería, 1968.

4. I make this reservation because García Márquez at times likes to make fun of those interviewing him: "Interviews are a new genre of literary fiction: I answer the questions with the same criterion with which I write a story." (Interview in *Panorama* 7, No. 128, October 7-12, 1969).

5. For a view of how Latin American intellectuals tend to see North American comic strips, see the recent study by the Chilean Ariel Dorfman, *Cómo leer al Pato Donald*, Santiago, Editorial Universitaria, 1972. It cannot surprise us that García Márquez makes, of all people, the henchmen of the mayor read such "literature." Dr. Giraldo reads Dickens.

The Double Inscription of the *Narrataire* in "Los funerales de la Mamá Grande"

David William Foster*

[For the first time people spoke of her and conceived of her without her rattan rocker, her afternoon stupors, and her mustard plasters, and they saw her ageless and pure, distilled by legend.] (p. 141)[1]

I

If ["Balthazar's Marvelous Afternoon"] may be characterized in terms of narrative irony at the expense of the characters with a concomitant complicity between narrator and implied reader, the title story of [*Big Mama's Funeral*] takes a step further in developing a complex image of the

*Reprinted by permission of the publisher, from *Studies in the Contemporary Spanish-American Short Story* (Columbia: University of Missouri Press, 1979), 51–62. Copyright 1979 by University of Missouri Press. All rights reserved.

narrataire or receiver of García Márquez's narratives. Although the story has been analyzed from many points of view — the use of exaggeration for satiric-comic effect; the distillation of the Colombian writer's denunciation of feudal society as embodied in the legendary frame of the all-powerful Mother Earth figure;[2] the use of a tone and devices that remind us of the traditional folktale, the interplay between history, legend, and fiction — no one has studied one of the most salient features of the text: the explicit projection of an image of the reader and the bifurcation of that image into two conflicting and non-complementary modes.

II

It is impossible to study all narratives in terms of the structural markers that identify the implied reader — the *narrataire*, as Gerald Prince has called him. These markers may range from specific vocabulary choices that suggest a particular type of reader, perhaps one far different in sociocultural formation from the characters being described (this is, in fact, an option that we associate with naturalistic fiction, which involves its own form of narrator-reader complicity), to overt asides to or invocations of the reader. (I will use "reader" to refer to someone actually addressed, *narrataire* to refer to the implied — and therefore ideal — reader of a text; clearly, the two may be one and the same in terms of the *écriture* of a particular narrative).

In García Márquez's fiction, the *narrataire* is particularly prominent structurally, and a novel like *Cien años de soledad* can only function on the basis of an implied reader who will, in his decoding of the structurally complex novel, identify himself (if only subconsciously at first) with the many characters who undertake to decipher Melquíades's manuscript. When manuscript and novel become the same text, character and narrative become the same entity, engaged in reading the same retrospective prophecy of their sociohistorical experience.

Yet, few of García Márquez's stories are explicitly addressed to a reader, and the fact that "Los funerales" does involve an audience is perhaps why this one text has received attention in terms of the conventions of the traditional folk raconteur. Actually, the explicit address occurs only in the opening lines of the story:

> [This is, for all the world's unbelievers, the true story of Big Mama, absolute sovereign of the Kingdom of Macondo, who lived for ninety-two years, and died in the odor of sanctity one Tuesday last September, and whose funeral was attended by the Pope.] (p. 127).

Indeed, one could argue that such a delivery to a presumed public is merely conventional and serves more to specify the self-image of the storyteller than that of the *narrataire*. In any case, what we can say is that there is unquestionably the implied specification of a single kind of *narrataire*: the openmouthed ingenue who will be impressed by the verbal flourishes that accompany the marvelous, extraordinary tale the raconteur is about to unfold: his wisdom and his superior talent will provide us with an instructive entertainment. Yet, any serious reading of the story (and García Márquez's texts are just entertaining enough as farfetched yarns to threaten cunningly the serious intent of determined reader-critics) quickly reveals that the story is meaningless if the *narrataire* is left identified exclusively with the reader who is overtly addressed in the first sentence.

The *écriture* of "Los funerales" depends on the interaction of two kinds of *narrataires*. One is the receptor of the folk narrative, one of the *incrédulos* for whom the details of the story are simply too far beyond his everyday experience to be assimilated in terms other than the fantastic and the marvelous. For this reader, the legend of Mamá Grande is palpable reality because it is simply his daily experience with the feudal society in which he lives, written in the grander terms of Mamá Grande as told impressively by a raconteur with superior information. In short, the "folktale *narrataire*" comes close to the implied reader of official writings — history books, constitutions, newspapers, self-serving speeches — that is, the reader of official myths and lies that become guiding truths by virtue of their cunning rhetoric.

The second *narrataire* of García Márquez's story is the reader who is supposed to be able to gauge the distance between official history, folk legend, and demythifying literature. In short, the reader who is able implicitly to discover the ways in which the purported raconteur's tale is not the exegesis of legend, with its own particular supplements to it, but the demythification of both legend and official history and the denunciation of the way in which the two intersect to the advantage of official myths.[3] Although this *narrataire* is never spoken to explicitly, both the closing comment of the narrator's introduction and the closing remarks of his story may be taken as postulating the need for the emergence of the "critical *narrataire*" as opposed to the passive receptor of folk legends:

> [Now that the nation, which was shaken to its vitals, has recovered its balance; now that the bagpipers of San Jacinto, the smugglers of Guajira, the rice planters of Sinú, the prostitutes of Caucamayal, the wizards of Sierpe, and the banana laborers of Aracataca have folded up their tents to recover from the exhausting vigil and have regained their serenity, and the President of the Republic and his Ministers and all those who represented the public and supernatural powers at the most magnificent funeral recorded in the annals of history have regained control of their estates; now that the Holy Pontiff has risen up to Heaven in body and soul; and now that it is impossible to walk around in Macondo because of the empty bottles, the cigarette butts, the gnawed bones, the cans and rags and excrement that the crowd which came to the burial left behind; now is the time to place a stool against the front door and relate from the beginning the details of this national commotion, before the historians have time to get to it.] (p. 127)

. . . Now the Supreme Pontiff could ascend to Heaven in body and soul, his mission on earth fulfilled, and the President of the Republic could sit down and govern according to his good judgment, and the queens of all things that have been or ever will be could marry and be happy and conceive and give birth to many sons, and the common people could set up their tents where they damn well pleased in the limitless domains of Big Mama, because the only one who could oppose them and had enough power to do so had begun to rot beneath a lead plinth. The only thing left then was for somebody to place a stool against the doorway to tell this story, lesson and example for future generations, so that not one of the world's disbelievers would be left who did not know the story of Big Mama, because tomorrow, Wednesday, the garbage men will come and sweep up the trash from her funeral, forever and ever.] (pp. 146–47).

In this sense, "Los funerales" may be viewed as a metanarrative that functions on two levels, one straightforward and one that is self-ironizing and, therefore, self-critical. Since these two levels are contained within the same narrative, they cannot be easily separated and must be identified as present in the form of certain markers or features that signal the underlying tension between two *narrataires* of the same overt utterances. The insistence on the need for this text, on the need for someone [to place a stool against the doorway to tell the story], as opposed to the already existing legend on the one hand and the oblique suggestion of what the historian will do with the material on the other, results in two strategic insistences on story versus legend-history in addition to the juxtaposition established in the opening paragraphs of the text. On the occasion of the description of the repercussions at the highest levels of government of Mamá Grande's death, the narrator notes how the event must be assimilated into official history:

[The events of that night and the following events would later be identified as a historic lesson. Not only because of the Christian spirit which inspired the most lofty personages of public power, but also because of the abnegation with which unlike interests and conflicting judgments were conciliated in the common goal of burying the illustrious body. For many years Big Mama had guaranteed the social peace and political harmony of her empire, by virtue of the three trunks full of forged electoral certificates which formed part of her secret estate.] (p. 139)

Indeed, it is only when the lawyers and constitutional lawmakers have succeeded in harmonizing Mamá Grande's death, which had occurred months before, with the highest purposes of the state that the funeral is allowed to proceed with all due ceremony:

. . . Then the full awareness of his historical destiny dawned on him (the President), and he decreed nine days of national mourning, posthumous honors for Big Mama at the rank appropriate for a heroine who had died for the fatherland on the field of battle. As he stated in the dramatic address he delivered that morning to his compatriots over the national radio and television network, the Nation's Leader trusted that the funeral rites for Big Mama would set a new example for the world.] (p. 140)

Clearly, the event, which is part of legend on the narrative legend of the people, who live on the margin (and at the mercy of) officialdom, has been made into history to serve the demands of the latter. The text, as literature (*historia literaria* versus *historia oficial*), is able to challenge that process through the creation of a secondary, critical *narrataire*. It is the latter, of course, who is able to gauge the ironic incongruency of the following segment of narrative:

[So much had been said that the discussions crossed the borders, traversed the ocean, and blew like an omen through the pontifical apartments at Castelgandolfo. Recovered from the drowsiness of the sleepy days of August, the Supreme Pontiff was at the window watching the lake where the divers were searching for the head of a decapitated young girl. For the last few weeks the evening newspapers had been full of nothing else, and the Supreme Pontiff could not ignore an enigma located such a short distance from his summer residence. But that evening, in an unforeseen substitution, the newspapers exchanged the photographs of the possible victims for that of one single twenty-year-old woman, marked off with black margins. "Big Mama," exclaimed the Supreme Pontiff, recognizing immediately the hazy daguerrotype which many years before had been offered to him on the occasion of his ascent to the Throne of Saint Peter. "Big Mama," exclaimed in chorus the members of the College of Cardinals in their private apartments, and for the third time in twenty centuries there was an hour of confusion, chagrin, and bustle in the limitless empire of Christendom, until the Supreme Pontiff was installed in his long black limousine en route to Big Mama's fantastic and distant funeral.] (pp. 141–42)

The third occasion on which the narrator refers to the tension between history, legend, and story is in the closing paragraph of the text, the last lines of which have already been quoted. What has not been quoted is the long period that precedes the sentence (itself a "majestic" period) that begins ["Now the Supreme Pontiff could . . ."]. This period, which is structured in terms of a series of phrases beginning with ["Nobody"] and followed by verbs of perception ["saw," "noticed," "noticed"] definitively established the juxtaposition between the receptors of legend—the masses of people who are able only to experience the sense of relief in the fact that, at last, it is all over—and the critical *narrataire* who, because he is the receptor of ["this story, lesson and example for future generations"], is able, precisely, to see how the *historia* [*literaria*] is, in fact, a legitimate ["lesson and example"]. It may well be that García Márquez, like many a committed Latin-American writer who would want the audience of legend retold with the flourishes of folktale to become the critical reader able to perceive the dreadful sense of an extraordinary event, would want his literature and the image of narrative that it embodies to function as a process for the formation of the latter out of the former. Nevertheless, the text, while it does incorporate a metacommentary on the nature of narrative, does not do so regarding textual *narrataires*, and the only way in which we can speak of the interplay between the folk receptor and the critical reader is by projecting the narrative circuit suggested by what metacommentary is included in "Los funerales." To the extent that the verbal texture of García Márquez's text is stylistically bivalent — an echo of traditional, entertaining folktales versus explicit references to the story as a gesture of demythification — we may speak of the presence of dual *narrataires*, one for each level of style. To the extent that the image of narrative as demythification in the end asserts itself at the expense of innocuous popular legend (and oppressive official history), we may speak equally of the suppression of the first type of *narrataire* by the second, critical one. It is only in this sense that we can maintain that García Márquez's story, despite the presence of traits taken from the "charming" tradition of popular folk narratives, does in fact conclude by postulating the bases of its own appropriate demythifying readings and the image of the critical reader capable of undertaking the process. At the same time, both *narrataires* allow García Márquez to relate his story in terms of innocuous tales that, because they reduce historical events to legend, deprive events of the opportunity to serve as ["lesson and example for future generations"], a function that is alleged necessary if the people are ever to attain any significant degree of revolutionary self-knowledge. Thus, the writer both mocks a form of ineffectual narrative on significant "epic" events (in both a routine and a Brechtian sense of the word) and proposes, through the medium of his parody, what he considers to be an appropriately critical telling — and, hence, reading — of historical occurrences.

III

It remains, then, to describe the *écriture* of "Los funerales" by which the image of one type of *narrataire* — the openmouthed *incrédulo* ["incredulous one"] — is supplanted by another, the critical *incrédulo*. In short, how does the story mock its own pseudo-folktale format to suggest a more appropriate level of narrative story?

There appear to be at least five rhetorical processes by which it is possible to gauge the implied rejection of one reader in favor of another: (1) exaggeration, (2) incredible circumstances, (3) remote or unusual practices, (4) ironic language, and (5) pejorative or satiric insinuations. It is notable that the most overt process is lacking: the overt address of one reader at the expense of the other. Since there is no direct address ever made to the proposed implied "appropriate" reader, it is necessary to identify him through the functional presence of the rhetorical processes listed. At the same time, it should be evident that these processes overlap in nature and presumed effect. The only reason that we are justified in speaking of different types is because we acknowledge that a literary text, for reasons of stylistic variety, is going to modulate its rhetorical pattern. Thus, rather than speaking of one basic device, we recognize several related but slightly different processes working together to accomplish an overall structural goal: the signalling of the two levels of implied *narrataires*.

Exaggeration is recognized as one of García Márquez's stock rhetorical plays, particularly when it is based on chaotic enumeration, coupled with what is essentially comic because of the inappropriateness of detail or the juxtaposition of unassociated details. Exaggeration in "Los funerales" helps to identify the alternate reader to the extent that, by distorting the details of the superficial narrative (the folktale), it suggests the absurdity of taking it at its face value. Throughout, the face value of the text is the folktale homage to the grandeur of Mamá Grande and an epic paeon to her majestic death. The implied "secret" text is the demythification of such a homage and the laying bare of how the legendary matriarch was the powerful embodiment of an oppressive social system, a woman to inspire hate rather than awe. The explicit text, when read by the implied folk *narrataire*, is marked by dignified respect. When read by the aroused *narrataire*, it is characterized by derisive ridicule. Exaggeration, like the other rhetorical processes that have been identified, functions as a key postulate of the text's *écriture* to signal the necessary, imperative transition from one reader to another. One example of exaggeration is the following passage, which speaks of the extent of Mamá Grande's domain:

> [The imminence of her death stirred the exhausting expectation. The dying woman's voice, accustomed to homage and obedience, was no louder than a bass organ pipe in the closed room, but it echoed throughout the most far-flung corners of the estate. No one was indifferent to her death. During this century, Big Mama had been Macondo's center of gravity, as had her parents in the past, in a dominance which covered two centuries. The town was founded on her surname. No one knew the origin, or the limits or the true value of her estate, but everyone was used to believing that Big Mama was the owner of the waters, running and still, of rain and drought, and of the district's roads, telegraph poles, leap years, and heat waves, and that she had furthermore a hereditary right over life and property. When she sat on her balcony in the cool afternoon air, with all the weight of her belly and authority squeezed into her old rattan rocker, she seemed, in truth, infinitely rich and powerful, the richest and most powerful matron in the world.] (pp. 129–30)

Or, in this passage, where the conjunction of details is incongruous and therefore self-mocking:

[The wealth of the subsoil, the territorial waters, the colors of the flag, national sovereignty, the traditional parties, the rights of man, civil rights, the nation's leadership, the right of appeal, Congressional hearings, letters of recommendation, historical records, free elections, beauty queens, transcendental speeches, large demonstrations, distinguished young ladies, polite gentlemen, punctilious military men, His Illustrious Eminence, the Supreme Court, goods whose importation was forbidden, liberal ladies, the meat problem, the purity of the language, setting a good example, the free but responsible press, the Athens of South America, public opinion, the lessons of democracy, Christian morality, the shortage of foreign exchange, the right of asylum, the Communist menace, the ship of state, the high cost of living, republican traditions, the underprivileged classes, statements of political support.

She didn't manage to finish. The laborious enumeration cut off her last breath. Drowning in the pandemonium of abstract formulas that for two centuries had constituted the moral justification of the family's power, Big Mama emitted a loud belch and expired.] (p. 137)

Many other passages could be cited (for example, the physician's remedies [p. 131], the legislator's deliberations [pp. 140–41], and the funeral procession [pp. 144–46]). Since comic exaggeration is one of the Colombian writer's stock devices, one that he takes from those folktales that likewise mock what they pretend to report seriously, it is not surprising that the text is replete with strategic — and effective — examples.

By *incredible circumstance* one refers to those conjunctions of incongruous detail whereby the particular need to demythify legend — at least when that legend can be seen by the *narrataire* to deviate significantly from a civilized norm — may be stressed. For example, the attendance at Mamá Grande's funeral by both the President of the Republic (made possible by only the most lengthy of constitutional "adjustments") and by the Holy Father (made possible by only the most arduous of transatlantic crossings in his ["long black gondola"] [The Pope's traditional black Mercedes Benz 600?]) is an outrageous inflation of the honors due a local matriarch, no matter how symbolic of a feudal status quo. Hence, the description that has already been transcribed of how the Pontiff learns of the woman's death and undertakes his unheard of journey to the New World, a journey that the forewarned reader will immediately correlate with the visit by Pope Paul to Colombia in the mid-sixties, the first visit to the New World by a pope.

On the other hand, *remote or unusual practices* refers to a circumstance that, by its very nature, demands a reaction of incredulity. For example, we learn that the venerable matriarch, although endowed with the mammary attributes of a fecund Mother Earth figure, in fact, dies a virgin:

[Her hour had come. Seeing her in her linen bed, bedaubed with aloes up to her ears, under the dusty canopy of Oriental crepe, one could hardly detect any life in the thin respiration of her matriarchal breasts. Big Mama, who until she was fifty rejected the most passionate suitors, and who was well enough endowed by Nature to suckle her entire issue all by herself, was dying a virgin and childless. At the moment of extreme unction, Father Anthony Isabel had to ask for help in order to apply the oils to the palms of her hands, for Mama had clenched her fists. The nieces' assistance was useless. In the struggle, for the first time in a week, the dying woman pressed against her chest the hand bejeweled with precious stones and fixed her colorless look on her nieces, saying, "Highway robbers." Then she saw Father Anthony Isabel in his liturgical habit and the acolyte with the sacramental implements, and with calm conviction she murmured, "I am dying." Then she took off the ring with the huge diamond and gave it to Magdalena, the novice, to whom it belonged since she was the youngest heir. That was the end of a tradition: Magdalena had renounced her inheritance in favor of the Church.] (pp. 133–34)

The significance to a sociologically committed reader of the self-enforced sterility of the "mother" figure and her bestowal of the symbols of her matriarchy upon a niece who, by taking the nun's veil, has also denied herself a legitimate biological role is too obvious to require belaboring. Unlike Ursula but like the bitch-woman Fernanda in *Cien años de soledad*, Mamá Grande exercises power despite an illegitimate repudiation of a productive role in society: she controls the reins of material wealth without contributing to their production as either a human being or a woman. (This is not to be taken as a sexist assignment of a predetermined role to María del Rosario Castañeda y Montero: it is her "title" and her assumed role as supreme matriarch that defines a social role that she refuses to honor. Mamá Grande is, therefore, a false mother figure, as is the Virgin Mary by the implications of Mamá Grande's endowment to her niece.)[4]

Ironic language, which unquestionably is a correlative of exaggeration and the signalling of incredible circumstances, deserves specific identification as the verbal marker of the link between the overt and the secret text. It tells us, in essence, to contradict semantically what is being explicitly signified by the verbal signs of the text. The conclusion of the story is perhaps the best example of the functional use of irony in "Los funerales," for it is here that the narrator, although reaffirming the folk nature of his tale, delineates an underlying meaning — the attainment of a structure-breaking millenium in the debt of Mamá Grande that is to be set against both innocuous legend and oppressive official history. It is this delineation that most directly evokes what I have called the "appropriate narrative" demanded by the text, and irony is a particularly effective instrument in the process. At other places in the text, like for example when the importance of Mamá Grande's death is elevated to the status of a national crisis (["The social order had been brushed by death"] [p. 138]), verbal irony is useful for marking the disjuncture between the meanness of Mamá Grande's domain and the terms in which it is viewed by her partners in capricious power.[5] This disjuncture is particularly emphasized by the following type of irony, based as it is on the juxtaposition of the glorious and the mundane:

> [Such a noble goal was to conflict nevertheless with certain grave inconveniences. The judicial structure of the country, built by remote ancestors of Big Mama, was not prepared for events such as those which began to occur. Wise Doctors of Law, certified alchemists of the statutes, plunged into hermeneutics and syllogisms in search of the formula which would permit the President of the Republic to attend the funeral. The upper strata of politics, the clergy, the financiers lived through entire days of alarm. In the vast semicircle of Congress, rarefied by a century of abstract legislation, amid oil paintings of National Heroes and busts of Greek thinkers, the vocation of Big Mama reached unheard-of proportions, while her body filled with bubbles in the hot Macondo September.] (pp. 140–41)

Pejorative or satiric insinuations are, in a sense, the culmination of the foregoing elements in that they overtly refer to the demand for demythification. Appropriately, they allude specifically to matters concerning the social and political order incarnate in Mamá Grande's person. The long period that is the second paragraph of the story (p. 127) is full of indirect meanings. The series of clauses introduced by ["now that"] establishes a counterpoint between a present circumstance and an absent one, alternately past and future. Whether the past is at issue (presumably the one of the secure and inalterable legend, of the belief that Mamá Grande was immortal) or the future (the order to be built out of the collapse of a feudal autocracy held together by only the allegedly eternal matriarch; compare the closing paragraph of the text) is of secondary importance. What is important is that it is not that of the present, defined in terms of streets clogged by empty bottles and the memory of a hubbub reminiscent of a raunchy medieval fair. The text sardonically defines an alternate order by virtue of its not being what is explicitly described. Against the backdrop of the interplay between the text that speaks and the secret text that is silent, the narrator undertakes to weave his story. Ostensibly framed by the present circumstance, that story, in fact, elaborates a counterpoint between what can be stated openly (legend and official history) and what can be stated in absentia (demythificational narrative). It is also, by extension, a counterpoint between the two *narrataires*, the characterization of which has been the central concern of this study of the narrative *écriture* of "Los funerales."

IV

In closing his ecphrasis on Mamá Grande's funeral cortege, the narrator observes the following:

[In her coffin draped in purple, separated from reality by eight copper turnbuckles, Big Mama was at that moment too absorbed in her formaldehyde eternity to realize the magnitude of her grandeur. All the splendor that she had dreamed of on the balcony of her house during her heat-induced insomnia was fulfilled by those forty-eight glorious hours during which all the symbols of the age paid homage to her memory. The Supreme Pontiff himself, whom she in her delirium imagined floating above the gardens of the Vatican in a resplendent carriage, conquered the heat with a plaited palm fan, and honored with his Supreme Dignity the greatest funeral in the world.] (pp. 145–46)

It is clear that the series of events has been perceived in terms of two orders separated by an imbreachable abyss: on the one hand, Mamá Grande and the ego-centered legend that surrounds her and that she has in large measure created and perpetuated; on the other hand, the "reality" of the narrator, who is obliged to the series of events because of its oppressive sway as a sociopolitical occurrence, but who is committed also to exorcising its oppressive weight through the medium of his demythifying narrative. Once again, we can speak of the fundamental opposition postulated by the *écriture* of "Los funerales": the *narrataire* who accepts the legend in all of its eccentric array (for example, Mamá Grande's mighty burp as she expires, the Italian candies distributed to the children of the matriarch's fiefdom by the Holy Father) versus the *narrataire* who prevails in his understanding of the tragic absurdity of such a social order. The "shock of recognition," which reminds readers that few social orders if any are better than tragically absurd—and that Macondo's is so only to an extreme if accurate degree—is effected through the *écriture* of the dual implied *narrataires*. As I have already suggested, the use of a folktale style that validates the passive *narrataire* as the most immediate sense of the text only enhances the shock of recognition when unspoken text and the *narrataire* that it demands begin to emerge via the specific details of rhetorical inscription that have been discussed in this analysis.

Notes

1. García Márquez, "Los funerales de la Mamá Grande," in *Los funerales de la Mamá Grande*, 6th ed. (Buenos Aires: Editorial Sudamericana, 1969), pp. 125–47. All quotes are from this edition.

2. Although the last segment of his essay deals with ["the feudal society"], Mario Vargas Llosa places greater emphasis on the mythic-legendary quality of the story: "Los funerales de la Mamá Grande: exageración y perspectiva mítica," in his *García Márquez: Historia de un deicidio* (Barcelona: Barral Editores, 1971), pp. 398–419. The title of Vargas Llosa's monograph certainly stresses García Márquez's literature as implicitly demythificational. Judith Goetzinger, "The Emergence of Folk Myth in 'Los funerales de la Mamá Grande,' " *Revista de Estudios Hispánicos* 6 (1972); 237–48, despite the title of her paper, also realizes that the narrator is interested not in comic entertainment but in presenting a "powerful apocalyptical vision of total decay" (p. 248). It is, unfortunately, Ricardo Gullón's monograph that has done the most to suggest the image of García Márquez as a [charming

narrator]. See his *García Márquez o el olvidado arte de contar* (Madrid: Taurus, 1970); María Delia Rasetti, "Análisis del 'motivo' en *Los funerales de la Mamá Grande*," *Revista de Literaturas Hispánicas* 10 (1970):88–98; and Robert Sims, "The Creation of Myth in García Márquez' 'Los funerales de la Mamá Grande,'" *Hispania* 61 (1978): 14–23.

3. One of the major points made by René Jara in his essay on *Cien años de soledad* concerns the creation of an image of myth as a demythificational force. René Jara and Jaime Mejía, *Las claves del mito en García Márquez* (Valparaíso, Chile: Ediciones Universitarias de Valparaíso, 1972), part 1.

4. The best material concerning García Márquez's portrayal of a sterile feudal society is Josefina Ludmer's *Cien años de soledad: una interpretación* (Buenos Aires: Editorial Tiempo Contemporáneo, 1972).

5. For the writer's political concepts, see Gregory Lawrence, "Marx in Macondo," *Latin American Literary Review* 2:4 (1974):49–57.

Gabriel García Márquez (Colombia, 1928–)

D. P. Gallagher*

Gabriel García Márquez is a man who has so far dedicated his entire literary career to the writing of one novel. That is not to say that he has written only one book. It is rather that such short works as *La hojarasca* (*Chaff*, 1955), *El coronel no tiene quien le escriba* (*No One Writes to the Colonel*, 1961), and *La mala hora* ([*In*] '*The Evil Hour*,' 1962), and the short stories collected in *Los funerales de la Mamá Grande* [*Big Mama's Funeral*], 1962), though promising enough, can be seen now as warming up exercises for his masterpiece, *Cien años de soledad* (*One Hundred Years of Solitude*, 1967).[1] Nearly all his works explore a remote, swampy, imaginary town called Macondo, a backwater in the Colombian *ciénaga*, the region where García Márquez was brought up. The richly charted town of Macondo is García Márquez's fictional "world," his contribution to Latin American literature. Yet the Macondo whose hundred years of solitary history is recorded triumphantly in *Cien años de soledad* had to be built, brick by brick, in its creator's imagination. The earlier works serve this purpose of meticulous construction. For this reason I shall concentrate on the definitive novel. Indeed there is nothing of importance that can be said of it that cannot be applied to the previous works.

Of all the contemporary Latin American novels, none has captured the public imagination more than *Cien años de soledad*. It has sold hundreds of thousands of copies in Latin America and Spain, and many more in numerous translations. In Latin America it appears, remarkably, to appeal to most people who can read. Enthusiasm for it comes readily from university professors, but also, for example, from ladies who normally read Spanish translations of Agatha Christie. The enthusiasm, moreover, appears to be genuine. Why?

The main reason for the book's success may be that it can be read on many levels, and there is a superficial level on which it can be read of very obvious appeal. For this town of Macondo that García Márquez has been inventing for so many years is an extraordinarily dotty place, populated by endearingly eccentric people whose antics are, above all, *funny*. The novel is full of comic caricatures. Thus young Remedios, la bella, a member of the Buendía family whose trajectory over one hundred years is the principal topic of the novel:

> Until she was well along in puberty Santa Sofía de la Piedad had to bathe and dress her, and even when she could take care of herself it was necessary to keep an eye on her so that she would not paint little animals on the walls with a stick daubed in her own excrement. She reached twenty without knowing how to read or write, unable to use the silver at the table, wandering naked through the house because her nature rejected all manner of convention. When the young commander of the guard declared his love for her, she rejected him simply because his frivolity startled her. "See how simple he is," she told Amaranta. "He says that he is dying because of me, as if I were a bad case of colic."[2]

The dead-pan depiction of extraordinary people and extraordinary events is indeed one of the principal stratagems the book employs to achieve its comic effects. Events and personal characteristics are spectacularly *exaggerated*, made quite absurdly larger than life, yet in a style that takes the hyperbole for granted, as though it were a meticulous fact. Thus a young Buendía, Meme, brings sixty-eight friends back home from school for the holidays: "The night of their arrival the students carried on in such a way, trying to go to the bathroom before they went to bed, that at one o'clock in the morning the last ones were still going in. Fernada then bought seventy-two chamberpots but she only managed to change the nocturnal problem into a morning one, because from dawn on there was a long line of girls, each with her pot in her hand, waiting for her turn to wash it."[3] In the same vein, as though they were the most natural of facts, we are told of how a man (the itinerant gipsy sage Melquíades), returns to life after dying because he could not stand the loneliness of death, or of how Remedios, la bella, is lifted up to Heaven like the Virgin Mary. When José Arcadio, a senior Buendía, dies, a rain of tiny yellow flowers carpets the streets. And his mother, Ursula, learns of his death thanks to a thread of his blood that exits from his house into the street and, meticulously turning corners, travels relentlessly to Ursula's house, reaching the kitchen where Ursula "was getting ready to crack thirty-six eggs to make bread."[4]

These straightforward descriptions of the extraordinary are the hallmark of García Márquez's art. There is plenty of satisfaction to be derived from this book simply in the savouring of his joy in whimsy and much of the novel's appeal lies in the sense of liberation it inspires in one: liberation from a humdrum real world into a magical one that also happens to be funny. It also happens to be exotically tropical, of course, and part of the novel's success in France or Argentina, for example, may be due also to its differentness.

Yet the novel functions at far deeper levels. Like several other contemporary Latin American novelists García Márquez has discovered that it is possible to tell a compelling story in a novel yet also convey complex thoughts in it which do not disturb the story's rhythm.

A clue to one of the novel's more complex aims can be found in its occasional references to other Latin American novels. Thus one character claims to have witnessed the heroism of Artemio Cruz during the Mexican revolution:[5] Artemio Cruz is the eponymous hero of a novel by Carlos Fuentes. Another character stays in Paris in the same hotel room where "Rocamadour was to die":[6] Rocamadour is a baby who dies in a hotel room in Julio Cortázar's *Rayuela* [Hopscotch]. The main implications of these and several other instances where the characters have similar contact with characters in other novels will be discussed later. For the moment it should be merely stressed that these references show that García Márquez is assiduously *aware* of other Latin American writers. We shall see that *Cien años de soledad* is almost as much a reading of them as an exercise in original creativeness.

Sometimes García Márquez seems deliberately to be invading the "territory" of other writers. There are scenes which could almost have been written by Alejo Carpentier, others which could almost have been written by Borges or by Juan Rulfo. Take this description of a dream that José Arcadio Buendía[7] recurrently has:

> When he was alone, José Arcadio Buendía consoled himself with the dream of the infinite rooms. He dreamed that he was getting out of bed, opening the door and going into an identical room with the same bed with a wrought-iron head, the same wicker chair, and the same small picture of the Virgin of Help on the back wall. From that room he would go into another that was just the same, the door of which would open into another that was just the same . . . and so on to infinity. He liked to go from room to room, as in a gallery of parallel mirrors. . . .[8]

Borges has created labyrinths of a very similar kind. And who but Borges and the final Aureliano would read an English encyclopedia not for reference, but from beginning to end "as if it were a novel?"[9]

Messages to Borges are numerous in *Cien años de soledad*, and there are many others directed at Alejo Carpentier. What, then, is their purpose? Is García Márquez merely engaged in some Nabokovian game to be deciphered by some Latin American Mary Macarthy? I don't think so. I believe that he is attempting to suggest to his readers that one of the novel's fundamental aims is to tell us something about the nature of contemporary

Latin American writing on which we shall see that it acts as a kind of interpretative meditation. For the novel places many of the obsessions of contemporary Latin American writing in an illuminating context.

This it does in particular with regard to fantasy, which we have noted is one of the central ingredients of contemporary Latin American fiction. In the works of Borges, Bioy Casares, Sábato, Cortázar, Rulfo, José María Arguedas, Asturias, and Juan Carlos Onetti, to name but a few, fantasy is spectacularly evident. Why? It would seem to be one of the roles of *Cien años de soledad* to suggest several plausible reasons.

In the first place, the novel shows how there can be no continental agreement on what is real and what is fantastic in a continent where it is possible for a palaeolithic community to reside at an hour or two's flight from a vast, modern city. Backwardness of course need not be palaeolithic. A wholly isolated village in a Colombian swamp with religious beliefs almost unchanged from those imparted by the Spanish medieval Church is sure to have an appreciation of reality somewhat different from the one entertained by the inhabitants say of Bogotá. The Assumption of a local girl, the ability of a local priest effortlessly to levitate, a rain of yellow flowers — all these things are less astonishing for the people of Macondo than the "modern inventions" that reach the town from time to time, such as ice, magnets, magnifying glasses, false teeth, the cinema, and the railway. One's distinctions between fantasy and reality therefore depend a great deal on one's cultural assumptions. And in an isolated community, such distinctions are likely to be perceived from a particularly *ex-centric* perspective, should one wish, arbitrarily perhaps, to take modern Western civilization as a centre of reference.

Now modern Western civilization is represented in the novel by Bogotá and by an American Company that sets up a banana plantation in Macondo. But neither Bogotá nor the American company turns out to be a very reliable guide as to what is real and what is fantastic. Take the American banana plantation where José Arcadio Segundo initiates a strike. As a result of it some three thousand workers are massacred and their bodies are secretly whisked away one night on a vast train. José Arcadio Segundo witnesses the massacre, but the authorities deny it. The official version predominates, and years later it is possible to read in school textbooks in Colombia that there never even was a banana plantation in Macondo at all.[10]

For the Government and for the Americans reality is something then that you can cavalierly fabricate at your own convenience. So who can blame a mere citizen of Macondo for believing in the Assumption of a local beauty? And who can blame García Márquez for choosing to liberate himself from official lies by telling his own lies, or otherwise for choosing to exaggerate the Government's lies *ad absurdum*? Many of the fantasies of *Cien años de soledad* are indeed absurd but logical exaggerations of real situations. Thus if the Americans, backed by their lawyers — "those illusionists of the bar"[11] — can change reality (the lawyers had declared during the strike that there *were* no workers employed by the company), it follows that they are all powerful. So, in order to punish Macondo, they order a flood and as a result it rains in Macondo for "four years, eleven months, and two days."[12]

The exuberant use of hyperbole in the language of the novel can be seen, too, as a reaction to officialdom. *Cien años de soledad* is written in a style that reads very much like a travesty of historical narrative. The novel is full of precise yet inflated dates and numbers, of meticulous yet incredible descriptions. The resultant atmosphere is one of a parody of the cruder forms of traditional Latin American historical writing, in particular of the sort intended for schools, in which events are comically inflated as a result of nationalist or political bias. This kind of parody is evident in the title story of *Los funerales de Mamá Grande*, where we are told quite seriously, as though it were a historical fact, that the Pope once came to Macondo for a funeral.[13]

García Márquez's hostility to the "official version" is similar to Vargas Llosa's. But he expresses it in a very different manner. For whereas Vargas Llosa seeks to subvert the misleading linear sequence of historical narrative and to probe savagely for the truth behind the fantastic facades of authority, García Márquez emulates both and then exaggerates them to a point of absurdity:

> Coronel Aureliano Buendía organized thirty-two armed uprisings and he lost them all. He had seventeen male children by seventeen different women and they were exterminated one after the other on a single night before the oldest one had reached the age of thirty-five.[14] He survived fourteen attempts on his life, seventy-three ambushes and a firing squad. He lived through a dose of strychnine in his coffee that was enough to kill a horse. He refused the Order of Merit, which the President of the Republic awarded him. He rose to be Commander in Chief of the revolutionary forces, with jurisdiction and command from one border to the other, and the man most feared by the government, but he never let himself be photographed.[15]

García Márquez's version is hyperbolic, but not all that much so. The Colombian civil wars were very much larger than life. Colombian history is fantastic enough on its own, let alone once exaggerated or distorted by Colombian historians or (more genially) by García Márquez.

It may be objected that all this is very local. The novel successfully places both its own and other Latin American novels' fantasies into a political and cultural context. But is that context not one of merely local relevance, and is the whole exercise therefore not a very limited one? Has the novel, in short, any universal interest at all? I think it has, in the first place for the simple reason that Latin America has no monopoly of biased historians and mendacious politicians. Similarly, with regard to the dependence of our perception of reality upon cultural assumptions, it may be conjectured that an inhabitant of a Cotswold village has a view of what is real that is different from that of, say, the Queen. The differences may be greater in Latin America than in Europe. But in the end García Márquez may be writing a hyperbolic parody of a continent that looks itself from Europe like a hyperbolic parody — of things that are nevertheless all too familiar. García Márquez is, moreover, aware that the problem "What is real?" is not only a cultural one. He is always alert, for instance, to the extent to which our percepts are coloured by the state of our perceiving faculties at any given moment. Many of the fantasies described in *Cien años de soledad* are therefore the result of its characters' distorted or declining faculties of perception. Drunkenness, blindness, madness, and old age all play a part in the creation of fantasy. Thus old age and blindness impair the old matriarch Ursula's sense of time: " 'Fire!' she shouted once in a temper, and for an instant panic spread through the house, but what she was talking about was the burning of a barn that she had witnessed when she was four years old."[16]

There is yet another fundamental reason why García Márquez can feel free to deploy fantasy in his writing: it is that his books are indeed books, and there is nothing to stop anything happening in a book that its author is capable of imagining. We saw how Borges demonstrated that even the most realistic writing is fictive because all writing is. He showed, in his poem "El otro tigre,"[17] that a tiger evoked in a poem is a very different thing from the beast that paces the jungles of Bengal. So if you cannot reproduce a real tiger in a book why not write about a tiger with three legs, say, that reads Sanskrit and plays hockey? Both are fictive, but is one necessarily more fictive than the other, or less real within the fictive reality of a book? We may know that yellow flowers do not suddenly pour from the sky to carpet the streets in normal life but we cannot deny that they do in *Cien años de soledad* and, because they do, we have to recognize that they are a legitimate part of that book, of the world that book seeks to create and which is signified in its language. It follows, of course, too, that that world, the world of Macondo, is neither bigger nor smaller, lasts neither longer nor shorter than the sum of the book's pages. Macondo *is* the book, and when the book ends, so does Macondo.

This point is made on the last page of *Cien años de soledad*. For the past hundred years the Buendía family has been befriended by Melquíades, that itinerant gipsy sage who so expertly rose from the dead. Now Melquíades had once presented the Buendía family with a manuscript written in an apparently incomprehensible jargon. It is left to Aureliano Babilonia, the last adult Buendía, to discover that the manuscript is in Sanskrit. Yet even when Aureliano learns Sanskrit and translates the manuscript he discovers it to be written in an apparently undecipherable code. He finally cracks the code in the closing pages of the novel, and discovers that the manuscript is a savagely prophetic one, for it meticulously records the entire history of the Buendía family as it has been lived over the hundred years since the manuscript was written. On the last page, he reads of the cyclone that finally destroys Macondo, and as he reads, the cyclone itself begins to rage around him:

> Macondo was already a fearful whirlwind of dust and rubble being spun about by the wrath of the biblical hurricane when Aureliano skipped eleven pages so as not to lose time with facts he knew only too well, and he began to decipher the instant he was living, deciphering it as he lived it, prophesying himself in the act of deciphering the last page of the parchments, as if he were looking into a sleeping mirror. Then he skipped again to anticipate the predictions and ascertain the date and circumstance of his death. Before reaching the final line, however, he had already understood that he would never leave that room, for it was foreseen that the city of mirrors (or mirages) would be wiped out by the wind and exiled from the memory of men at the precise moment when Aureliano Babilonia would finish deciphering the parchments, and that everything written on them was unrepeatable since time immemorial and for ever more, because races condemned to one hundred years of solitude did not have a second opportunity on earth.[18]

In short, the manuscript written by Melquíades is *Cien años de soledad*, the novel we have been reading. That novel describes events, a place, people, but they only exist in so far as the novel exists: they are condemned to live according to the relentless passage of the novel's pages. They do not have "a second opportunity on earth" because they are "condemned to *One Hundred Years of Solitude*." When the writer, or the reader, reaches the last page, they themselves reach the threshold of their extermination. The blank space that follows the last word of the book signifies the void to which they are henceforth consigned. Rather than postulate an existence for them beyond the last word García Márquez underlines their total coexistence with the book by making the book itself signify their disappearance on its last page. Again, we are reminded of Borges, in particular of the memorable end to his story "La busca de Averroes" ("The search for Averroes," or "Averroes's search"). After "describing" (or creating) the medieval Arab scholar, Averroes, Borges concludes that: ". . . Averroes disappeared suddenly, as if fulminated by an invisible fire, and with him disappeared the houses and the unseen fountain and the books and the manuscript and the doves and the many dark-haired slave girls and the tremulous red-haired slave girl and Farach and Albucasim and the rose bushes and perhaps even the Guadalquivir. . . . (The moment I cease to believe in him, 'Averroes' disappears.)"[19]

Averroes, and every one of the story's props, are annulled by the blankness that follows the story's last sentence.

Borges's way of making his point is much simpler than García Márquez's. Why? Why does García Márquez go to such lengths as to conjure up a Sanskrit text written by a mysterious supernatural being which translated turns out to be in *code*, and then has to be deciphered? Let us attempt some guesses.

In the first place, Melquíades's supernatural aura, his apparent resistance to time, his magical powers (on one visit to Macondo he is a decrepit old man, next visit he is triumphantly rejuvenated)[20] confer upon him a mythical status in the novel. He is as timeless and mysterious as the gypsies themselves. Now what is significant is not only that he is a magical, mythical being but also that supposedly he, not García Márquez, has written the novel. The point being made therefore would seem to be that to write a novel is to mobilize powers outside of oneself that are moreover both timeless and magical. Melquíades in short is García Márquez's Muse, or perhaps his unconscious. He is the expression of the fatal fact that writing is not an autonomous exercise, of the fact that what is written *emerges* in a manner that the writer can neither fully control nor fully understand.

For many reasons *Cien años de soledad* was not written by García Márquez alone, despite the fact that his manipulation of a typewriter was a necessary condition for its emergence. For one, García Márquez has *drawn* on the folklore of the *ciénaga*: his novel could not exist if he had not been brought up in Aracataca, if he had not been able to imbibe its legends and experiences from childhood. Aracataca, moreover, did not emerge from nowhere. The complex history of the world before its foundation was a necessary precondition for its existence. Of this fact the book provides some suggestive reminders.

After giving birth, as predicted by Melquíades, to a monster, the final Buendía, Aureliano Babilonia, discovers that "Sir Francis Drake had attacked Riohacha only so that they could seek each other through the most intricate labyrinths of blood until they would engender the mythological animal that was to bring the line to an end."[21] Francis Drake's assault of Riohacha as it happens caused a somewhat distant ancestress of Aureliano Babilonia to be wounded in a manner that for reasons that are too complicated to enumerate set in motion the whole complex story of the book.[22] There could therefore have been no Macondo without Drake. One could add that there could have been no Macondo without Spain, and no Spain for that matter without Rome, no Rome without Greece, and so on to the beginning of time. Hence the immemorial nature of García Márquez's Muse, Melquíades. A book is not the mere invention of a particular man at a particular time. Its writing (like the sources of inspiration) is preconditioned by the collective experiences of mankind, indeed by the history of the universe. The Muse is immemorial therefore because immemorial experiences condition and inspire the writing of books. It is, finally, magical because novels are the product of the imagination, not merely of conscious observation. Not only can we imagine the most magical things; the imagination itself works in a magical way, for like magic, it is an "inexplicable or remarkable influence producing surprising results."[23]

But why is the novel purported to be a *Sanskrit* text that translates into *coded* Spanish? I think that the Sanskrit is a metaphor for language in general. One of those preconditions for the writing of *Cien años de soledad* that lie outside its author is the Spanish language. Yet the Spanish language itself, like Aracataca, did not emerge from nowhere. Like Sanskrit, it is an Indo-European language and its existence presupposes millennia of linguistic transformations. Just as the collective experiences of mankind and more specifically the discovery and history of America are a necessary condition for the existence of Aracataca and finally of Macondo, so the existence of language, and more specifically the Spanish language, is a necessary condition for the existence of the Caribbean Spanish spoken in Aracataca and finally of that text in which Macondo is signified.

It is not accidental that the Sanskrit text translates into a *code* that has to be deciphered. That code, I think, stands in the first place for the given language, what Saussure calls the *langue*, the system of word conventions and usages that is given to a writer and which is outside him. He did not create it and he must draw on it in order to formulate his particular text, his sentences, his speech or *parole*, the words he mobilizes from the whole gamut of given words in order to signify something. Where the *langue*, the given language, is the *code*, the *parole* is the *message*, the choice of sounds the writer makes in order to signify Macondo. In short *Cien años de soledad* was originally buried in mere language (Melquíades's "Sanskrit"); next it passed through the *Spanish* language (the translated *code*); finally it emerges as a text, a piece of writing that draws on the Spanish language in order to signify something — it is a message.

The final pages of *Cien años de soledad* are so suggestive that I have certainly not exhausted their implications. They are, for instance, suggestive not only of the preconditions and implications of writing but also of the nature of reading. For what better expression of the subjectivity of reading could there be than when Aureliano Babilonia finds that the sheets of the parchment he is deciphering are like mirrors? And there is moreover at any rate one other fundamental purpose that these final pages serve.

Let us go back to an earlier section of the book, when the citizens of Macondo are ravaged by a mysterious plague of insomnia. The most serious consequence of their malady is that they begin to lose their memory. Their difficulty in remembering things is ultimately such that they have to label objects in order not to forget what they are:

> With an inked brush he marked everything with its name: *table, chair, clock, door, wall, bed, pan.*[24] He went into the corral and marked the animals and plants: *cow, goat, pig, hen, cassava, banana.* Little by little, studying the infinite possibilities of a loss of memory, he realized that the day might come when things would be recognized by their

inscriptions but that no one would remember their use. Then he was more explicit. The sign that he hung on the neck of the cow was an exemplary proof of the way in which the inhabitants of Macondo were prepared to fight against loss of memory: *This is the cow. She must be milked every morning so that she will produce milk, and the milk must be boiled in order to be mixed with coffee and milk.* Thus they went on living in a reality that was slipping away, momentarily captured by words, but which would escape irremediably when they forgot the values of the written letters.[25]

This crisis of memory would seem to be a parable of a fundamental theme of the novel: the problem of preserving the past, the problem of the extent to which the preservation of the past depends on words. Now writing (like memory) is, as Borges's Funes knew, selective and simplifactory. A word is a mere sign in the place of what it is designed to designate. At the time of writing, a written text about a real event can of course always be compared with what it is aiming to describe. As a result of such comparison, the written sign will evoke rich contemporary associations. But generations later, when those associations have dispersed, there will be nothing left but the text. The *real* "values of the written letters" will have been forgotten, for a piece of historical writing cannot be compared to any real thing contemporary to it: it can only be compared to another piece of historical writing. History, in the end, is words; events in the past are confined to the words written about them. Since we cannot "remember" events that took place centuries ago, we must rely entirely on what is written about them. Those events *are* what is written about them. Similarly in the novel, when the plague of insomnia leads people to forget that a given object is a table, they must rely wholly on the label *table* to tell them what it is, and the object is subsumed in the word *table*. The oblivion suffered by the citizens of Macondo symbolizes the oblivion we all necessarily suffer with respect to previous generations; in both cases, an elusive reality (like the one that was "slipping away") is subsumed in the words that designate it, and should "the values of the written letters" be altogether forgotten there will be no more such reality.

Yet if the past is a series of texts it is, by definition, a series of fictions, because all writing is fictional in the sense that it never tells the whole truth, but rather another truth: the tiger on the page is not the tiger of the jungle. Colombia's past is as much a fiction as *Cien años de soledad*, all the more so of course because it is contained in words that were written, like the textbook that denies that Macondo ever had a banana plantation, with the deliberate aim to deceive. So the final pages of *Cien años de soledad*, by showing us how Macondo can exist only within the pages of the book that depicts it, also symbolizes the fact that Colombia's past only exists within the books that have been written about it. Like the history of Macondo, the history of Colombia is a verbal fiction. The "city of mirrors (or mirages)" is in the end a symbol of a "country of mirrors (or mirages)."

It should be noted that this "city of mirrors" was *dreamt* by José Arcadio Buendía the night before he founded it: "José Arcadio Buendía dreamt that night that right there a noisy city, with houses having mirror walls rose up."[26] So *Cien años de soledad* is a novel about a *dream* of a city — or of a country — that proved to be an illusion: as insubstantial as an image in a mirror, as unreal as a fiction. What was that dream all about? It was the dream that perhaps all founding fathers have — a dream of greatness, of progress, of excellence, the Utopian dream that accompanies all acts of foundation. In this sense, the history of Macondo again symbolizes the history of Colombia, or of Latin America: the foundation of Macondo re-enacts the foundation of Bogotá or Lima or Santiago by the first *conquistadores*. What did the dreams of foundation come to? In Macondo, as in Colombia and elsewhere, to nothing much. In the words of Carlos Fuentes, "the Utopia of foundation [was] exploited, degraded, and finally assassinated by the epic of history, activity, commerce, and crime."[27]

There was much degrading "activity," but it led nowhere. It got trapped in a labyrinth of temporal cycles. As in *Conversación en la Catedral* and so many other Latin American novels the view of history offered by *Cien años de soledad* is ultimately a cyclical one. Everything in the end repeats itself and nothing really progresses: Macondo is sometimes on the up, sometimes in the doldrums, but never is there any consistent *development*. The Buendías themselves, all of them called Aureliano, José Arcadio, Amaranta, or Ursula are almost interchangeable. There are different types of Buendía, but there is little to choose between two of the same type even if separated by half a century. The longest-lived Buendía, the family matriarch Ursula, is best qualified to observe the extent to which the family is trapped in a cyclical labyrinth: "once again she shuddered with the evidence that time was not passing, as she had just admitted, but that it was turning in a circle."[28]

Once again, García Márquez provides a *context* for a characteristic phenomenon of Latin American literature: in this case for the sense that things repeat themselves cyclically that is so typical of contemporary Latin American writing. For it is possible to discern from the history of Macondo why such a vision is so frequently entertained.

There are political reasons, similar to those depicted in Vargas Llosa's *Conversación en la Catedral*, where a great deal of teeming political activity seemed to lead nowhere, where even revolutions came and went but made no lasting change. Similarly political activity leads nowhere very much in *Cien años de soledad*, however hectic it may be. This is most notoriously the case in the generations of civil wars between liberals and conservatives. They fight relentlessly, but the issues at stake are scarcely discernible, and their quarrels change nothing fundamental.

The phenomenon of economic boom, such as the one that attends Macondo with the advent of the banana plantation is another possible reason why a cyclical view of history predominates in Latin American writing. All over the continent there have always been booms of this kind — rubber booms, nitrate booms, gold booms, silver booms — which have provided a cycle of momentary prosperity inevitably followed by one of depression, because the mineral has run out, or foreigners have invented a cheaper synthetic alternative, or world markets have sunk.

There are, finally, many *natural* justifications for a cyclical vision of history in Latin American literature, and many of them are paraded in this novel. Natural disasters such as floods, droughts, and, not least, cyclones impose perpetual cycles of destruction and reconstruction on Macondo. Like Alejo Carpentier (and in a style that sometimes seems to be parodying his) García Márquez describes the tenuously equal battle man must fight against nature when in the tropics. Perpetual vigilance is necessary in order to keep vegetation from enveloping a house, and to keep on the right side of "the age-old war between man and ant."[29] It is significant that in the end, the last infant Buendía is devoured by ants a few hours after he is born and a few minutes before the cyclone destroys Macondo. Man's presence in Macondo, his history there, has turned out to be desperately fleeting. Only nature is permanent. Ultimately it is the cyclical rhythm of nature that predominates.

The cycles imposed by nature invalidate historical development, make history all the more an illusion, a fiction. Like Vargas Llosa's novels, *Cien años de soledad*, is as we have seen, full of the *appearance* of historical action, of apparent movement through time. Throughout the novel — on every page almost — we indeed meet adverbial phrases that suggest temporal progression: "thirty years later," "it was then that," "afterwards." Yet then we ask ourselves "thirty years later than what?" "when is then?" For this movement through time always withers in the novel's aura of timelessness: it is an illusion that only temporarily distracts from the fact that nothing changes.

Like Vargas Llosa's heroes, even the most active Buendías are ultimately charging at windmills. For their often hectic actions are not only meaningless in the face of the cyclical labyrinth that envelops them, but also fleeting and doomed to be effaced even from memory. Thus only a few decades after his death, no one has ever even heard of Coronel Aureliano Buendía in Macondo,[30] despite the thirty-two rebellions he perpetrated in his heyday!

Latin America of course need have no monopoly on cyclical time: it is possible to be a Borges and suspect that things repeat themselves *everywhere*. Indeed the cycles that Macondo travels through have deliberate biblical reverberations, as though to imply that it has all happened before, that these repetitions have been repeated elsewhere. Thus José Arcadio Buendía commits a *crime* as a result of which he and his wife are *banished* and go in search of a new world. They then *found* a *dynasty* and a city which, after decades of progress, is destroyed by a *flood*. Of course the

Latin American reverberations of this mythical sequence are as obvious as the biblical ones: many of the early colonizers left Spain under a cloud in the hope both of escaping from the past and of laying the foundations of a future in the New World. But the first colonizers had several things in common with the inhabitants of the Book of Genesis. For instance, they too were faced with the basic task of *naming* flora and fauna that they had not hitherto encountered. This task is re-enacted in *Cien años de soledad*: "At that time Macondo was a village of twenty adobe houses. . . . The world was so recent that many things lacked names, and in order to indicate them it was necessary to point."[31] Again, we are reminded of how relative historical time is in Latin America. For it is possible for people to be living at the beginning of History there in the twentieth century. And time is cyclical, therefore, not only because a given society may be trapped in temporal cycles but also because the historical processes of one society may be repeated in another centuries later.

Like other mythical dynasties, the Buendía dynasty is tribulated by the fact that its founding pair was incestuous: the first José Arcadio and the first Ursula were cousins. The Buendías believe that the issues of incestuous relationships are born with the tail of a pig, and although the children of José Arcadio and Ursula are born clear of this symptom, generations of Buendías throughout the novel are warned that such is the consequence of incest.

Incest is indeed a recurring concern of the novel, and it is a constant temptation for the novel's characters despite its supposedly terrible consequences. José Arcadio's son, José Arcadio, marries a woman, Rebeca, who is supposedly his cousin, although no one knows why. The first José Arcadio's daughter, Amaranta, is quite stubbornly incestuous: she first of all earns the love of her nephew, Aureliano José, who had never imagined one could marry an aunt until he heard "some old man tell the tale of the man who had married his aunt, who was also his cousin, and whose son ended up by being his own grandfather."[32] Although they do not marry, Amaranta, undeterred, later experiences sexual desire even for her little great-great-nephew, José Arcadio, every time she bathes him.[33]

Yet none of these incestuous relationships have issue. It is not until the end of the book that an incestuous pair have a child when the Aureliano who deciphers the Sanskrit text and his aunt, Amaranta Ursula, end up by producing the dreaded monster, the final Aureliano, who is born with the tail of a pig.

The incest taboo is of course normally thought to exist in primitive societies because incest precludes communication between various groups of kin, and is therefore a hindrance to social cohesion. If women are kept in the family for sexual ends and not offered as wives to other groups of kin, the opportunity is lost of cementing an alliance with another family through a binding marriage contract. Now it should not be forgotten that the novel is, as the title reminds us, a novel about one hundred years of *solitude*, and therefore it is about a failure to communicate, a failure to establish social relationships that bedevils all of its characters. Every single character in the novel is a victim of appalling loneliness, and many of its characters end their lives in total isolation: *locked* for years in a room, *tied* for years to a tree, or long *forgotten* in a deserted house. What is the cause of this loneliness? Not to forget the obvious, one reason can be found for it in the isolation of Macondo itself, in the isolation of a forgotten Colombian backwater. Yet why then is there no solidarity at least *within* Macondo? And what part does incest play herein?

In the case of Amaranta, incestuous leanings certainly spell an especially bitter fruitlessness and loneliness, for it is hard for her to share her passions with anyone. José Arcadio, married to Rebeca, commits suicide, and Rebeca lives out her lonely widowhood in an empty house. Interestingly, neither Rebeca nor Amaranta can somehow bring themselves to marry an Italian outsider, Pietro Crespi, who courts each in turn and with whom either one might have been far better fulfilled. They reject him for wholly mysterious, but clearly compelling, reasons. And it is the careless *introspection* of the final incestuous pair, Aureliano and Amaranta Ursula, that enables nature, attended by the final army of ants, to take over. In this instance, incest quite clearly precipitates social breakdown. For it is the pair's lack of interest in anything but each other that causes them to be overrun by their environment.

Yet normal marriages are no more successful, tending to have claustrophobic effects on those who embark on them, and it is free love that turns out to be most fulfilling. This is particularly the case of Aureliano Segundo's relationship with one Petra Cotes (to whom he regularly escapes from his wife): every time they copulate, their livestock miraculously multiplies. It is as though the book were implying that sexual liberation heralded progress and prosperity. Conversely, it is the Buendías' rigid prohibition of female sexual freedom that indirectly precipitates the final destructive incest. Aureliano, the son of Renata Buendía, has been *hidden* from the world throughout his life because he was conceived out of wedlock with an unsuitable outsider. The family hide him because they are ashamed of him, and dispatch his mother to a convent. Brought up in secret in the Buendía mansion, Aureliano is never told of his origins, and Amaranta Ursula, who is his mother's sister, never learns of them either, because the guilty secret is kept even from members of the family. Although Aureliano and Amaranta Ursula *suspect* that they are related, it can be argued that their incest is indirectly caused by their family's taboo on female sexual freedom: for if they had not brought up Aureliano in isolation he might have achieved contact with other females, and if he had known for certain who he was, he might have stayed clear of his aunt.

Incest ultimately would seem to be just the extreme symptom of the real force behind the Buendías' failure to communicate: their claustrophobic introspectiveness. For the Buendías are one of those dominating, demanding, self-contained, and self-centered families you often find in Latin America, one of those families whose autarchic nature makes contact with anyone outside almost impossible. The family's irresistible magnetic power is frequently depicted in the novel: we remember José Arcadio's blood which, when he dies, trickles relentlessly round corners until it returns to the family fold, more precisely to the matriarch, Ursula. Coronel Aureliano has seventeen bastard sons during his campaigns: all inexplicably find their way to Macondo. The tragedy of each of the characters is that he cannot break away from the family fold: whenever anyone does, he compulsively returns to it.

If Latin America were made up of strings of introspective, uncommunicative families like the Buendías, it would not be surprising that the social cohesion necessary for a constructive history should not come about. I am not sure if the novel is trying to make this perhaps rather questionable and perhaps even absurd point. I think it is certainly a novel about the failure of Latin American history, and certainly a novel about the loneliness that a claustrophobic family results in, just as it is a novel about reality and a novel about writing. It may be foolish to attempt to tie everything in it together and perhaps more sensible to be merely grateful not only that it contains so many richly disparate ingredients but also that it weathers them with such entertaining fluency.

Readers of chapter 8 will wonder if there could have been a *Cien años de soledad* without Borges. I doubt there could have been. The novel's built-in reminders that what one is reading is a fiction, its disturbing suggestions that life may be no less of a fiction, its vision of the world as endless repetition, its deployment of messages to other writers, particularly of messages that deliberately confuse "fact" and "fiction," its conversion of writing into a sort of "reading" of other literatures — all these things are Borges's familiar stamping ground. Yet García Márquez is no plagiarist, not only because his novel, in its every detail, *feels* so different from Borges's work, there being little similarity between García Márquez's Caribbean exuberance and Borges's rather English understatements, but also because though García Márquez follows Borges very closely, he somehow modifies him and throws fresh light upon him. As he does with contemporary literature of fantasy in general, he provides him with a very Latin American context. *Cien años de soledad* is a very Latin American *reading* of Borges, for it discovers Borges's relevance to Latin America — the relevance of his cyclical vision of time to the cyclical nature of Latin American history, the relevance of his sense that life is a dream, a fiction, to the dream-like nature of Latin American politics, the relevance of his sense that the past is inseparable from the fictive words that narrate it to the tragic fact that Latin America's past is inseparable from the deliberately distorted words that have claimed to record it, the relevance, finally of Borges's demonstrations that our perceptions of things depend on our previous assumptions about them to the fact that in a continent shared by so many cultures there can be no common continental perception of anything.

Notes

1. The quotations in this chapter have been taken from Gregory Rabassa's translation of *Cien años de soledad*, *One Hundred Years of Solitude*. New York and London, 1970. The page references refer to the passages' original location.

2. *Cien años de soledad*, Buenos Aires, 1967, p. 172.

3. pp. 223–4.

4. p. 118.

5. p. 254.

6. p. 342.

7. The father of the José Arcadio whose death was heralded by a rain of yellow flowers. All Buendía males are called José Arcadio or Aureliano, a confusing fact whose significance will be discussed later.

8. p. 124.

9. p. 316.

10. p. 329.

11. p. 256.

12. p. 267.

13. *Los funerales*, Buenos Aires, 1967, pp. 141–2.

14. This is not exactly so: one survives until much later (cf. p. 317). There are many clearly deliberate anomalies of this kind in the book which, we shall see later, questions the reliability of its own written words as relentlessly as it questions the reliability of the written words of, say, official historians.

15. *Cien años*, p. 74.

16. p. 290.

17. *Obra poética*, 1967, pp. 191–3.

18. *Cien años*, pp. 350–1.

19. *El Aleph*, Buenos Aires, 1971, pp. 100–1. Translation quoted from *Labyrinths*, Penguin, 1970, pp. 187–8.

20. *Cien años*, p. 14.

21. p. 350.

22. p. 24.

23. C.O.D.

24. This joke is by courtesy of the English language. It is not in the original.

25. p. 47.

26. p. 28.

27. Carlos Fuentes, *La nueva novela hispanoamericana*, Mexico, 1969, p. 61.

28. *Cien años*, pp. 284–5.

29. p. 345.

30. p. 329.

31. p. 9.

32. p. 132.

33. pp. 236–7.

Gabriel García Márquez and the Lost Art of Storytelling

Ricardo Gullón*

SPACE AND TONE

When speaking of the excellence of A *Hundred Years of Solitude*, it is not enough to say that Gabriel García Márquez has invented an original imaginary world; and yet it should not be forgotten that this is precisely what he has done. The invention is in itself a remarkable achievement, and in our day even unusual. It would not be idle to remind ourselves of something so well-known that it is usually forgotten, namely, that the creation of space in fiction is similar to that of sacred space insofar as it implies a transformation of chaos into cosmos and the imposition of order. The first impulse to accomplishing an act of creation is like the laying of a foundation, the tracing of boundaries, the making of a reservation (in the American sense of the word) where the fictional will develop.

That fictional space alternately communicates and does not communicate with the outside world, that is, with Life, is easy to understand when we consider the analogy that exists between fictional and sacred space. What has been introduced into, and assimilated by sacred and fictional space has form, whereas what remains outside does not and because of its lack of form continues to appear chaotic. For this and other reasons Gabriel García Márquez is correct in giving us the details of how the foundation is laid together with the foundation itself as indispensable parts of the novel. Macondo becomes and then *is* "the World." In that world the characters are born and from it they overflow. Everything is contained in that world and within its boundaries all the prodigious events occur. Things further removed are less dense, less consistent, almost misty, at times formless.

One wonders how García Márquez came to create a world so similar to our everyday one and yet so totally different from it. Technically, he is a realist in the presentation of both the real and the unreal. He somehow skillfully handles a reality in which the limits of the real and the fantastic fade away quite naturally.

*Reprinted from *Diacritics* 1, no. 1 (1971):27–32. Translated by José G. Sanchez. Reprinted by permission of the journal.

This feat requires analysis of his resources, beginning with the one which seems to me the most important—narrative tone. García Márquez intuitively grasped the vital relationship that exists between space and tone when he noticed that tone could serve as the main unifying force in the novel. Tone belongs by all rights to the narrator's voice, and the narrator is the Narrator: someone who is removed from his narrative; who knows all there is to know about the events; who reports them as a reporter would— calm and untouched, without comment, and without passing moral judgments on what has happened. He does not doubt or question events or facts. For him there is no difference between what is likely and what is not; he fulfills his mission—his duty—of telling all, speaking as naturally of the dead as he does of the living, associating with the greatest of ease the intangible with the tangible. His steadfastness reveals itself in his un-changing, constant tone. From the first page to the last he maintains the same tone levels, without fluctuation or variation.

Prodigious events and miracles mingle with references to village and household events. The narrator never allows it to become evident, by interjection or amazement, that there may be a substantial difference between the extraordinary and the commonplace. For example, there is a character who wakes up a ghost (whom he does not see) as he urinates on him. Phantoms may sleep and do other things that make one forget their state, just as the living may at any moment take flight without anyone's attaching the slightest importance to it. In García Márquez' novel, they all communicate easily. And why shouldn't they? They live side by side— immersed in an atmosphere which shelters them indiscriminately, making them equals. In the novel's space, proven and fabulous events are equally true, a fact which all great fiction should show.

In the *Odyssey* the Sirens are neither more nor less real than Ulysses. Understanding this fact, García Márquez breaks with the literary conven-tions of realism. Yet he does not stray from the tradition or from fictional reality. And his authentic presentation of events (that is to say, his tone) allows him to dispense with explanations and justifications. There is no need to justify the fact that a character dies, or appears to die, and later comes back to life, or appears to, twenty, a hundred, or five hundred years later; there is no reason to follow the clock's chronology, or the calendar's, when the only really important time is the novel's own time. One hundred years of solitude? Might it not be a hundred centuries? Might not the novel's own time be time in its totality, absolute, beginning with the awakening of humanity and ending with its expiration? Would it not be possible to calculate mathematically what the world is, put it in a nutshell and with it all of history, from Genesis to the Apocalypse?

The novel has the circular and dynamic structure of a gyrating wheel. The narrator has seen that wheel turn, and his way of relating the events which he came to see in the wheel's constant turning serves as a unifying force. Narrative authenticity becomes more readily perceptible when what is related oscillates between impossible and everyday occurrences. As an example of this we have José Arcadio Buendía telling Prudencio Aguilar's obstinate ghost (it insists on appearing and reappearing) to go to hell, just as he would have told a bothersome neighbor.

The narration of events, we are told, was recorded twice. First, in a language unintelligible to the Macondo inhabitants (Sanscrit) by Melquíades, before they actually took place; as prophet-chronicler, he forsees what is to come (unless he has seen it in some other turn of the wheel) and anticipates it in his story. Second, by the narrator (in Spanish), after the events have occurred; he relates the past, recognizing it as such, and on the first page predicts the execution of Colonel Aureliano Buendía, which will not actually take place for years or centuries. Could the narrator be Melquíades' double, or in the terms of this novel, his reincarnation? In any case, we know that there is no discrepancy between his version and the immortal man's; one is a facsimile of the other, the result of a miracle similar to Pierre Ménard's when he unwittingly wrote a *Quixote* identical to Cervantes'. When we read on the last page that Aureliano IV deciphers Melquíades' parchments, we discover that the novel was contained in them — that they are in fact the novel — which is why they cannot be deciphered until the novel ends. The ancient papers do not allow their meaning to become clear until the prophecies are fulfilled, and the narrator describes that fulfillment step by step. He limits himself to the business of narrating: he neither predicts the future nor possesses the key to the past. Melquíades duplicates him and in some ways anticipates him; a mythical and legendary figure, he possesses special powers, and in the novel he plays multiple roles.

We do not know at the beginning what the difference consists of, even though we are aware of Melquíades' uprootedness, his readiness to be absent. We come to feel that he is only passing through Macondo. This gives him the special attribute of a being without a beginning or an end. He is not reincarnated in other people; he reappears after his spurious deaths, and when he withdraws from the novel, he does so because he has played out his role of prophet and scribe. Melquíades is successively and simultaneously alchemist, adventurer, experimenter, scientist, encyclopedic sage; he is mortal and immortal, a resurrected being. But most important, he is the wanderer who circulates freely through the space of the novel and beyond, crossing without effort the boundaries between one world and another. He serves as link and messenger between the living and the dead.

In the novel only the narrator's voice is heard; such is the demand of tonal unity. Through it the reader apprehends everything the characters say or think, their dialogues and monologues. The narrative voice is, as the tone suggests, friendly and familiar; it is a voice which instills confidence in the listener and succeeds in making itself heard and accepted without objections. The relationship between the narrative voice (that is, the narrator) and the reader is also one of familiarity, and therefore a close one. Events occur and characters parade before the reader in the most natural manner, nearby, and seemingly at the same spatial and psychological distance from him.

The narrator's speaking unfazedly, calmly (even when describing tragic events), does not prevent him from becoming a center of consciousness. Quite the contrary. The distance between the narrator and what he narrates reinforces his objectivity and allows him to speak without judging. What is said is ethically qualified because of the way it is said. The characters derive their consistency from the word and the consciousness from which that word springs; the imagery and a unique use of adjectives allow the reader to detect a value judgment which has not been formulated, but merely insinuated. When the army enters Macondo to end the great strike, the narrator says: "Its many-headed dragon-breathing impregnated the midday sunlight with pestilent vapors."

The extremely reduced distance between the reader and the characters, due to the intimacy of the narrative voice, practically disappears when a character, living his normal everyday life, performs the minute actions so familiar to the reader himself. Colonel Aureliano, without ceasing to be a kind of retired mythological figure, urinates at certain times during the day. The Colonel's regularity brings him closer to the reader, who thereby more readily identifies with him and tolerates everything else said about him in that and previous chapters.

The central character is Úrsula Iguarán, wife of José Arcadio Buendía; together they make up the first couple. Ursula is both a mother and The Mother, and is present throughout most of the novel. She articulates some of the key observations; her "normal" domestic activities, constructive and incessant, create a center where decisive events happen and others slowly germinate. That center is charged with the unique atmosphere which Ursula radiates. Ursula's function is to impregnate the fictional space with everyday realities so that the marvelous may enter it smoothly. Thus stabilized and "normalized," the novelistic space assimilates prodigious things and converts them into acceptable phenomena which the reader can easily admit.

García Márquez' success in creating such an atmosphere is more evident if we contrast that atmosphere to the backdrops of Gothic novels and other such narratives. Poe's castles, cemeteries, shadows, thunder, and phantasmagoria produce the opposite effects of those in *A Hundred Years of Solitude*; instead of fusing the extraordinary with the ordinary, such backdrops mark boundaries too sharply, thereby opposing the real to the unreal and preventing them from communicating; in Gothic tales "real" life is distinct from the fantastic episodes related.

There is still more to say about space in the novel. The Buendía house and the city of Macondo are representations of a vast universe where everything has its proper place, including time. Primordial space, which precedes creation, is not organized until the creator comes and gives objects names: "The world was so new that many things lacked names, and in order to refer to them one had to point them out." José Arcadio Buendía is the first to take space and conceptualize it, grasping it intellectually in all its fullness: "When he became expert in the use of his tools, he developed an idea of space which enabled him to sail unknown seas, visit uninhabited lands and engage in relationships with magnificent beings without ever having to leave the room." Together, José Arcadio's imagined space and Ursula's familiar space embrace everything that has ever existed or exists, from nothingness to infinity.

At least one critic, Emmanuel Carballo, has suggested the possibility that Macondo might be an equivalent of Spanish America. But it would be a mistake to narrow the scope of the novel to specific places. Though the novel may suggest parts of Colombia, it clearly transcends physical particularizing and offers instead a parable of creation, man's history and human nature.

The circular structure of the novel leads the reader from the chaos and void where creation occurs to the chaos and void where all ends and is resolved. The presence of a well-defined, concrete geographical space (Macondo) does not lessen its universality; it reinforces it. And the circularity is compatible with the plot, which moves forward in linear development, never retroceding, yet also searches constantly for its origins. The book contains no index and its chapters have no titles; it is a chain of reiterations; it is continuity itself. Names are constantly repeated. There is always a new beginning, a returning — I would almost say a reincarnation — of the characters, whose overwhelming personalities reappear continuously in accordance with the design-destiny of their names: the José Arcadios, the Aurelianos, the Remedios, the Amarantas and the Ursulas. Pilar Ternera, at once priestess and lust incarnate, knows that "the history of the Buendía family [is] a chain of irreparable repetitions, a gyrating wheel that would have continued turning forever had it not been for the gradual and inevitable wearing out of its axle." The gyrating wheel in the quotation is a suitable structural image for this novel. Because Melquíades is both magician and seer, the wheel is superfluous for him; he needs but look into the crystal ball, for in it he sees time in its totality — without duration, without past, without future. In a magical realm, events and worlds appear with a simultaneity and density that, we are told, may be captured only at the moment of death. It is no accident that Melquíades' documents guard their secrets, which may be deciphered only when the narrative concludes.

The wheel never stops; its constant motion, linking the beginning to the end, is visible in the case of Ursula. Her old age is and is not like that of others. As the years — centuries — pass, she becomes progressively smaller, "becoming mummified while alive to the point that, during her last months, she was a mere prune lost in the folds of her nightgown." That powerful image is anticipated when the narrator indicates that Ursula was becoming so "foetus-like" that she looked like "a newborn old lady." Nor is she the only one who ends up the way she started. The signs of repetition multiply in the course of the novel: at the end, the gypsies who had appeared at the beginning (years or centuries earlier) return to the village and bring once again the wonders that had earlier produced such widespread awe: the magnet, the gigantic magnifying glass, the false teeth. These objects are symbols of what is permanent in change or of what changes without ceasing to be identical to what it was. The Arab merchants are where they were before and where they will be again, "sitting in the same place and in the same posture as their parents and grandparents, taciturn, fearless, invulnerable to time."

When Aureliano II returns to the house of his mistress, Petra Cotes, after the flood, he finds her worn out, aged, and sickly, but also beginning anew, preparing once again to engage in the activities that helped make their fortune. She was "writing numbers on scraps of paper for a raffle." Later, Ursula finds José Arcadio II in Melquíades' room and is surprised to find herself repeating something that Colonel Aureliano had said to her much earlier when she told him what José Arcadio had just told her. This is the moment of dreadful realization: "time did not pass . . . ; it went around in circles."

RHYTHM

The contrast between tone and rhythm, which is characteristic of *A Hundred Years of Solitude*, is one more reason why this novel attracts, convinces and seduces the reader. If the familiar tone makes the suppression of limits between the real and the imaginary tolerable, the rhythm complements it by contrast: vertiginous beneath the apparent calm, the rhythm injects the narrative with a dynamic force that might seem incongruous with the tone. Yet this is not so: the narrator does not allow his pace to be affected by the accumulation of events. Rather, he concentrates, summarizes and equalizes them in his constant talespinning. The kaleidoscope turns, slowly shaping very different situations. So many things are compressed into the space of a few pages that one might say the narrator has overdone it. But no, he has merely reduced things to their essentials — condensed them without sacrificing vitality — and connected them through imperceptible transitions. Events accumulate naturally because of the natural tone. The transition from one delirious state to the next occurs as smoothly as the switch from the unreal to the real. Delirium is presented as trivial reality; in a state of hallucination, Amaranta is not surprised to see death sitting beside her, sewing in the hall. Reality, by logical contrast, is delirious. Wars succeed each other so rapidly that war eventually becomes a way of life. The gringos come, fleece and devour the country, destroying everything, like a plague, and then disappear. The killing of Colonel Aureliano's seventeen sons is a clear case of an event that occurs on the borderline of reality. The event lacks versimilitude yet it *is* "real" and is told with the tonal objectivity and quick rhythm that García Márquez blends so well. In a single page the inhuman killing begins and ends.

This curious rhythm-tone symbiosis implies complete mastery of condensatory techniques, from the oxymoron to synesthesia. An example of the former: "the enchanted region" that José Arcadio Buendía explored when Macondo was founded and where banana plantations were to prosper later, "*was* a marsh of putrefied stumps." The verb "was" (which I have italicized) links the contradictory terms of the sentence. Synesthetic imagery ("delicate breeze of light") enlarges the frame of reference. Similarly, the use of paradox permits transitions to be made with verbal economy: "Ursula allowed decreptitude to drag her into the depths of darkness where only José Arcadio Buendía's ghost continued to be visible under the chestnut tree." Equally effective in the process of condensation is the systematic use of anachronisms, for they unite distant moments of time. By locating in one moment what happened in another, the author is able to stretch the temporal boundaries of his novel in a few lines: "Every time Ursula flew off the handle with rage because of her husband's follies, she skipped over three hundred years and cursed the day Francis Drake attacked Riohacha."

A sustained synthesis, A Hundred Years of Solitude covers centuries, perhaps millenia. On the first page alone we find prehistory and Arcadia (whence the "Adam" of the story — Arcadio — takes his name); then come Genesis and the journey to the "un"-promised land; the founding of the city; the plagues that devastate Macondo (insomnia and forgetfulness); the resurrection of Melquíades; and the Flood (which lasts four years, eleven months and two days), imposed as a punishment for man's sins, especially for the greed and pride of the directors of the Yankee banana company who spoil the regularity of the rainy seasons with their agricultural methods. The book contains all of History, synthesizing it in symbolic episodes such as the finding of the Spanish galleon or the arrival of the Magistrate, who brings with him the seeds of violence (of authority) that will later destroy José Arcadio's "Arcadia." Contemporary history is represented in the exemplary episodes of the corruption engendered by American banana interests; the capitalist exploitation; the poor people's strike and their execution by an Army that represents "the Law," that is, the violence which those in power (the uniformed executioners) use against the weak; the sinister black men who "legalize" the spoils; the falsification of the truth by a Government of assassins. And at the end, completing the circle, is the Apocalypse, announced from the pulpit by Father Antonio Isabel, who reads the omens as dead birds rain down, scouring the village (this episode is told in detail in the short story "A Day After Saturday" in *Mamá Grande's Funeral*); a Biblical hurricane razes Macondo when the prophecies are fulfilled on the last page.

This feat of condensation takes place in 350 pages. They are taut, although somewhat slackened by the monochord tone; and they are dense, for individual and collective destinies are meshed. Each particular character's life and vital concerns are interrelated with the collective life of the town from the beginning: together they search for Arcadia; together they undertake expeditions and live the fleeting moments of paradise and the eternity of hell. Plague and war afflict them equally, just as the flood blinds them all and violence from without strikes them all. The structural curve is identical for the hero and the masses, and their fall is simultaneous, which is why these fabulous and mythified heroes never cease to be "representative."

THEME

Solitude, the novel's central theme, knits personal destinies closely. Whatever their essence, all the characters are born condemned to suffer it. It is a universal law and no one, not even Ursula, the Mother who lives for others, is spared it; her final blindness plunges her into "the impenetrable loneliness of decreptitude." The most obvious example, emphasized by the symbolism of the act, is Colonel Aureliano's order to have traced around him a chalk circle which no one may cross. His is the solitude of power, and in that solitude, as the narrator says, Colonel Aureliano is completely isolated. Later we read that "he locked himself in, as it were, and his family ended up thinking of him as if he had died." This line sums up the meaning of solitude by equating it with death.

Perhaps it is here that the novel — correctly read — yields its meaning and the reason why the living characters can co-exist and converse so naturally with the dead ones. Whoever lives his solitude as these people do, incapable of communication with the other alive-dead souls, is at the same distance from other people as he is from the dead-alive, or dead. Solitude is a common denominator that tinges them with a common sadness; it both unites and separates them as one may note in the relationship between Aureliano IV and José Arcadio IV: "That bond between the two loners of the same family was far from being a friendly one; it allowed them both to bear better that fathomless solitude which simultaneously brought them together and separated them." Aureliano IV is not at all interested in escaping from the confinement to which his grandmother has condemned him. He is content to live within himself, stubborn in his will to unravel the meaning of Melquíades' parchments: it is the duty of a loner.

Solitude is a vocation imposed by birth, in accordance with a law; it is an indelible mark. The successive Aurelianos and Arcadios have in common the family's "solitary look"; Aureliano IV has been "from the beginning of the world and forever branded by the pockmarks of solitude." The solitude of silence is a prison and a refuge. When Mauricio Babilonia is wounded, his lover Meme withdraws in "stony" silence and much later dies of old age without ever having uttered another word. In this case, solitude is a form of desperation, and in the case of Aureliano II, it is even more extreme; he surrenders to the "bitter solitude of drunken sprees." He loses himself in them in order to escape the solitude of Fernanda, the stern wife who, as an outsider and foreigner to Macondo, attempts to force the chains of isolation on their home and village. Fernanda wishes to live entombed, faithful "to the paternal decree to be buried alive," as her father had done and as she herself demands of her daughter and grandson. Rebeca does the same thing, but for different reasons: she shoots and kills the thief who attempted to force the door to her place of confinement. (The visit to Macondo by the dead boy's mother is told in "The Tuesday Afternoon Siesta" in *Mamá Grande's Funeral*.)

In the case of José Arcadio Buendía, the solitude of madness is accompanied by the failure of language. He suddenly begins to speak in a strange language (which we later learn is Latin) incomprehensible to those around him. He will live for years or centuries tied to the trunk of a chestnut tree in the courtyard, and after his death he will continue to inhabit the same place with a ghostly life scarcely different from his former one. No less incomprehensible, although in a quite different way, is Remedios the Beautiful, impervious "to the language of man," always "wandering in the desert of solitude" and finally rising out of fictional time and space into oblivion.

Amaranta's solitude is that of rancor and death in life. She lives alone with her hate and solely for it. Her communication with Death is normal and no different from that which she has with people around her. Death is neither more nor less than "a woman dressed in blue, with long hair, of a somewhat antiquated appearance and bearing a certain resemblance to Pilar Ternera," who sews by her side and who one day asks her "to please thread a needle for her." Knowing the date of her own departure, she offers herself as messenger to the inhabitants of Macondo to carry news from the living to the dead, thus redeeming the wretched solitude of her hate. Her offer is accepted without objection: "The news that Amaranta Buendía was setting sail for the twilight zone carrying the mail of death spread through Macondo before noon, and by around three in the afternoon there was already a big box filled with letters in the room. Those who were not able to write spoke their messages, which Amaranta jotted down in her notebook with the name and date of death of the addressee." No one doubts that the requests will be carried out.

The Buendías are not the only ones who live as recluses. So do the veterans, whittling away their useless old age waiting for the promised government check that never comes. (In *The Colonel Has No One to Write*

Him García Márquez has elaborated on this hopeless waiting.) There is only one way for mortal beings to transcend this common solitude: through love. But love during these hundred years (or centuries) is precarious and always in danger of ending in a catastrophe like the ones that undermine the lives of Amaranta, Rebeca, Mauricio, Meme. Amaranta Ursula and Aureliano IV believe they have conquered solitude by forgetting themselves in frantic love, an erotic passion in which the family's last energies are consumed. Around them the world is destroyed and returned to dust. In Macondo, "forgotten even by the birds [. . .] it was difficult to breathe," but the lovers reconstruct for their passion the fatal solitude that consumes everything, withdrawing "through the solitude of love" into the house that is being devoured by ants — before they devour the last of the Aurelianos. They are the last living creatures in this fictional space: "in an empty universe where love [is] the only daily and eternal reality," in a world where they hear no voices other than those of their dead parents, grandparents, and great-grandparents, they achieve peace, persuaded that death itself will not be able to separate them. The birth of Aureliano V is the end of the novel; in him the prophecies of destruction are fulfilled, and Macondo, reduced to dust, disappears forever and with it the memory of those who made and inhabited it.

MOTIF AND HYPERBOLE

Among the unifying devices utilized by García Márquez, the reiteration of certain motifs is important. The motifs reappear at certain intervals and unite various parts of the novel, thus reinforcing the feeling of circularity (the sinister black men, charged with preparing and justifying the Government's pillage; the distant, invisible doctors with whom Fernanda communicates). One motif, of particular interest, accentuates the futility of human actions, and can be seen in the Buendía family's peculiar custom or vice of making things only to destroy them afterwards. Aureliano I falls into this characteristic mode of repetition, as the narrator observes, when instead of selling the little gold fish he makes, he melts them down to remake them and thus continues incessantly. Memories come back to Ursula in a similar way. José Arcadio Buendía keeps busy reading and rereading Melquíades' parchments. Amaranta sews and unsews buttons, and alternately weaves and unweaves her shroud to retard the coming of death. These are solitary games, designed to regain lost time; they are also the novelist's technique of indirectly expressing small but significant details in order to press the creative process.

There is a kind of justifiable excess in the novel, a systematic distortion by means of hyperbole that fits the author's design: a design to create a world of fiction so perfect as to make it ideal. Events and figures contain dimensions, as they should. The novel's beginning is Genesis; its end is the Apocalypse; rain is equivalent to the Flood; wars are War.

García Márquez' weakness for hyperbole is decisive when it comes to characterization. Being verbal inventions, the characters necessarily owe their substance to the way in which the author arranges his words; the traditional hypothesis that the novelist faithfully describes characters who exist previous to the narrative is a metaphor that suggests, at length, the autonomy of the character.

Hyperbole may produce a comic effect, as when Aureliano IV runs about the house "balancing a beer bottle on his inconceivable sex organ," or it may yield lyrical imagery: "His mistress was so close to him and so completely disarmed that Aureliano could perceive the deep murmur of her bones." Again, it may induce a fantastic vision: "The atmosphere was so humid that fish could have come in the doors and exited by the windows, swimming through the air in the rooms." Such hyperboles might be read as metaphors; but in context they should be accepted literally, because of the levelling off between reality and unreality which is characteristic of *One Hundred Years of Solitude*.

A systematic study of the imagery (and the symbols, such as the plague of insomnia and forgetfulness or the indelible ash crosses that single out the Aurelianos for death) would show that it points towards that levelling and indeed contributes to it. The excesses of the Buendías are passed on from one generation to the next. Aureliano II is a Gargantuan, capable of devouring a whole calf; José Arcadio II, who went around the world sixty-five times and like Ray Bradbury's illustrated man had his whole body tattooed, became a cannibal when the moment demanded it. His overindulgence in bed or at the table knew no bounds. "His farts wilted the flowers," reads the expressive image.

War and the general strike are culminations of horror in the novel — nightmares that actually happen yet retain their delirious quality. There is no doubt about their function in the novel. The narrator, as he relates them, erases any differences that might have existed, indeed destroys the very idea of a possible barrier between the real and the imaginary. In the natural order of things, such nightmares fall within the realm of the possible — they are readily accepted as "historical" and natural events, and for the assassins they are even honorable — but in the novel they are more, rather than less, fantastic and incredible, in their naked brutality, than are specters and monsters. Whoever thinks they can be explained will easily accept the plague of insomnia or the rain of dead birds. There is no substantial difference between those horrors and these unnatural events, even though only the former are man-made. Narrative objectivity undergoes no change, not even when in the end the false version of the story must be told (a falsification occasioned by the criminal's desire to erase all traces of the crime and by man's refusal to recognize the monstrosity of the real).

As García Márquez completes his last fictional circles, he illuminates their and the novel's meaning. The difference between Márquez and other contemporary novelists lies in the fact that the latter may disperse themselves in a welter of techniques: he does not. His need to tell a story is so strong that it transcends the devices he uses to satisfy that need. Technique is not a mere game; it is something to be made use of. At its best, it serves only to relate the story. Should the novelist get lost in his own creation, it is so he might find himself in it, in that imaginary world which is Macondo — the Macondo which has been compared to Faulkner's Yoknapatawpha county, if for no other reason than that both are relatively pure fictional regions, absolute inventions like Goriot's Paris or Fortunata's Madrid; inventions that are reserved for artists like Márquez who know how to revitalize the ancient and almost forgotten art of storytelling, reserved for those who practice it with the complex simplicity the genre demands.

Foreshadowing as Technique and Theme in *One Hundred Years of Solitude*
Biruté Ciplijauskaité*

The constant use of foreshadowing and premonition stands out as one of the basic structural elements of *One Hundred Years of Solitude*. All such elements, including cyclical reiteration, paradox and parallelism, are tightly interwoven with the main themes of the book; as a consequence, they can be studied as integral parts of the "story" as well as of the "discourse," where syntactic and semantic aspects are interrelated. A major portion of the book obeys the rule of ambiguity which Todorov stresses as an important element of "fantastic literature,"[1] more generally referred to as "magic realism" when applied to the Latin American novel and short story.

The realm of the fantastic, affirms Todorov, lies between the real-explicable and the supernatural, with a continuous fluctuation of boundaries and an uncertainty intensified by the total absence of the narrator's guiding point of view. García Márquez suggests that this will also be a characteristic of his book: on the first page, stressing the importance of imagination in José Arcadio Buendía, the founder of Macondo, he writes, "his imagination always went beyond the genius of nature and even beyond miracles and magic."[2] He causes the whole story to "float" by disrupting the natural temporal sequence and making even spatial relations uncertain.[3] The constant intertwining of the real and material with the fantastic and spiritual fosters ambiguity and permits a myth to be

*Reprinted from *Books Abroad* 47, no. 3 (Summer 1973):479–84. Copyright 1973 by the University of Oklahoma Press. Reprinted by permission.

born. (According to García Márquez, a similar blend was present in the atmosphere in which he grew up: "For lack of something better, Aracataca lived on myths, ghosts, solitude and nostalgia.")[4] Technically, the use of ellipsis together with chronological leaps, both forward and backward, produces a seldom-experienced density of statement which invites both literal and symbolical readings.[5] (García Márquez said once he would have liked to be the author of *La peste* whose economy of devices he admired. If one considers that the density achieved by Camus represents a chronicle of the human destiny of a city during a period of nine months, one may be even more surprised to find that García Márquez compresses into a similar number of pages the hundred-year history of a whole tribe and, figuratively, a whole continent. The absurd arrived at has the same poignancy in both authors; the difference in the presentation derives from the rational and civilized character of the French and the overflowing vitality of the Latin Americans.) Repetitions with variations are extremely effective in producing this density: the variants convey essential developments and at the same time establish paradigmatic relations within and between the symbolic patterns of the text. Vargas Llosa emphasizes the incantational value of these frequently repeated patterns. In addition, their purely formal function overflows into the semantic aspect (Pilar Ternera appears periodically in her role of consoler).

Ambiguity in the novel is further intensified by the transposition and confusion of senses and sensations (Melquíades speaks "lighting up with his deep organ voice the darkest reaches of the imagination" [p. 6]; Rebeca "spits hieroglyphics" [*escupe jeroglíficos*, p. 44] José Arcadio sees a "route that . . . could only lead to the past" [p. 11] and then perceives the sea colored with disillusionment). Such devices as synesthesia, oxymoron and the like in most cases allow more than one interpretation. As Todorov points out, the fantastic often originates in hyperbole and metaphor— both of which abound in *One Hundred Years of Solitude*.

Structurally, the fantastic element helps to create and maintain suspense; its semantic function, asserts Todorov, is its very presence in the work. And what could be more fantastic in the case of *One Hundred Years of Solitude*, asks Vargas Llosa, if not the fact that it is a story of a story told in reverse? An unusual aspect of it—with a distinctly twentieth-century flavor—is that it contains within itself not the account of its writing, but rather one of its reading and interpretation. Thus, all events in the novel gain added significance as clues for a final deciphering. A structuralist can easily discover a careful system of signs and codes in this never-totally-revealed universe full of premonitions.

Vargas Llosa took nearly seven hundred pages to outline a few essential characteristics of García Márquez's work. It would seem vain to attempt here a complete analysis of even one aspect. The role of foreshadowing is of primary importance in the novel, and only a long essay could do it justice. These lines will barely serve as an introduction to what begins the book as technique and ends it as theme. It should be noted that throughout the greater part of the story a single character may embody both technique and theme. The very first image the reader encounters, one periodically reiterated, provides a glimpse of the future (which then is not fulfilled): Colonel Aureliano Buendía in front of a firing squad. Aureliano is the first and the greatest seer of the Buendía family, and one who attains mythical stature. His supernatural qualities are suggested when Ursula hears him cry in her womb; his first spoken words are a premonition: "the boiling pot is going to spill" ([la] olla de caldo hirviendo . . ." "se va a caer" [p. 15]). At this point, with the introduction of the husband's and the wife's characters the dichotomy in their reactions becomes clear: what frightens Ursula seems a "natural phenomenon" to José Arcadio. Much later, while awaiting his execution, Aureliano formulates what could be considered a theory of premonitions, which is related to a vital theme of the novel: the natural versus the artificial. Amazed at the fact that on this occasion he has no premonition of his pending execution, he concludes that only a natural death warrants a supernatural sign. As it happens no one dares carry out the orders leading to his "artificial" end; thus, the lack of a premonition of death in his mind becomes in the mind of the reader a foreshadowing of life.

Another interesting use of the foreshadowing technique is found in the account of Amaranta's death. In this case, a premonition takes on human form and visits her personally, leaving exact instructions. This fantastic situation is even further exploited as it is raised to the level of superstition: knowing she is to die, Amaranta announces publicly her willingness to collect and deliver the "mail for the dead" on behalf of the whole village. An even greater degree of complexity is achieved by the narrator's comment that "it seemed a farce" (p. 239). The imperfect tense and, in Todorov's terms, the "modalization" lead one to assume that it was *not* a farce. The paradox is taken further, however: it is Amaranta herself who, looking and feeling perfectly well, directs to the very end the preparations for her own funeral.

It might be noted that the manner of presentation of each premonition exemplifies the basic technique of the novel itself: in rhythmically repeated "fore-flashes" of the main characters' deaths is included a short synopsis of the strongest emotions and impressions of their lives. The same interruptive technique is used throughout the novel to record cardinal stages in the life and death of the tribe and the whole village. The opening sentence of the novel renders Aureliano's first distinctly remembered impression as he awaits his last; as the book closes, the last Aureliano in the family line receives the final impression of his life as he reads about the first. Life and literature become one, and both seem destined to sink into oblivion.

The importance of foreshadowing becomes evident when we analyze the first chapter more closely. In it can be found most of the major themes and devices of the novel. Like the entire book, the introductory chapter forms a perfectly circular structure, a circle that runs counter to the clock. There is also a complete integration of various temporal levels: what the colonel glimpses of the past in the first sentence (which is itself a fore-flash) closes the chapter as a living experience in the present tense. Fire and ice unite as opposites, forming a paradox, a device constantly used throughout the novel. The importance of the word — the Verb, the Creation — is stressed at both the opening and the close: Macondo is so new to the world that names have to be invented to designate objects, says the narrator in his first description of the town. At the end of the chapter we see José Arcadio groping for words when confronted with what for him is a new phenomenon — ice. The novel itself closes with a character reading the last line, which for the first time releases the book's full meaning.

The circle — and the premonition — can also be found in the symbol of the child with a tail. What appears in the first chapter as superstitious fear (thereby opening the gates to the realm of the fantastic) is finally justified in the last. The whole novel in some way anticipates the fulfillment of this oracle. Another use of foreshadowing can be found in the first pages: i.e., the prediction by Melquíades that the whole tribe of Buendías will be extinguished. Melquíades's life comes full circle within the limits of this chapter: it starts with his first arrival in Macondo and ends with the news about his death, just as the book itself develops from the arrival of the Buendías in Macondo to the written news of their final extinction.

It may be worthwhile to note that the first character introduced in this book is Melquíades, a fantastic figure constantly fluctuating between the real and the supernatural: he "was a gloomy man, enveloped in a sad aura, with an Asiatic look that seemed to know what there was on the other side of things. . . . But in spite of his immense wisdom and his mysterious breadth, he had a human burden, an earthly condition that kept him involved in the small problems of daily life" (p. 6). The physical description of him, in turn, intensifies the temporal distortion: he wears "a velvet vest across which the patina of centuries had skated" (p. 6). And one of the first "wonders" he brings is called "*fierros*," not "*hierros mágicos*," an archaic form of the word which also suggests his agelessness. While indulging in magic, he is able to give the most lucid explanations about recent progress in the scientific world. (One of the most delightful examples is his conversation with Ursula about his being a demon, where he explains to her the odor of the devil from a chemical point of view.) His blindness and the increased lucidity it brings about foreshadow Ursula's last years when the role of intuition is emphasized. It leads, moreover, to another principle theme in the novel: that of insanity versus sanity, which is developed with regard to several members of the family.

Melquíades bears within himself the main theme of the novel: he returns from the kingdom of the dead, renouncing immortality, because he is unable to endure solitude. The book closes with the reading of his scriptures. Only at this point does the reader realize that Melquíades was not only a character but the narrator himself.[6] In one of his first appearances in the novel, he even gives a definition of what the book turns out to be—"fantastic stories" (p. 6)—suggesting, moreover, that there are always several interpretations to a phenomenon: on the same page we see him through four different pairs of eyes, interpreted four different ways. Thus, the figure of Melquíades points to everything in this novel being a language of signs and patterns, a "récit indiciel" with intricate metaphorical relationships.[7]

The first chapter makes full use of such structural elements as paradox, which is essential in the presentation of the theme of the absurd (José Arcadio sets out to look for the sea, gets lost in the jungle and founds Macondo; while seeking to communicate with the city, he discovers the sea; Ursula, seeking her son, discovers the road to civilization); parallelism (José Arcadio as a symbol of the village and Ursula, of the home); antithesis (José Arcadio embodying imagination, Ursula embodying common and practical sense; the two sons who become archetypes for the entire descendency divided between an emphasis on physical enjoyment of life and the anguish of imagination); repetition as the essence of the story, summarized by Pilar Ternera at the end: "the history of the family was a machine with unavoidable repetitions" (p. 402). The repetition may be associated with the symbol of mirrors perceived by José Arcadio in the dream which determines the founding of Macondo, transposed once we understand that the mirrors do not reproduce the image an infinite number of times but instead a mirage which is impossible to repeat.

A favorite device of realistic novelists, the use of historical figures, is not disdained by García Márquez but used with a dose of ambiguity. The figure of Francis Drake, evoked at the very first, is rendered with a new emphasis: "he had gone crocodile hunting with cannons and . . . he repaired them and stuffed them with straw to bring to Queen Elizabeth" (p. 10).

Many secondary themes are also introduced in this chapter and later developed more fully: the first notion of religion is, significantly, mixed with superstition; the only reference to the civil government is especially important for it underscores its inefficiency. José Arcadio's desire to invent a "memory machine" is a precursor of the long episode of the "insomnia plague"; his interest in developing arms for "solar warfare" hints at the future revolution and the mythical exploits of Colonel Aureliano Buendía. The principles of self-government and equality are established by José Arcadio's distribution of land and sun, thus introducing the important roles nature and climatic conditions are to play.[8] José Arcadio's expedition wrestling with the fierce forces of the jungle provides one of the earliest glimpses of the jungle's power and makes convincing its final invasion of the Buendías' family house in the last chapter.

Nature also serves to introduce the eternal dichotomy between the natural state of man and civilized man, illustrated in the first chapter by the two tribes of gypsies. The first are simple and honest and want to share their knowledge. Those that follow, "purveyors of amusement," come to cheat and loot. The theme of solitude and isolation is opposed to that of friendship and is brought out by emphasizing the desire to communicate, which is as strong in individual characters as it is within the village community as a whole.

There is, finally, in the first pages of the novel an early intimation of one of the most exuberant of the later episodes: Aureliano Segundo's "papering" the walls of his house with money clearly echoes José Arcadio's announcement in the first chapter that "we'll have gold enough and more to pave the floors of the house" (p. 2). (The paradox attached to the theme of gold is that we see José Arcadio on the first page and Aureliano Segundo toward the end of the book desperately searching for it without success while at the peak of the fortune a saint's figure [to whom Ursula lights candles and prays] is discovered containing a treasure of gold. A further paradox can be seen in the fact that Ursula's hiding place is indicated in the first chapter and later repeated, but when the whole house and garden are dug up during the search, nobody looks under her bed.) A strong parallelism can be observed between the fall and rise of the family and of the village, which is symbolized at the end of the book by the return of the first tribe of gypsies we met in Chapter I: The development of the village has completed a full circle between the two comings, and the villagers have returned to a state where they can again be awed by innocent, primitive magic.

A powerful imagination is the prime characteristic defining José Arcadio. It too comes full circle: in the first chapter we see him teaching his children by "forcing the limits of his imagination to extremes" (p. 16), interrupting his task only to greet the arrival of gypsies who bring even more imaginary inventions. At the end, the last descendants receive instruction from Aureliano Segundo who uses an English encyclopedia without being able to read it; he draws on his imagination to invent instructions.

There is a distinct gradation among the first "wonders" acquired by José Arcadio from the gypsies, a gradation further developed in later chapters. He begins by exploring the fields around Macondo with a magnet in search of gold for personal purposes (prosperity that will be achieved through Ursula's fabrication of candied animals and later through the proliferation of real animals during Aureliano Segundo's reign); then he passes on to convert a magnifying glass into a weapon of war (war will eventually involve the whole country through his son's revolutionary opposition to the government); with the compass and the sextant his imagination crosses seas and frontiers — as his last descendants will do in actuality. Finally, alchemy transports him to a realm of irreality, which is later repeated as several members of the family end their lives "liberated" from the limits of time, space and social convention.

Only the all-important element of time remains to be examined in the first chapter. Again a technique is introduced which is used throughout the novel. The compression of time is evident: fourteen years of life are packed into fourteen pages. This is achieved mainly by fragmenting and juggling various temporal levels, a process which can be summarized as follows: future with the present, in which five different stages are marked by the successive arrivals of the gypsies, introducing the great theme of transformations; the past alone, which contains allusions to an even more remote past; and present, past and future together. On all these levels, further divisions as well as interrelations between real time and imaginary time could be established. One remark by Ursula deserves mention: almost ready to die, she complains that "time was slower before." In fact, José Arcadio and his men need four days to conquer twelve kilometers in the first chapter; in the last, Gaston is contemplating the establishment of airmail service to Macondo. The speed of events becomes frantic at the end, when the sudden whirlwind of destruction prevents Aureliano Babilonia (note the change in name) from finishing the deciphering of the manuscript. Almost at the exact center of the novel Ursula utters, "it's as if time had turned around and we were back at the beginning" (p. 169). From this point on, one can add to the reading in progression another reading in regression. The tempo increases, but the quickened passing of time only brings omens of degeneration and destruction. All human efforts are revealed to be futile, all hopes absurd in the face of the ultimate predestination. But precisely at this point, where written time ends, the cycle is reinitiated—in the reader's imagination.

Notes

1. The following works by Tzvetan Todorov are referred to: "Les catégories du récit littéraire," *Communications*, 8, 1966, pp. 125–51; *Literatura y significación*, Barcelona, 1971; *Introduction a la littérature fantastique*. Paris, 1970.

2. *One Hundred Years of Solitude*, Gregory Rabassa, tr., New York, Harper & Row, 1970, p. 2. All quotations are taken from this edition.

3. Mario Vargas Llosa draws attention to this technique in his *Historia de un deicidio*, Barcelona, 1971, p. 145. After his exhaustive study there remain few unexplored aspects in García Márquez's work.

4. M. Vargas Llosa, "García Márquez: de Aracataca a Macondo," *9 asedios a García Márquez*, Santiago de Chile, 1969.

5. See R. Barthes on "distaxie et integration," "Introduction à l'analyse structurale des récits," *Communications*, 8, 1966, pp. 1–27.

6. Also in *La peste* Rieux is revealed as the author only at the very end of the chronicle.

7. See R. Barthes, *op. cit.*

8. Camus takes great pain to describe the geographic and climatic conditions of Oran in the first chapter of *La peste*.

One Hundred Years of Solitude:
The Last Three Pages
Emir Rodríguez Monegal*

The last three pages of *One Hundred Years of Solitude* contains one of the keys to the book, one which gives access to its total fictionality. In three pages, Aureliano Babilonia, after having seen the corpse of his monstrous son carried away by "all of the ants in the world," has a sudden revelation. He remembers something he once read in an obscure and indecipherable manuscript: "*The first of the line is tied to a tree and the last is being eaten by ants*" (*One Hundred Years of Solitude*, p. 420). The text belongs to the manuscript left behind by Melquíades, a text inserted into the novel like the play-within-the-play in the third act of *Hamlet*. The sudden revelation decides Aureliano's destiny: leaving everything out, he will lock himself in a room to read for the first time in its entirety Melquíades's book; he will then be able to decipher the sense of his destiny and the destiny of his family, of which he is the only survivor. If the reading of the coded parchments had been impossible before, now (after the revelation) he reads them as easily "as if they had been written in Spanish." What Aureliano reads is summed up by the author in these words:

> It was the history of the family, written by Melquíades, down to the most trivial details, one hundred years ahead of time. He had written it in Sanskrit, which was his mother tongue, and he had encoded the even lines in the private cipher of the Emperor Augustus and the odd ones in a Lacedemonian military code. The final protection, which Aureliano had begun to glimpse when he let himself be confused by the love of Amaranta Ursula, was based on the fact that Melquíades had not put events in the order of man's conventional time, but had concentrated a century of daily episodes in such a way that they coexisted in one instant. (p. 421)

While Aureliano reads the history of his family and discovers that he had been engendered by people of whose existence he had a very vague idea, or none at all; while he reads that Amaranta Ursula is his aunt and not his sister (as he feared with delicious horror while possessing her voraciously), and that the son with the pig's tail whom they engendered is not only their offspring but that of a whole line which extends to them through "the most intricate labyrinths of blood," Macondo, the town surrounding the house in which Aureliano is reading, is being assailed by a wind that will erase it from the face of the earth. The reading of the book of destiny takes place at the very moment when destiny closes the book of life.

Outside, the wind destroys everything. Inside, Aureliano remains trapped in the hypnotic reading of a text which not only escapes time because it was written one hundred years ago and tells what is happening

*Reprinted from *Books Abroad* 47, no. 3 (Summer 1973):485–89. Copyright 1973 by the University of Oklahoma Press. Reprinted by permission.

now but which is also outside of time because it telescopes a whole century into a single moment. Inside, Aureliano discovers the immortality of the text. Outside, the wind (a metaphor of time) will destroy Macondo, yet in the timeless world of Melquíades's parchments, nothing ever dies, nothing is destroyed, everything is present.

THE MAGIC ROOM

The reading of Melquíades's book being simultaneous with the destruction of Macondo by an apocalyptic wind is only a textual simultaneity. In the reality of the fiction, the reading is done outside time and thus the wind that levels Macondo cannot touch the reader. The end of García Márquez's book is very explicit:

> Macondo was already a fearful whirlwind of dust and rubble being spun about by the wrath of the biblical hurricane when Aureliano skipped eleven pages so as not to lose time with facts he knew only too well, and he began to decipher the instant that he was living, deciphering it as he lived it, prophesying himself in the act of deciphering the last page of the parchments, as if he were looking into a speaking mirror. Then he skipped again to anticipate the predictions and ascertain the date and circumstances of his death. Before reaching the final line, however, he had already understood that he would never leave that room, for it was foreseen that the city of mirrors (or mirages) would be wiped out by the wind and exiled from the memory of men at the precise moment when Aureliano Babilonia would finish deciphering the parchments, and that everything written on them was unrepeatable since time immemorial and forever more, because races condemned to one hundred years of solitude did not have a second opportunity on earth. (p. 422)

Aureliano is thus trapped in a magic room in which time has stopped forever. It is the same room in which José Arcadio Segundo had taught him to read, Melquíades's room still haunted by the presence of the immortal gypsy: "In the small isolated room where the arid air never penetrated, nor the dust, nor the heat, both had the atavistic vision of an old man, his back to the window, wearing a hat with a brim like the wings of a crow who spoke about the world many years before they had been born. Both described at the same time how it was always March there and always Monday . . ." (p. 355). In that magic room, where neither the wind nor the dust nor the heat had ever come, time itself never comes. Now that Aureliano has locked himself up in that room to decode his destiny in Melquíades's parchments, he discovers perhaps that he too is trapped there forever. Like the magician who dreams a man (a son) in Borges's masterful story, "The Circular Ruins," this Aureliano of the city of mirrors, or mirages, discovers on the last page that he too is a ghost who has been dreamed by another man. He is trapped in a labyrinth of words, written one hundred years before and in Sanskrit, by the Magus.

AN ALEPH OF TIME

The connection of *One Hundred Years of Solitude*'s last three pages with Borges's fiction is not casual. Where else can one find texts which contain similar magic and textual connotations? Where else can one find a similar profusion of fantasy and hyperbole? Only in Borges does one find the same labyrinths made of unending or circular time, the secret scriptures of gods, cities obliterated by time to their very ashes, immortal men forever trapped in the lines of a text which turns upon itself in such an obsessive, oneiric way.

Borges's fiction helps to understand a decisive aspect of *One Hundred Years of Solitude*, i.e., the simultaneity of its times. The key lies in one of its sentences. Upon discovering the parchments, Aureliano understands that "Melquíades had not put events in the order of man's conventional time, but had concentrated a century of daily episodes in such a way that they coexisted in one instant" (p. 421). Melquíades had created an Aleph made of time. In Borges's story of the same title, the Aleph is made of space: " 'The Aleph?' I repeated. 'Yes, the only place on earth where all places are — seen from every angle, each standing clear, without any confusion or blending' " (*The Aleph*, p. 23). A few pages later, when the narrator finally sees the Aleph, he says, "I saw the Aleph from every point and angle, and in the Aleph I saw the earth and in the earth the Aleph and in the Aleph the earth . . ." (p. 28). The coexistence of one hundred years in a single moment of time makes Melquíades's book into an emblem of the Aleph. As in Borges's story, the book contains the world and the world contains the book, in a mirror-like way.

It is not necessary to resort to the Kabbalah (which has so much influenced this aspect of Borges's fiction) nor to the better known example of Nostradamus's prophecies (which García Márquez does mention), nor even to Mallarmé's famous dictum that everything culminates in a book, to discover that this concept which connects the book and the world is at the core of the basic religions of the West, as Borges has shown in his famous essay, "On the Cult of Books" (in *Other Inquisitions*, 1952). Borges's essay concludes as follows: "According to Mallarmé, the world exists to culminate in a book; according to Bloy, we are the versicles or words or letters of a magic book, and that incessant book is the only thing in the world: or rather, it is the world" (p. 120). It is obvious that García Márquez arrives at this concept in his novel not only through the reading of the Bible (as has been suggested by some critics) but also through Borges and his total reading of literature as text. On the level Melquíades's parchments are situated, his book is an Aleph image of the world, and the word (as in St. John's Gospel) is the instrument of creation. In the Beginning was the Verb. Which brings the argument back to a point already discussed. Instead of being completely destroyed, the world of Macondo is partially saved from time. On the last page, the wind does not annihilate the whole of Macondo because there is still one room untouched. Time is finally stopped in its tracks to become eternally fixed in the very act of creation. That is, in the act of reading. (To decipher a text is to create it.)

In skipping through Melquíades's book, while outside the wind erases Macondo forever, Aureliano perhaps discovers what the other reader (*the* reader) has discovered a while back: that he and the room in which he reads are immune to the destructions of time because they have always lived in another dimension, that of the speaking mirror of a book. A mirror which is also a mirage, composed of solitude and sudden revelation, but above all of the immortality which the word confers.

It is poetic justice that the last name of the character to whom this revelation is destined is Babilonia, in double homage to Borges's "The Lottery in Babylon" and "The Library of Babel." For who but a man with such a name could have triumphantly decoded the Babelic cipher of Melquíades's parchments. From the Biblical confusion of languages to the discovery of the key to language, Aureliano Babilonia solves the mystery and reads (for the first time in its entirety) the book. Needless to say, the book he reads is, emblematically, the same in which he lives, *One Hundred Years of Solitude*. Melquíades's reader and García Márquez's reader complete the same task at the same time. Both decode the same text, the same Aleph.

The simultaneity of readings reinforces the concept of the world as a book. While Aureliano Babilonia discovers that his own destiny and that of his lineage are enclosed in a book, the reader discovers that the book Aureliano is reading and Macondo itself are enclosed in yet another book, which is the Book. The true destiny of Aureliano Babilonia is not to be forever trapped in Melquíades's magic room (as he had been virtually enclosed from the very beginning in the Magus's parchments) but to be trapped in the pages of this other Book. His destiny is the circular immortality of all creatures of fiction.

THE TOTAL FICTION

Melquíades is not the only magus which the Book postulates. It has already been insinuated, I think, that Melquíades has a role in relation to the author that is similar to the one Aureliano occupies in relation to the reader. This paves the way to a reading of the Book as total fiction: a fiction in which even the author is incorporated into the text not as a secondary character (there is a "Gabriel," a friend of Aureliano, who could represent him) but as the author of the parchments. Beneath the mask of Melquíades it is possible to recognize the face of García Márquez: the Magus is a persona of the author. Like the latter, the author has written the complete story of *One Hundred Years of Solitude* before that story had been read and deciphered by its readers. It would be possible to stretch the parallel a bit further. I would like, however, to suggest another reading which the Book indicates. One must look beyond the text into the author's biography for the elements which appear (metamorphosed) in the novel. Some anecdotes help to place García Márquez's childhood in the same pathetic dimension of the last Aureliano's. He too was a child abandoned by his parents who lived an almost ghostly existence in the big rambling house of his grandparents. Even though many details do not coincide (García Márquez's parents would come back to reclaim him), the basic initial situation, the one which generates the symbols, is the same. García Márquez has told of his admiration for his grandfather, the prototype of Colonel Aureliano Buendía, and he has also told of his grandmother's tales, she being the model of the fabulous Ursula Iguarán and the person to whom he owes the fantastic turn of his best fiction and above all the gift of the spoken language in his stories. His grandparents are at the origin of his fiction. But it is the abandonment by his parents that created the basic situation in which his whole fiction is rooted.

Knowing this, how is it possible to resist the temptation to recognize in Aureliano, the last of his lineage, in that child who runs naked and wild through his grandparents' house, deserted by his parents, an alter ego of his author, even though this Gabriel is no bastard nor has ever had carnal relations with his aunt, nor has engendered a son with pig's tail, nor is the last of a line condemned to one hundred years of solitude? The truth of the emblematic figure outshines the mere truth of detail.

Accepting this, it is possible then to see in Melquíades, in that extra-lucid and kabbalistic gentleman, the same child who is now situated in another dimension of time: after he has grown up and seen the world and returned to his place of origin to write in Sanskrit (that is, in his mother tongue), the history of his ancestors, the fabulous history of his lineage. Because to become an author is to become a magus.

Aureliano reading Melquíades's parchments in Melquíades's magic room (the same room, by the way, in which he learned to read) becomes Melquíades, that is, he becomes the author. When Aureliano decodes his life and destiny in the parchments he is like the author (any author) when he reaches the end of his book: only then can he read it in its entirety. Now Aureliano can read what he has lived as the author can read the text which he was destined to write. The character and the author not only share a common biographical experience, they have come to share the same complex specular operation of the writing-and-reading and writing of a text which is a speaking mirror. An operation, on the other hand, of perfect circularity. So that we finally reach the last tautology of this novel, which like all stories, ends up biting its tail. In the end is the beginning.

If the last Aureliano discovers on the last page that he won't be able to leave the magic room any more because that room is the last reality that remains to him in a world obliterated by the wind, it is not only because he has finally accepted being condemned to solitude but because perhaps on a non-conscious level he has accepted his reality as a creature forever lost in a world of mirages, of a being who inhabits a world of total fiction. But within that world, the wind that destroys the rest of Macondo in the last two pages does not touch Aureliano, petrified forever in the last line in the act of reading. Because that wind (like everything else in the Book) is made of words and is enclosed in a solid object made of pages that one can turn back to begin (once more and so on to infinity) the reading. What really ends on the last page of the Book is only the first reading. It is enough to turn back the pages for time to begin to run again, for the figures of the old and deceased to come to life, for the fable to recommence. It's enough to read, or re-read.

Gabriel García Márquez's "Eréndira" and the Brothers Grimm
Joel Hancock*

Since the first publication of *Nursery and Household Tales* in 1812, the fairy tales collected by Jacob and Wilhelm Grimm have endured in popularity. Originating in the oral tradition, the old folk stories — once the main staple of entertainment for adults — are now published in sumptuous volumes with beautiful illustrations and directed to a younger public. The influence of the tradition is significant: numerous variations of the old tales have appeared, and many contemporary writers such as Andersen, Wilde, St. Exupéry, Thurber, Dodgson, Tolkien, and Sendak, to name a few, have each in his own way, expanded the form. The Grimm brothers' influence has long been prominent in other arts also, in such well-known works as the opera and ballet versions of "Cinderella," "Hansel and Gretel," "Rumpelstiltskin," "Sleeping Beauty," and "The Beauty and the Beast." Countless more reworkings enrich the theatre, films, and puppetry.[1] Elements from fairy tales can be identified in writings by authors who ostensibly are far removed from the tradition, such as Franz Kafka.[2] The impact has been felt in Latin American literature as well. Jean Franco observed that the mixture of violence and fairytale is increasingly common in contemporary fiction."[3] She offers a specific example in her review of Gabriel García Márquez's *The Autumn of the Patriarch*, claiming that the novel "can be read as a series of entertaining fairy tales which have the undertow of violence found (for instance) in the *Arabian Nights*."[4] My purpose in this paper will be to elucidate certain elements and narrative structures in a story by Gabriel García Márquez as representative of those

*Reprinted from *Studies in 20th Century Literature* 3 (1978):45–52. Reprinted by permission of the journal.

morphologies which Vladímir Propp delineates for the genre of the fairy tale.

There is no doubt that García Márquez is keenly interested in children's literature. During the period between the publication of *One Hundred Years of Solitude* (1967) and the writing of *The Autumn of the Patriarch*, he composed several short stories, some of which carried the sub-heading "story for children."[5] In 1978, the tales appeared in English translation in *Innocent Eréndira and Other Stories*, a collection of eleven stories and one novella.[6] The volume's featured work is "The Incredible and Sad Tale of Innocent Eréndira and Her Heartless Grandmother," an awesome title which alludes to the cries of hawkers at county fairs.[7] It is a long narrative which has enjoyed more critical attention than its companion pieces and has been diversely labled as an "historia rosada," a parody of melodrama, a fanciful boutade, and a work so complex that the question of influences could be discussed indefinitely.[8] Numerous features of the story are illuminated when it is examined in the light of the structures and themes of the fairy tale, and especially in the tradition of the brothers Grimm.[9] Dimensions of special interest are the structural organization of the narrative, the portrayal of characters, and certain motifs, all of which are strongly reminiscent of Grimm's *Fairy Tales*.

Any discussion of the form of a fairy tale would do well to consider the now classical work by Vladímir Propp, *Morphology of the Folktale*,[10] which is undoubtedly the most thorough and influential examination of the genre. Conceived as a description of fairy tales according to the characteristic elements and their relationship to one another, the study upholds as one of its basic premises that "all fairy tales are of one type with regard to their structure" (p. 23): it further offers a classification of what Propp terms "functions of dramatis personae" (pp. 25–65). A close look at the form of "Innocent Eréndira" reveals that many of Propp's "functions" can be discerned, suggesting that it does indeed have the organizational framework of a fairy tale.

Most fairy tales, says Propp, begin with an "initial situation" (p. 25), a statement that introduces the protagonists and suggests what direction the story might take. For example, the Grimm brothers' "Rapunzel" opens: "There were once a man and a woman who had long in vain wished for a child."[11] In "Innocent Eréndira" the ominous first sentence is likewise in keeping with this pattern: "Eréndira was bathing her grandmother when the wind of her misfortune began to blow" (p. 1). The reader has thus met the two main characters and has been warned that a catastrophe is imminent. The synoptic opening is then followed, Propp affirms, by an "interdiction" (p. 26) that tends to be a prohibition or a warning: "if by tomorrow morning early you have not spun this straw into gold, you shall die," in "Rumpelstiltskin";[12] or Jorinda's advice to Joringel, "take care that you do not go too near the castle";[13] or the King's prohibitive decrees in "Faithful John," "the last chamber in the gallery shall you not show."[14] In

"Innocent Eréndira," the interdiction is seen in the grandmother's command, "Before going to bed make sure everything is in perfect order,"[15] to which Eréndira replies, "Yes, grandmother" (p. 1). According to Propp, one function results from another, and thus a logical development is a "violation of the interdiction," (p. 27). In Eréndira's case, she does not heed the warning. Fatigued from the abusive burden of her daily chores, Eréndira falls into bed without extinguishing the candles. That night a wind overturns the candelabra and the mansion is burned to the ground, thus fulfilling the presentiment voiced in the initial sentence.

Customarily, at this point a villain decrees some extreme and cruel punishment. In a Grimm's fairy tale it could be a devil, stepmother, animal, evil queen, or such. In Eréndira's case, the antagonist is the grandmother who announces, "life won't be long enough for you to pay me back for this mishap" (p. 7). She imposes a penalty and begins its execution: Eréndira must dedicate her life to large-scale prostitution and repay all damages. According to Propp, "the harm or injury caused by the villain" (p. 30) is the most important of all functions because it generates the rest of the action. This is certainly true in "Eréndira." Throughout most of the story the reader finds the young girl in her tent carrying out the terms of her sentence. The grandmother's edict—forcing the child into "filthy business"—is harsh and excessive; it is nonetheless in keeping with the tradition where the villainous deeds are varied and severe: banishment, enslavement, bewitchment, mutilation, and cannibalism, to name a few.

Once the villain has imposed the punishment, the stage is set for the appearance of the hero. In "Eréndira," the male lead is Ulises, a handsome lad who is on a trip through the desert with his father. Intrigued by the stories of Eréndira's beauty, he visits the tent where she is conducting her business affairs and experiences his sexual initiation in a night of passion. Smitten with love, he later decides to follow Eréndira and elope with her. Their first attempt fails when the grandmother, assisted by the military, overtakes the couple and retrieves the girl. Eréndira is returned to her degradation, this time chained to the bed. Soon she becomes the most sought-after prostitute in the area and, consequently, hated and humiliated by her sisters-in-trade. The opulence and carnivalesque splendor of Eréndira's surroundings contrast with her desperation. This situation calls forth another series of "functions" peculiar to fairy tales.

According to Propp, "misfortune is made known and the hero is approached with a request" (p. 36). The motif is very common in the Grimm brothers. In "Iron Henry," a prince-turned-frog comes to the aid of a forlorn princess; a young girl is saved from hard work by three deformed women in "The Three Spinners"; handsome princes rescue the "Goose-Girl," "Snow White," and "Sleeping Beauty." The formula is similarly adhered to in the story by García Márquez. Eréndira beckons Ulises through mental telepathy:

Eréndira looked at her (the grandmother) from the bed with intense eyes that in the shadows resembled those of a cat. Then she went to bed like a person who had drowned, her arms on her breast and her eyes open, and she called with all the strength of her inner voice:
"Ulises!"
Ulises woke up suddenly in the house on the orange plantation. He had heard Eréndira's voice so clearly that he was looking for her in the shadows of the room. After an instant of reflection, he made a bundle of his clothing and shoes and left the bedroom (p. 49).

The communication leads to three other Proppian functions: "the hero decides upon counteraction" (p. 38), "the hero leaves home" (p. 39), and "the hero is led to the whereabouts" (p. 50). Ulises ponders the question for a second, then packs his clothes and informs his father of his departure. Although the trip across the desert is arduous, Ulises arrives safely, as if magically delivered: "On that occasion Ulises didn't have to ask anyone where Eréndira was. He crossed the desert hiding in passing trucks, stealing to eat and sleep, until he found the tent in another seaside town. Eréndira was asleep chained to the slat and in the same position of a drowned person on the beach from which she had called him" (p. 50).

Fairy tales must inevitably conclude with a confrontation in which the hero defeats the villain, thus delivering the victim to safety. Propp assigns three separate functions to these events: "the hero and villain join in combat" (p. 51), "the villain is defeated" (p. 53), and "the initial misfortune or lack is liquidated" (p. 53). Ulises decides to kill the grandmother in order to liberate Eréndira. The task is not easy and requires three attempts. First, Ulises presents the old woman with a cake laced with arsenic which has only a soporific effect. Next, Ulises resorts to dynamite, but the detonation merely inflicts surface burns. In desperation, Ulises turns to a knife and finally accomplishes his task. Free at last, Eréndira picks up the vest containing the profits of the business which the grandmother had converted into gold and flees toward the sea, never to return.

Hence, the happy ending, at least for Eréndira. The closing sentence has the effect of implying that she lived "happily ever after," a formula ending which typifies most of the Grimm fairy tales: "Without turning her head she ran past the saltpeter pits, the talcum craters, the torpor of the shacks, until the natural science of the sea ended and the desert began, but she still kept on running with the gold vest beyond the arid winds and the never-ending sunsets and she was never heard of again nor was the slightest trace of her misfortune ever found" (p. 59).

Just as the structure of García Márquez's story adheres to that of a fairy tale, so do the descriptions and development of the major characters. It is interesting to observe that the dominant figures in the story — Eréndira and her grandmother — are female. Such is the case also for the majority of tales from the Grimm brothers' collection, according to the well-known Swiss folklorist Max Lüthi who cites Sleeping Beauty, Snow White, Little Red Riding Hood, Rapunzel, The Princess in Disguise, and Goldmarie as the most celebrated fairy tale figures.[16]

Eréndira shares common ground with the personages listed above. When the story opens, she is barely fourteen years old, "and was languid, soft-boned, and too meek for her age" (p. 1). An orphan of illegitimate birth, Eréndira lives as a servant with her grandmother, accepting orders with stoic passivity. She is Cinderella, inhumanly abused as she performs her household chores of bathing and dressing the grandmother, sweeping and mopping floors, washing rugs, cooking meals, polishing crystal, caring for plants and pets, ironing clothes, and winding clocks—this last endeavor taking six hours of her time. Her exploitation reaches its peak when she is forced into prostitution, servicing large hordes of men each day. With the growth of Eréndira's clientele, the fame of her beauty spreads throughout the land. There is no doubt that she is miserable under her grandmother's tutelage, the only happy moments of her life being those during a brief period of captivity in a convent.

With Eréndira the Cinderella figure, her grandmother is squarely within the tradition of the cruel stepmothers so prevalent in fairy tales. Physically, she is a grotesque figure, a tattooed woman of elephantine proportions whose make-up and apparel complete the caricature of her appearance. Her enslavement and treatment of Eréndira is brutal, and her dealings with customers and business associates is equally cold-blooded. At the height of success in what has become a thriving capitalistic venture, the woman and her domain are engulfed in an atmosphere of revelry. Side-shows and concessions surround the central circus tent. But, as in all Grimm fairy tales, the wicked witch must come to her end, and she does in an appropriately gory fashion. The grandmother's death follows the formula of violent demise met by the stepmothers in "The Twelve Brothers" and "The Juniper Tree," or the queen in "Snow White."

More difficult to accommodate to the scheme is the male protagonist. Ulises' handsome appearance qualifies him as a hero—"a gilded adolescent with lonely maritime eyes and with the appearance of a furtive angel" (p. 16)—but his actions and the outcome deviate from the expected pattern.[17] In a review which appeared shortly after the story was published, Carlos Meneses portrays Ulises as a kind of anti-Prince Charming.[18] The critic indicates that Ulises is the son of a Dutch smuggler, which is far from royalty; he steals from his father to pay for Eréndira's pleasure; he is inexperienced in love; and he becomes an assassin. These objections may apply to a traditional fairy tale, but not necessarily to a contemporary one. A white horse could not survive the Colombian desert, and certainly a Prince Charming is obligated to destroy the villain. Ulises is in fact somewhat unaggressive and innocent, and in this regard is closer to the Dummlings or simpletons seen in Grimm brothers' fairy tales. Lüthi calls the type the negative or passive hero: "The preference of modern literature for the passive hero . . . is not without parallel in the fairy tale . . . (which also) has a partiality for the negative hero; the insignificant, the neglected, the helpless."[19] Nonetheless, one must agree that Ulises fails when it comes to Propp's final and perhaps most important function: the hero is married and ascends the throne" (p. 63). Eréndira does not share her final bliss; Ulises is left "lying face down on the beach, weeping from solitude and fear" (p. 59).[20]

A motif commonly found in fairy tales is the notion of successive ordeals. In the stories compiled by the Grimm brothers, the characters often participate in a series of labors or trials. Heroes must prove their valor by performing courageous deeds. They are compelled to unravel a sequence of riddles, or be subjected to what Propp terms "tests, interrogations, or attacks" (p. 39). An instance of this is seen in Ulises' efforts to kill the grandmother, successful only after the third attempt. Eréndira's introduction to sex also illustrates the theme. Three men — a widower, a trucker, and a mailman — are forced on her in rapid succession.

Cruelty, violence, scabrous sex, and gore are common-place items in the story by García Márquez. The description of the grandmother's death is a prime example:

> Ulises managed to free the knife and stab her a second time in the side. The grandmother let out a hidden moan and hugged her attacker with more strength. Ulises gave her a third stab, without pity, and a spurt of blood, released by high pressure, sprinkled his face: it was oily blood, shiny and green, just like mint honey. . . . Huge, monolithic, roaring with pain and rage, the grandmother grasped Ulises' body. Her arms, her legs, even her hairless skull were green with blood. Her enormous bellows-breathing, upset by the first rattles of death, filled the whole area. Ulises managed to free his arms with the weapon once more, opened a cut in her belly, and an explosion of blood soaked him in green from head to toe. The grandmother tried to reach the open air which she needed in order to live now and fell face down. Ulises got away from the lifeless arms and without pausing a moment gave the vast fallen body a final thrust (pp. 57–58).

The graphic account of this murder has antecedents in Grimm brothers' fairy tales such as "The Juniper Tree" which combines murder, decapitation, mutilation, and cannibalism;[21] or the original "Cinderella," where the two stepsisters are punished for their wickedness when birds peck out their eyes.

Alternating with these incidents of blood and brutality are García Márquez's characteristic incursions in the world of fantasy, the so-called "magical realism." When Ulises touches glass, for example, it turns blue because he is in love. Similarly, when the grandmother is deep in slumber, she lucidly describes luminous manta rays floating in the air and live sponges causing children to cry so they can soak up the tears. These events have clear parallels in fairy tales. In fact, Marthe Robert identifies the combination of reality and imagination as an essential element in Grimm's fairy tales: "To be sure, the fairy tale abolishes natural laws just as it pleases; but it remains well in contact with flesh and blood."[22] This definition is clearly applicable to "Innocent Eréndira" where the alliance of fantasy and objectivity serves to enhance the implicit observations, satire, even criticisms of society.

As I have tried to show, elements of the fairy tale are conspicuous throughout "The Incredible and Sad Tale of Innocent Eréndira and Her Heartless Grandmother": the frame of the story; the description and development of the characters; the role of ingredients such as cruelty and bloodshed; the mixing of reality and fantasy; and the other features here identified as properties of the fairy tale. García Márquez tells his story with the charm and simplicity peculiar to the popular narratives. With his unique and idiosyncratic style he has earned his entry into the company of the great line of anonymous tellers of the fairy tale and of the fellow authors mentioned earlier: Wilde, St. Exupéry, Thurber, Tolkien, Sendak.

Notes

1. Fairy tales as subjects for creations in the other arts are discussed by Julius E. Heuscher, *A Psychiatric Study of Myths and Fairy Tales* (Springfield, Illinois: Charles C. Thomas Publisher, 1974), pp. 75–77.

2. The "anti-fairy tales" of Kafka and their similarities with fairy tales are treated by Max Lüthi, *Once Upon a Time* (New York: Frederick Ungar Publishing Company, 1970), pp. 145–46.

3. Jean Franco, "Rumour at the Top," *Times Literary Supplement*, October 10, 1975, p. 1172.

4. *Ibid.*

5. This information is provided by Mario Vargas Llosa, *Historia de un deicidio* (Barcelona: Barral Editores, 1971), p. 617.

6. Gabriel García Márquez, *Innocent Eréndira and Other Stories*, trans. Gregory Rabassa (New York: Harper Row, 1978). Hereafter, references to this work will be cited in the text.

7. Vargas Llosa, p. 628.

8. These four opinions are mentioned respectively by: Carlos Meneses, "*La increíble y triste historia de la cándida Eréndira y de su abuela desalmada*," *Sin Nombre*, IV, 1 (julio-septiembre 1973), pp. 81–84; William L. Siemens, "Gabriel García Márquez and the Tainted Hero," *Philological Papers* (West Virginia University Bulletin), vol. 21 (December 1974), p. 95; Ricardo Cano Gaviria. "*La increíble y triste historia de la cándida Eréndira y de su abuela desalmada*," *Libre*, 4 (1972), pp. 118–19; and Roger M. Peel, "Gabriel García Márquez y *La increíble y triste historia de la cándida Eréndira y de su abuela desalmada*," *Estudios de Literatura Hispanoamericana en Honor a José J. Arrom*, Andrew P. Debicki and Enrique Pupo-Walker, eds. (Chapel Hill: University of North Carolina Studies in Languages and Literatures, 1974), p. 287.

9. A brief, anonymous review, "The Marvellous and the Monetary," *Times Literary Supplement*, September 29, 1972, p. 1140, suggests that the story has the apparatus of a fairy tale.

10. Vladímir Propp, *Morphology of the Folktale* (Austin: University of Texas Press, 1968). Hereafter, references to this work will be cited in the text.

11. "Rapunzel," *The Complete Grimms' Fairy Tales* (New York: Random House, 1972), p. 73.

12. "Rumpelstiltskin," *The Complète Grimm's Fairy Tales*, p. 265.

13. "Jordina and Joringel," *The Complete Grimm's Fairy Tales*, p. 339.

14. "Faithful John," *The Complete Grimm's Fairy Tales*, p. 43.

15. This sentence is omitted in the English version. The translation from the original is mine.

16. Lüthi, pp. 135–36.

17. Allusions to the protagonist of the Homeric epic are clearly evident. Ulises and the classical prototypical hero show similarities in name and physical description. Both men also travel extensively, confront obstacles and undertake specific labors imposed on them. Parallelism between this story and the epic tradition could be examined in another study.

18. Meneses, pp. 81–84.

19. Lüthi, p. 145.

20. Since there are no other characters of real substance, it would be difficult to analyze them in terms of types found in fairy tales. There is one other, perhaps remote, point of contact: most of the minor figures are identified in terms of their occupation or conditions which reminds us of the widowers, millers, fishermen, and tailors who abound in the Grimms' stories. In the García Márquez text we have the example of Eréndira's first series of sexual encounters with a widower, a trucker, and a mailman.

21. Heuscher, p. 148, discusses in his chapter on "The Juniper Tree" the appropriateness of some fairy tales for young people: "Many fairy tales are only sadistic fare for children and must, therefore, be withheld or carefully expurgated."

22. Marthe Robert, "The Grimm Brothers," *Yale French Studies*, 43 (1967), p. 55.

The Voyage beyond the Map: "El ahogado más hermoso del mundo"

Mary E. Davis*

Since the publication in 1972 of Gabriel García Márquez' penultimate collection of short stories, critics have been hard pressed to analyze the enigmatic, fabulous tales that make up the group. Several stories are developed from the tension between the sea and the land, the latter almost always being a boring place inhabited by citizens of limited imagination. In several cases, unusual apparitions from the sea provoke traumatic explosions of imagination in one or many of the inhabitants of an otherwise staid region.

Certainly no reader of García Márquez is surprised to encounter fabulous beings immersed in what is otherwise ordinary reality. The difference then, between an earlier work like *Cien anos de Soledad* and

*Reprinted from *Kentucky Romance Quarterly* 26, no. 2 (1979):25–33 by permission of the journal.

La increíble y triste historia de la cándida Eréndira y de su abuela desalmada reveals itself in the greater complexity of heroic figures that work themselves into the text, thereby providing the author with the perfect tool for interweaving many levels of reality simultaneously. In the course of reading the collection, one meets characters named Pelayo, a peripatetic angel with no name, a patriarch Jacob, Sir Walter Raleigh, a sea captain resplendent in his dress uniform, a fascinating Laura, the magician Blacamán, Holofernes, Lautaro (the model for Ercilla's Caupolicán), William Dampier, two Amadises, Ulysses, and Francis Drake. Adding to the dislocation of reality are apparitions of a phantom ship, oranges with diamonds growing naturally inside, Eréndira's malevolent grandmother, whose blood is as green as a dragon's, a whole city submerged beneath the sea, paper animals that come alive, and money that flies through the air like butterflies.

As a whole, the stories create a fabulous environment, and the Caribbean becomes as prodigious a sea as the Mediterranean was for Homer. Gradually the land areas around it become permeated with beings from other times and other civilizations. The original inhabitants are disturbed by the heroic characters, and at the end of the story, nothing is as it was before. Forced to see themselves and their world as they are, some natives seize the opportunity to change, so that their world begins to adjust itself to the heroic demands of the travelers from other realms.

One of the most enigmatic stories in the collection, "El ahogado más hermoso del mundo" ["The Handsomest Drowned Man in the World"], illustrates the manner in which García Márquez utilizes a heroic figure to revolutionize mundane reality. To achieve the appropriate reaction from the reader to the disparate elements in the story, García Márquez creates a constant tension between a small fishing village and the sea which borders it. The tension heightens as the story progresses, and it remains unresolved at the open-ended conclusion. The meaning of the story must be developed in the mind of the reader, for it is not readily apparent from the various elements of the plot.

As the story progresses, both the nature of the village and that of the drowned man who washes up on a nearby beach are gradually revealed. The village is small, and its few inhabitants live in houses rapidly constructed of boards. In this village devoid of beauty, patios are filled with rocks rather than with flowers. The physical poverty of the village functions as an objective correlative of the capacity of soul of its natives. There is hope, however, for the village does contain children, who welcome the drowned man to their village as one of their own.

As the drowned man first appears, floating in the sea, the children on the beach pretend that he might be an enemy ship or a whale. When at last he washes ashore, he turns out to be a dead man, all covered with marine animals and residue from shipwrecks. The children play "funeral" with him all afternoon, burying him in the sand, then digging him up

Locations - Central Library

__ A	Art & Music		372-6520
__ B	Business & Economics		372-6552
__ C	Children's		372-6532
__ FILMS	Art & Music		372-6520
__ G	Government Documents		372-6534
__ H	History & Travel		372-6537
__ L	Literature & Language		372-6540
__ P	Popular Library (browsing only)		
__ S	Sociology, Religion & Sports		372-6555
__ SC	Special Collections		372-6648
__ T	Technology & Science		372-6570
__ MIL	Municipal Info. Lib. (300 City Hall)		673-3029

Locations - Community Libraries

__ EL	East Lake		724-4561
__ FR	Franklin		874-1667
__ HO	Hosmer		824-4848
__ LH	Linden Hills		922-2600
__ NK	Nokomis		729-5989
__ NR	North Regional		522-3333
__ NE	Northeast		789-1800
__ PB	Pierre Bottineau		379-2609
__ RO	Roosevelt		724-1298
__ SE	Southeast		378-1816
__ SU	Sumner		374-5642
__ WA	Walker		823-8688
__ WN	Washburn		825-4863
__ WP	Webber Park		522-3182

Note: R or **REF** means that the item is **reference** and cannot be checked out of the library.

JUV means that the item is **juvenile** (children's) material.

again. Eventually an adult notices their unusual toy, gives a shout of alarm, and the men carry the drowned man to the nearest house.

The men react quite differently to the dead man. Although they do not doubt he is a man, they refuse to accept him as one of them. Worried that he may be from their village, they look from man to man and realize that they are complete. The rest of the story illustrates how ironic is García Márquez' use of "complete" in this village. The men do notice the Homeric size of the stranger. He is heavy as a horse and will not fit into any house in the village. Leaving the body sprawled on the beach, the men leave to investigate his identity in nearby villages.

The women clean the body and, as they see the face for the first time, they are, literally, breathless. The drowned man is the most perfect being they have ever seen, and their poor imagination cannot accommodate him. They proceed, in a scene reminding the reader of the remotest, matriarchal period of man's past, to surround him in a circle on the beach. As the usually calm sea roars and seems anxious, the women sew clumsy garments for the drowned man. Fantasizing about his sexual prowess, the women indulge in a series of mental voyages: ["They were lost in those labyrinths of fantasy . . ."][1]

Since the women have exercised their imagination rarely in the past, they must proceed from the known (their village) to the miraculous (the drowned man's effect on the village). They imagine how their village would have to become if a being as fabulous as the ["drowned man"] were to live there. They compare their boring lives with husbands who fish every night to the spectacular possibilities provided by such a splendid man (["the best built man they had ever seen"] [page. 501]) The drowned man would have magical powers to call fish from the water, cause water to gush from rocks, and to plant flowers even in a rock wall.

Not content with an anonymous dead man, the women name him Stephen. After he has been dressed, curiously enough, as a huge baby, and given a martyr's name, the sea calms, as though satisfied. The women take their second mental voyage, speculating about the personality of Stephen. Because of his size, he would have been uncomfortable in their village. The women realize how innately hostile the group is to anything different, and they fear he would have been considered ["the big boob"] or ["the handsome fool"] (p. 53). By this time Stephen has assumed so much personality that he hardly seems dead, and the women cover his face so that the rising sun will not bother him.

Returning from a frustrating night, the men do not understand the fascination of the huge body for their wives. They jealously fear comparison with him and only want to throw him back into the sea with an anchor tied to his ankles. After they see Stephen's face, however, his beauty convinces them of the sincerity of his manner of being (which García Márquez ironically twists into "modo de estar" [way of life] [p. 55]).

The funeral rites for Stephen are resplendent with flowers. The village elects honorary parents and other relatives for Stephen, so that through this ritual everyone is now related to everyone else. After his body is returned to the sea, Stephen's memory causes the village to rebuild houses, plant roses, and paint with bright colors. Even more important, the villagers now realize that they are incomplete and always will be. The faculty of soul which they had so dreadfully lacked has begun to develop, however, and imagination, stimulated by so powerful a trauma as Stephen's visit, can hardly be prevented from expanding.

Through this résumé of the events of the story, the expansion of consciousness provoked by a visitor from afar reveals itself in four stages. The first is manifest in the children, who naturally participate in supernatural reality. The women gradually traverse the second stage, in which their atrophied interior lives begin to bloom for the first time. The men grudgingly participate in the third stage, which combines a vision of sublime beauty with the ritual enactment of the burial of the hero. The last, and most significant, stage is that of the whole community. During the last seconds of Stephen's presence, they see their village as it really is and determine to change it to fit their new self. The validity of their communal vision is manifest in the fame the village gains, a fame always connected with the legend of Stephen.

How does García Márquez justify the reversal of a way of life within the span of twenty-four hours? He convinces the reader that Stephen transforms the village through the introduction and constant reinforcement of heroic constructs. Four modes of heroic allusion interact throughout the text. The most complex group of allusions refers to what may be termed the classical construct of the hero, as he appears in Homer and other ancient writers. The most puzzling attributes of Stephen result from a configuration of traits traditionally connected with Quetzalcoatl. Then there follows a group of figures representing the Renaissance man: Sir Walter Raleigh, Gulliver, and a nameless sea captain. Finally, operating throughout the story are both subtle and obvious allusions to Odysseus. In order to create as complex an image as possible within the persona of Odysseus, García Márquez bases his hero on a composite of the various interpretations of Homer's hero that have grown up through the centuries.

It should be emphasized at this point that the separation of these modes is a purely artificial one to facilitate analysis; within the story all the heroic allusions work together constantly. A further peculiarity of the narration should be noted: the reader never sees Stephen either with his own eyes or through the means of strictly omniscient narration. Stephen is seen through the eyes and minds of other characters. This aspect of the narration makes it easier for the reader to accept the fabulous story; he remembers that, after all, the information comes through the limited sensibility of a fishing village.

Readers of García Márquez are accustomed to being teased by the devious Colombian. He often leaves clues on the surface of the text to alert the reader to look for other, hidden ones below the surface. True to his configuration as a classical hero, Stephen arrives mysteriously; his enormous size causes the children to confuse him with a ship and a whale, entities which connect him with Odysseus and Jonah. The first description of the drowned man emphasizes how long he has been at sea, the region classically inhabited by sirens, gods, and nymphs. García Márquez decorates Stephen with remains of shipwrecks (many times connected with Odysseus) and *medusas*, a subtle reference to Perseus' famous exploit, killing the terrifying Gorgon. Within the story, Stephen's presence rescues the village from inertia, a condition comparable to that of those who beheld the Medusa's awful visage. Stephen's size and beauty gradually reveal themselves. The men react to carrying him as the Lulliputians did to Gulliver — with frustrated bewilderment. As the process of cleaning the body begins, the villagers are amazed by Stephen's skin: [". . . his skin was covered with a crust of scales and mud"] (p. 49). His skin is like the tattooing of ancient Tibetan monks, whose skin was considered part of the parchment of God.

The women attribute to the giant the personality of dignified arrogance, a characteristic which reminds one of Zeus and almost all the Greek heroes. The highly charged eroticism provoked by Stephen's size is also reminiscent of the amorous adventures of Zeus, as well as of the sexual trials of Odysseus. The women's thoughts revolve around the Homeric size of Stephen's (hypothetical) bed, and García Márquez slyly directs the reader's memory back to the close of the *Odyssey*, as Penelope uses the characteristics of Odysseus' bed to ascertain the identity of the stranger who claims to be her husband.

The particular gestalt of the women, the sea, and the subtle eroticism presents, in a modernized version, a reworking of elements commonly found in myths of Dionysos. This "lately-come god"[2] was infamous among the Hellenes for the incredible mental states he produced among his female followers. García Márquez has utilized only a few of Dionysos' attributes: his connection with the sea, his provocation of ecstasy among women, the eroticism which becomes the vehicle for mental voyages, the disruption of normal life, the natural resistance of males to such disruption, particularly when it threatens marital harmony, and, finally, the ceremonial use of flowers and the sometimes peculiar religious trinkets in the decoration of Stephen's body for burial. Within the story, the village women never succumb to that customary, terrifying transformation from Dionysos' nurses into irrational maenads. The function of the Dionysian aspects of Stephen's visit to the village is to provoke an ecstatic change. Rather than inciting madness and death, Stephen causes a change in self-awareness which reveals itself in the esthetic reversal of the village.

Stephen's godlike qualities are constantly reinforced by his relationship to the sea. The Caribbean usually is calm in the area of the village, but on the Tuesday night the women spend sewing around Stephen on the beach, they notice that the sea had never seemed so distressed. The empathy between Stephen and the anxious sea becomes prophetic. Stephen is a product of the sea, whether he is a man or a god, and the sea that produced him will receive him again. The cyclical nature of this relationship reveals itself in Stephen's strange clothes. The women find it difficult to construct clothing large enough for the giant, so that his apparel is amazingly like that of a baby (a "sietemesino"). It is as if the brief period in the village provides Stephen with a chance to reincarnate himself before he returns to the sea for another voyage.

The new clothes were necessary because the old ones were in rags, torn [". . . as if he had sailed through labyrinths of coral"] (p. 50). Stephen's body, however, is intact, and his ability to thread labyrinths reminds the reader of Theseus. By connecting "laberintos" and "dédalos" with Stephen's passage through the sea, García Márquez emphasizes the ritualistic nature of the relationship between Stephen and the village, a ritual in that it means something beyond the scope of the actions themselves. Stephen's facility in escaping the confines of the liquid labyrinth reveals to the villagers the actual process behind the ancient usages of these forms of entrapment: "Eliade notes that the essential mission of the maze was to defend the 'Centre'—that it was, in fact, an initiation into sanctity, immortality and absolute reality and, as such, equivalent to other 'trials' such as the fight with the dragon. At the same time, the labyrinth may be interpreted as an apprenticeship for the neophyte who would learn to distinguish the proper path leading to the land of the Dead."[3]

The time of Stephen's visit is presented as a sacred time.[4] Although he washes up on Tuesday, he is always called the ["one who died on Wednesday"] thereby connecting him with the day controlled by Hermes, the messenger of the gods, who taught Odysseus' grandfather Autolycus to be an eloquent and skillful thief. Stephen's appearance, then, is the message from the gods or a visit of a god himself. When the women meditate upon the social difficulties for one of such size, they call Stephen ["the handsome fool"], bringing to mind ancient folk beliefs that the fool enjoys special protection of the gods and can be expected to utter prophetic statements. Stephen says nothing; his presence is the message.

The funeral ceremony provides García Márquez with the last ritual in the story. The flowers and the wailing of the women give a peculiarly primitive aspect to the funeral, reiterating that grandness within simplicity that marks Beowulf's funeral and the many leave-takings in the *Illiad*. The storyteller ironically twists the *llanto* into an alluring melody, as he relates that ["Some sailors who heard the weeping in the distance lost their sense of direction, and people heard of one who had himself tied to the mainmast, recalling ancient fables about sirens"] (pp. 55–6). This last allusion connects Stephen's funeral to Odysseus' trial with Circe and, simultaneously, suggests the power of art to transform reality, to create beauty from sadness.

A constant feature of García Márquez' style has been his fusion of Greek, Spanish, and American literary models and mythology. The most exotic aspects of Stephen's visit to the village correlate with the widely disseminated myth of Quetzalcoatl, the pre-Columbian god worshipped by several tribes of Central America and Mexico. Like Stephen, Quetzalcoatl arrived from the sea and brought a new civilizing influence upon the various forms of culture which he encountered. A new vision of beauty, of human relationships, and of time itself derived from Quetzalcoatl's emphasis upon self-sacrifice rather than the commonly accepted sacrifice of others. Indigenous resistance to Quetzalcoatl's revolutionary influence took the form of a magician, who, in the course of his epic struggle against the peaceful god, was able to make dead bodies incredibly heavy.[5] Stephen, it will be remembered, seemed impossibly heavy to the men who carried his body from the shore. Within Aztec mythology, Quetzalcoatl is at times called Ehecatl, the lord of the wind; it is therefore not surprising that the wind should rage and the sea be troubled on the night of Stephen's appearance.

Quetzalcoatl was a man as well as a god, and as a man he was defeated by the magician. As he abandoned the coast of America (to vanish on a "boat" of sea serpents), Quetzalcoatl made his last contribution to pre-Columbian mythology: he forecast the arrival of new gods, new deliverers, who would arrive by the same route he was taking. This prediction not only aided Hernán Cortés' conquest of the Aztec kingdom, but it also created an atmosphere of Messianic expectation that the future held something better than the present.

As the Spanish conquerors entered the Aztec capital Tenochtitlán, they saw at the summit of a central pyramid a statue representing Queztzalcoatl, a statue which fused the form of a man with a bird's head[6] (the fusion of elements reiterated but altered by García Márquez). Decorative details of the statue included marine birds, snail shells, and flowers—all often considered intermediate forms between the sea and the land. The idol was dressed in a curious, conical hat (like the medieval one to designate fools or heretics), and its lower regions were covered by a loin cloth resembling a large diaper. The women's clumsy clothes for Stephen and their mental identification of him with a fool therefore oddly resemble the Aztec representation of Quetzalcoatl.

Toltec, Aztec, and Mayan mythology all connect Quetzalcoatl with the circuit of the planet Venus, and, thereby, make his religion easily acceptable to women, children, and astrologers. As the result of this astrological connection, Quetzalcoatl may reappear in whatever form he chooses, but he will, like Venus, return cyclically. His appearance always denotes change, a revolution often represented esthetically as a fusion of opposites: defeat / victory, sacrifice / new life, and the blending of older traditions with a new dynamic.[7]

The three heroes from the Age of Exploration are not treated as expansively. Sir Walter Raleigh appears as a possibility for the identity of Stephen. The English gentleman-pirate, complete with parrot and harquebus, is dressed for one of his several raids in the Caribbean. Gulliver is alluded to when the village struggles with the giant on the beach, but he is never mentioned by name. The sea captain at the end of the story is decorated with a dress uniform, astrolabe, and even a polar star. He speaks fourteen languages, twice the magical number of seven. His function, like that of Sir Walter Raleigh and of Stephen himself, is to point toward the horizon, to that area of experience beyond known reality.

With this characteristic, we come to the modern concept of the figure of Odysseus, who, because of the ambiguity of his original presentation, has invited constant additions to his personality. García Márquez demands the reader to remember more than an aged hero doomed to return to Ithaca and (in Tennyson's words) an aged wife. He makes use of Dante's condemnation of Odysseus as the eternal wanderer, one who nevertheless fascinated the Florentine as he spoke to him from a towering flame (Canto 26 of the *Inferno*). Dante criticized the pursuit of forbidden knowledge for its own sake, but García Márquez uses his Odysseus to represent a way of knowing, which, once understood, must continue to point the villagers toward new horizons.

Tennyson in his dramatic monologue has Ulysses speak as a reckless navigator, never satisfied with home and hearth; his hero maintains: ". . . I am become a name; For always roaming with a hungry heart."[8] García Márquez' most obvious tribute to Tennyson appears in his use of the dramatic monologue; Stephen "speaks" to the men in a part of their mental voyage (p. 55), using in his monologue all the humorous deceit for which his Homeric prototype was famous.

Finally, García Márquez's presentation of Odysseus owes its distinctive qualities to James Joyce. Stephen's name immediately reminds one of Stephen Hero, Joyce's early protagonist, who later is amplified into Stephen Dedalus in *A Portrait of the Artist as a Young Man*. Joyce's continual identification with Daedalus, the artificer of labyrinths, finds an echo in García Márquez' combination of mythology from the New World and from the Old, of remote times with a present timelessness. His isolated fishing village becomes a sacred / profane precinct as did Dublin and the plains of Troy.

The composite nature of the heroic figure, the secularization of the revolution of consciousness, the compression and explosion of narrative time — all are developed along Joycean patterns. Stephen moves in a world in which spiritual problems (the lack of soul) are presented as psychological (lack of imagination). This is precisely the contribution of Joyce to

Odysseus' development, for "In place of this spiritual dimension Joyce substitutes the heroic dimension. Bloom's pattern and archetype is Ulysses, not Christ. His lost Eden is the heroic world . . . , not Adam's Paradise."[9]

The sonorous quality of García Márquez' prose is as important as it was for Joyce. Meant to be read aloud, the fictions of both writers function as incantations or charms designed to produce epiphany, the term Joyce applied to that sudden illumination of the imagination which effects one's concept of reality. García Márquez shares with Joyce a preference for open form, a refusal of closure, a deliberate provocation of the reader to create for himself the meaning of the narrative elements.

Joyce and García Márquez both use art as a way to create other realities and as a critique of reality as it is. Rather than concentrate on pessimistic destruction of the mundane world, they seize elements from that world to show the psychic possibilities of the human imagination. Open form is, itself, an attempt to reveal the dramatic, often unforeseen qualities of imaginative life, all too often characterized by unfulfilled longing and interrupted dream: "By dwelling upon that interrupted nuance, that unconsummated moment, that unrealized possibility, Joyce renews our apprehension of reality, strengthens our sympathy with our fellow creatures, and leaves us in awe before the mystery of created things."[10] In his combination of Homeric and modern aspects of Odysseus' personality with pre-Columbian heroic constructs, García Márquez creates still another embodiment of the archetype of man's refusal to accept reality as it is. His villagers, incited by a lively dead man, completely change from within, and their new self is reflected in their village, famous for the legend of Stephen, the martyr whose death stimulates new life.

Notes

1. Gabriel García Márquez, *La increíble y triste historia de la cándida Eréndira y de su abuela desalmada* (Buenos Aires: Editorial Sudamericana, 1972), p. 51. All subsequent citations are to this edition and appear within the text.

2. Pentheus' epithet for Dionysos in the *Bacchae*, quoted by W. K. C. Guthrie in *The Greeks and Their Gods* (Boston: Beacon Press, 1955), p. 153.

3. Quoted by J. E. Cirlot in *A Dictionary of Symbols* (New York: Philosophical Library, 1962), p. 167.

4. Sacred time being that temporal span within which another reality manifests itself. See Mircea Eliade, *The Sacred and the Profane* (New York: Harcourt, Brace and World, 1959), p. 11.

5. Jacques Soustelle in *La vida cotidiana de los aztecas en vísperas de la conquista* (México: Fondo de Cultura Económica, 1970), p. 165, relates the tale of the body enchanted by the magician Tezcatlipoca. Through his evil power the body acquired a supernatural weight.

6. The statue of Quetzalcoatl is described in baroque detail by Fray Diego Durán, *Book of the Gods and Rites and the Ancient Calendar* (Norman: University of Oklahoma Press, 1971), pp. 130–31.

7. Quetzalcoatl's fundamental position within the development of both the structure of society and the abstract justification for the forms the society manifests is explicated by R. C. Padden in *The Hummingbird and the Hawk* (Columbus: Ohio State University Press, 1967). He maintains that ". . . a survival of the ancient Quetzalcoatl cult . . . remained as the moral basis of society and a point of philosophical departure" (pp. 28–9).

8. From Alfred Lord Tennyson's "Ulysses," written in 1833, lines 11 and 12.

9. W. B. Stanford, *The Ulysess Theme* (Oxford: Basil Blackwell, 1954), p. 213.

10. Harry Levin in his introduction to *The Portable James Joyce* (New York: Viking Press, 1946), p. 16.

The Autumn of the Patriarch: Text and Culture

Julio Ortega*

The complexity of *The Autumn of the Patriarch* has not gone unnoticed by its readers, several of whom have sought to account for its power of persuasion,[1] but this complexity still requires further methodical analyses capable of following the debate on Latin-American history and culture rekindled by Gabriel García Márquez through his writing. The notable international success of García Márquez's novels should not make us believe, however, as has easily occurred in the case of Borges, that the values of a work are measured by its international dissemination. These values are revealed, instead, in the capacity of the work to reshape the notions and perceptions of our own literary tradition and cultural space. The extraordinary dimension of García Márquez's writings emerges not only from his widely recognized mastery of storytelling, but also from the fruitful participation of his works in the reformulation of a Latin-American literature capable of resolving its peculiarity and its universality, capable of accounting through fiction for the experience and consciousness of the culture that generates it. Czech novelist Milan Kundera has stated that "to speak of the end of the novel is a local preoccupation of West European writers, notably the French. It's absurd to talk about it to a writer from my part of Europe, or from Latin America. How can one possibly mumble about the death of the novel and have on one's bookshelf *One Hundred Years of Solitude* by Gabriel García Márquez ?"[2] To go just a bit further, we would add that in his works García Márquez also gives account of the constitutive process of the Latin-American cultural consciousness by having articulated through them one form of its privileged realization. The following notes seek to illustrate this debate from the perspective of a semiological approach to the literary text within the sphere of culture.[3]

*Reprinted by permission of publisher and author, from *Poetics of Change: The New Spanish-American Narrative*, trans. Galen D. Greaser (Austin: University of Texas Press, 1984), 96–119. Copyright © 1984 by the University of Texas Press. All rights reserved.

THE CODE OF POLITICS

The Autumn of the Patriarch is, in effect, a novel about a Latin-
American dictator, but it is also a novel about the Latin-American people
who suffer this paradigmatic tyrant. Just as the nameless patriarch of the
novel is the sum of all the dictators of a space centered in the Caribbean,
but including the city of Comodoro Rivadavia, and also of the name,
facts, and products (coca, rubber, tobacco) of several Latin-American
countries, so too the collective narrator of the novel is a sum of popular
voices. The history of Latin America is thus reconstructed in the dialogue
between this collective narrator and that nameless power. This process of
communication, generated in the production of a writing, functions first
of all as a political code, in other words, as the information modeled by
the deciphering of power.

The political code implies recognition of the norms that shape the
historical consensus. But here this consensus involves a distortion: history
has been usurped by the dictatorial power. Political tyranny — with its
violence, arbitrariness, and indulgence — replaces history, and the discourse of history is then in fact only a discourse of power. In the process of
its production by a collective consciousness, this discourse models its own
deciphering of the distortion, but not before recording — and the novel
illustrating — the unmistakable functioning of the code of repressive power.

This code provides ample proof of its absolute domination. Its
coherency is systematic and implies an underlying model of political and
economic oppression, but its unrestrained expansion is no less systematic in
the exercise of a terrifying hyperbole of power. These hyperbolic repercussions are magnified at the level of popular culture, where the arbitrariness
of the absolute dictator and his outlandish popular image merge in the
carnivalization of power fostered by the text.

In the first place, then, the political code emerges from the harsh
evidence of our colonial and dependent condition. One of the sources of
this dictatorial power is the colonial phase of our history; the other is its
imperialistic phase. Patricio Aragonés states it clearly: "everyone says that
you're president of nobody and that you're not on the throne because of
your big guns but because the English sat you there and the gringos
kept you there with the pair of balls on their battleship." Dependency is a
vicious circle, a state of permanent crisis: "we had used up our last
resources, bled by the age-old necessity of accepting loans in order to pay
the interest on the foreign debt ever since the wars of independence and
then other loans to pay the interest on back interest, always in return for
something general sir, first the quinine and tobacco monopolies for the
English, then the rubber and cocoa monopoly for the Dutch, then the
concession for the upland railroad and river navigation to the Germans,
and everything for the gringos through the secret agreements."

The text extends this process of denationalization in the hyperbole of the Caribbean Sea transferred to the Arizona desert, but the internal consequences of this power structure are equally verifiable. The first of these is repression, and here repression reveals the anti-national, surrogate function of the dictatorship:

> [they] begged us in the name of the nation to rush into the street shouting out with the gringos to stop the implementation of the theft, they incited us to sack and burn the stores and mansions of foreigners, they offered us ready cash to go out and protest under the protection of the troops who were solidly behind the people in opposition to the act of aggression, but no one went out general sir, because nobody had forgotten that one other time they had told us the same thing on their word of honor as soldiers and still they shot them down in a massacre under the pretext that agitators had infiltrated and opened fire against the troops.

Violence is, of course, the political practice of this barbarous power: "they're going to fall on you like a pack of dogs to collect from you in one case for the killings at Santa María del Altar, in another for the prisoners thrown into the moat of the harbor fort to be eaten by crocodiles, in another for the people you skin alive and send their hides to their families as a lesson."

As always, this violence is institutionalized in a force inherent to repressive governments: "he made him absolute master of a secret empire within his own private empire, an invisible service of repression and extermination that not only lacked an official identity but was even difficult to conceive of in its real existence, because no one was responsible for its acts, nor did it have a name or a location in the world, and yet it was a fearsome truth that had been imposed by terror over other organs of repression of the state."

Just as this systematic model of power shapes the political code, other sources form the dictator's ferocious, pathetic, and delirious repertoire. These sources are the facts and stories about Latin-American dictators — and also about Franco — that have been documented or are spread as opinions, jokes, or versions. At this level, seminal in its own right, the text finds a means of access to the popular version of the dictatorship, that is to say, to the interpretation of power in terms of the popular culture. So that even though we may discover features that seem to evoke a specific dictator and situations that appear to be based on the experiences of certain other tyrants, the decisive element in the configuration of this character is the fact that through this proliferating and ubiquitous figure the text generates the carnivalized mythology of power.[4] The political code is thus transformed into a different code, that of popular culture.

Within the context of colonial domination, and focusing on the monumental figure of the dictator as a hyperbole of power, the text is produced as the totalized space of a reading of history. Here history is tantamount to politics; the total historical experience, from the discovery of America by the colonial enterprise of Columbus to the geographical plunder of imperialism, is rendered by the text as a travesty. The text demands the occupation of this historical space as an overall model denouncing the profound disruption of the Latin-American political experience. This is why it unfolds in a recurrent time — in which the act of the colonial origin is also the anticipation of a no less colonial future — rather than in a chronological time. Beginning with pre-Columbian times and continuing through the decades of financial imperialism, the code of power has been the same. Its figure is thus not a single person but, instead, all our dictators. The following image conjugates the historical moments: [he] opened the window that looked out onto the sea so that perhaps he might discover some new light to shed on the mix-up they had told him about, and he saw the usual battleship, anchored in the shadowy sea, he saw the three caravels." History is viewed as anachronism and anticipation; its origin and its present time occur simultaneously in the spectacle of the text, in the scene of a writing that is tantamount to the space of consciousness.

The functioning of the political code does not stop there, however. Its connotative power is certainly much greater and involves other, less explicit, levels of the text. Turning again to the nameless patriarch, for example, the very fact of his namelessness implies the possession of all names, not only because he derives from our most visible tyrants, but because he transcends history through his encompassing historicity. We know that occasional protests and rebellions are silenced, and we also know that the tyrant is a figure agonizing in his loneliness and old age, but here power is not only the government or its authoritarian form, it is something more sordid and fundamental: the distortion of all communal norms, the perpetual model of domination. Thus the archetypal dimension of the patriarch occupies history and distorts it. Viewed from the perspective of the collective narrative, of popular legend, his figure acquires a mythologizing dimension; it is projected back to the origin and is the representation of power. Hence it also occupies language, imposing between words and things a conditioning that is simultaneously arbitrary and systematic.

"Bendición Alvarado didn't bring me into the world to pay heed to basins but to command, and after all I am who I am, and not you, so give thanks to God that this was only a game," the patriarch warns. At times, a religious substratum is clearly visible as an ironic referent in the novel. This is not intended to indicate that the omnipotent patriarch has also expropriated the repertoires of faith, but to illustrate in this textual caricature of it the comic license that total power attributes to itself. The point to be noted in this case, however, is the brazen tautology of the "I." "I am who I am"; that is to say, the loss of a name is the subject's gain inasmuch as his individuation is not contained in a name but in the representation of his archetypal person totalized by power. *"I am not you"*; in other words, you have a name, and that name, like your person, belongs to the absolute power. As distorted by this dictatorial power, politics implies the abolition of the "other," the shattering of the "you." Later, in the delirium of his old age, we read that "one night [the patriarch] had written my name is Zacarías, he read it again under the fleeting light of the beacon, he read it over and over and the name repeated so many times ended by seeming remote and alien to him, God damn it, he said to himself, tearing up the strip of paper, I'm me, he said to himself." The dictatorship is likewise a pronominal distortion. The patriarch, who does not require a name of his own, has occupied a grammatical category with his person and refused to make a distinction between it and himself, revealing the evil root of his appropriation of all names. In effect, the patriarch is defined not only in the hyperboles of the collective narrative, but also in the successive nominal repertoires that, through description, enumeration, and the associative and conjunctive text itself, pour out a sort of holocaust of names, images that consume themselves in the great devouring space of power. This power thus appears to be infinite. All names are attributable to it in the unending description of its attributes, in the sinister resurrection of its profound arbitrariness, and in the total occupation of our history. This operation contains within it, however, the end of absolute power, because the narrative turns back on itself from its reconstructive present, from its common voice, from the day of the delirious dictator's death.

When the ferocious Sáenz de la Barra establishes an even more implacable system of repression within the dictatorship, power itself reveals the tyrant's impunity: "you aren't the government, general, you are the power." But is he? The patriarch has been equally ferocious, but for some reason he feels that his notion of power has been carried to an extreme by this henchman. For the henchman total repression "was the only power possible in the lethargy of death which in other times had been his Sunday market paradise." In other words, power is cyclical, it establishes itself as a natural order, and its own excesses must insure its restoration, its continuity. Sáenz de la Barra's rationality is a literal power that lacks continuity: an evasion of power. The patriarch's arbitrariness, on the other hand, is rooted in a power naturalized by his manipulation of that "Sunday marketplace."

No name: all attributes. The names of the world write the properties of the omnipotent dictator, thus modeling the nature of his usurping power. This is, then, a constructive process that gives rise to myth in language. The movement of language generates the mythological construction of the patriarch as the representation of power. His origins, feats, loves, deaths, and resurrections are sustained by a mythologizing discursive process in which the names substantiate his archetypal figure.[5]

Power is thus established as a natural order, but it is perceived as a naturalized disorder. The political code of a distorting absolutism implies, in the end, a modeling of reality, and this modeling occurs within the sphere of culture, whose own popular order adopts, assimilates, and responds to the perpetuated violence. The model of politics thus competes closely with the model of culture, attempting to subject, manipulate, and incorporate it.

This is why the political code of tyranny replaces ideologies — the religious conceptions, for example — and itself expands as an undeclared ideology. Its legitimization is an act of force and terror, but it also includes the arbitrariness of its domination: it is self-sufficient as an occupying power. Its normative practice induces a reduction of history and regulates the consensus. Its judgments imply an unrestricted appraisal and hierarchization deriving from the use and abuse of power, and, for this same reason, it represents the subjugating occupation of the life of an entire people. Proceeding as a natural power, the political code of tyranny seeks to appear as the expression of a culture when in fact it operates as its negation. But in this tension it reveals, precisely, its most intense conflict, because the questioning of the dictatorship from the juncture of popular culture is a debate between a reality humanized by a model of consensus and a distortion imposed by an authoritarian model. Thus, even though a people may live the naturalized disorder of the dictatorship as an ideological order, it is in the workings of its own culture model that this order is finally dismantled and defeated. In other words, culture as a way of knowing resolves and counters the ignorance promoted by the political distortion,[6] which brings us to the code of culture.

THE CODE OF POPULAR CULTURE

We know that traditional political regimes attempt to reinforce the basic forms of social life, the relations of production, and the divisions among social groups. We know also that culture is part of the dynamics of history, contributing to the perpetuation or transformation of society.[7] Within this dynamics *The Autumn of the Patriarch* acts in the productive and critical sense that characterizes the popular culture that sustains it. Through its semantic operations in a specific cultural field, this literary text functions at the same time as a *text of culture*. From the point of view of semiology, this text represents a "condensed program" of Spanish-American culture.[8]

If, as Lotman contends, culture is the aggregate of information and also the means for organizing and preserving it — which implies a social conflict hinging on the "struggle for information" — then *popular culture* represents a specific form of the functioning of this information based on the communication that the collective speaker emits and receives, a process that models the historic experience in the collective memory.[9]

These forms of communication are a repertoire signifying a process of signification. They also imply a system of displacements, reductions, parodies, and, in general, a carnivalizing practice—through the masquerade, the feast, laughter, etc.—that celebrates the perpetuity of the people and emerges as a natural occupation of the public space, as Bakhtin has amply documented.[10] The dissolving power of that energy responds in this way to the malaise of history and liberates in consciousness a place of identity. Indeed, in our cultural reality the depredations perpetrated by the internal domination to which we have been subjected are a long history of violence against the sources of our Latin-American culture, whose popular formations have often been distorted and almost always eroded. Nevertheless, struggling against a tradition of ethnocentric violence, it has confronted, adapted, and revised its own versions of its conflictive and still unresolved origin. This, then, is the dimension of popular culture that we find in *The Autumn of the Patriarch* as a code receiving, processing, and generating the writing of the spectacle of power. The semantic forms of popular culture are elaborated and resolved as an articulating syntax in writing. In other words, the carnivalization of the text gives an account of the conflictive interaction of a history formulated as communication.

At the first death of the patriarch, which is the death of his double, Patricio Aragonés, the funeral ceremony soon becomes an outpouring of jubilation, which the patriarch observes "horrified with the idea of being quartered and devoured by dogs and vultures amidst the delirious howls and the roar of fireworks celebrating the carnival of my death." The carnival expresses the joy of popular liberation, but it also predominates in the production of the text itself through the circular point of view of an account that begins with the still questioned, but consummated, death of the dictator. But along with the carnivalized popular culture that contaminates the totalized account of the text, there is also a populist exercise of power acting as the natural form of its imposition. This is the false carnival of power, in other words, the manipulation of disorder as an order seeking to dominate the popular culture. This can be observed in the following passage: "and still he governed as if he knew he was predestined never to die, for at that time it did not look like a presidential palace but rather a marketplace . . . because no one knew who was who or by whom in that palace with open doors in the grand disorder of which it was impossible to locate the government. The man of the house not only participated in that marketplace disaster but he had set it up himself and ruled over it."

On its own, writing places in the account of the speakers the summary judgment of dictatorial power given by popular culture. The same process is reflected in the following sequence:

> everything had been a farce, your excellency, a carnival apparatus that he himself had put together without really thinking about it when he decided that the corpse of his mother should be displayed for public veneration on a catafalque of ice long before anyone thought about the

merits of her sainthood and only to contradict the evil tongues that said you were rotting away before you died, a circus trick which he had fallen into himself without knowing it ever since they came to him with the news general sir that his mother Bendición Alvarado was performing miracles and he had ordered her body carried in a magnificent procession into the most unknown corners of his vast statueless country.

In each case the text carnivalizes the information, but at the same time it distinguishes the tensions that are popular in origin from the manipulations of power. In this incident the despot reveals his frustrated project of replacing the popular version of the religious order. The farce reveals the comic paradox of the manipulation: "they had paid eighty pesos to a gypsy woman who pretended to give birth in the middle of the street to a two-headed monster as punishment for having said that the miracles had been set up by the government." This feigned childbirth, an event from the lore of the public square, is manipulated in this instance by the established power, but now it is clearly false, so that for the public it becomes a dual spectacle.

The spectacle of power develops in the text as a conflictive production, rather than simply as a polar production, and it is only in the textual totalization of this polyvalent writing, as we shall later see, that it is finally resolved as an inclusive and continuous integration. The popular view of the patriarch, even within culture, implies an ambivalent movement: the gathering of information discloses this movement, but the sense of the movement is discerned only when the information is processed. The patriarch is not always perceived as monstrous — as he is to our consciousness as readers — while he is still a source of information that must be assumed, processed, and modeled; and the text does not shy away from this first evidence, which it resolves in the end. The text includes this evidence ("it's him, she exclaimed with surprise, hurray for the stud, she shouted, hurray, shouted the men, the women, the children") because it discloses the deep fear and impotence felt by the people in the presence of power. The same thing occurs in a later incident: "long live the stud, they shouted, blessed be the one who comes in the name of truth, they shouted." Here the religious allusion is given an ironic twist by the text. Thus the patriarch's death, which begins the liberation of consciousness, creates a certain perplexity: "and yet we didn't believe it now that it was true, and not because we really didn't believe it but because we no longer wanted it to be true, we had ended up not understanding what would become of us without him, what would becomes of our lives after him." Some readers have almost resented the fascination exerted by the patriarch, but this is part of the ambivalence of the information gathered in the text and it is resolved in the integrating judgment suggested by the collective narrator.[11] This, then, is a work about information. From the perspective of social life information is emitted and recognized in the terms of a precarious and oppressed condition; from the standpoint of the uses of power it seeks to impose itself as the natural order of alienation; but from the point of view of the accounts of popular culture it is processed and elaborated as knowledge and response. Writing brings out these distinctions, formalizing their occurrence as a spectacle and carnivalizing their textual proliferation. Within this communicative network a reading of history is progressively being shaped as a promise of culture.[12]

Whereas for the Americans the country is a "nigger whorehouse," for the patriarch it is a "brothel of idolators." But the tyrant's opinion of the people is also paradoxical: "he was left with the undeserved burden of truth . . . in this nation which I didn't choose willingly but which was given me as an established fact in the way you have seen it which is as it has always been since time immemorial with this feeling of unreality, with this smell of shit, with this unhistoried people who don't believe in anything except life."

From the point of view of the people this criticism is a virtue. Stripped of history, the only possibility left to the people is to reaffirm their own existence, and, therefore, the awareness of their fulfillment is based on the deciphering of that history. Naturally, the energy of the popular culture is what sustains the life of a community, and within it the scars of underdevelopment are clearly the product of the erosion suffered by that culture. In this novel the code of popular culture encourages a productive conversion: transferred to a textual practice, this practice sustains the fulfillment achieved. This conversion acts through systematic humor, crushing irony, numbing sarcasm, and hyperbolic paradox, thus creating the current of earthy, unrestricted, and reducing humor that also pervades the creative joy of *One Hundred Years of Solitude*, although in *The Autumn of the Patriarch* humor has an added analytical dimension, inasmuch as this novel is a reflection on a political tragedy approached from the perspective of cultural comedy. The humor is certainly Rabelaisian to some extent, but it is above all a characteristically Spanish-American popular humor that creates here a system of expansive communication based on its festive oralness. It is not surprising, then, that when Manuela Sánchez disappears, humor becomes a chorus of voices, popular songs, and a dance of writing: "they told him that she'd been seen in the madness of Papa Montero's wake, tricky, lowlife rumba bunch." Here the information is duplicated within its popular source, going toward and returning from the rhythm captured from a carnivalized culture.

In contrast with the sordid origins of power, the origins of the people are a carnivalization, as suggested by the festive reconstruction of Columbus's landing. Despite the interaction of the codes of political power and popular culture, the writing of the text and the discourse of culture is articulated by the general difference between them. From the pedestal of power the patriarch trusts in "the final argument that it didn't matter whether something back then was true or not, God damn it, it will be with time"; but from the reality of popular culture there is a more stable truth and a fuller certainty. The myth of the patriarch within the narrative is constructed, quite clearly, by the popular culture, but in this same act it openly carnivalizes him, transforming him into a parody of power that is no less terrible, certainly, but which at least is discernible in terms of a repertoire of its own. This is the point of view explored by writing as it releases the detailed store of information that is always processed by the cultural code.

THE MYTHOLOGICAL CODE

The disjunctions of the political and cultural codes are resolved in the mythological code. This code accounts, of course, for the other two, but it also permits those significant internal tensions to be discerned in a symbolic field of forces that produce an ulterior consciousness.

It is here that the absence of information opens a cultural void, a loss of identity, in which the myth of the origin of power emerges: "there was no one who doubted the legitimacy of his history, or anyone who could have disclosed or denied it because we couldn't even establish the identity of his body, there was no other nation except the one that had been made by him in his own image and likeness where space was changed and time corrected by the designs of his absolute will, reconstituted by him ever since the most uncertain origins of his memory." This origin fuses history and cosmology as a fatalistic determinism: a model of the origin occupies reality and, therefore, replaces history. Reality is divided into a *before* corresponding to primitive times ("the times of the Spaniards were like when God ruled more than the government, the evil times of the nation") and into an interminable *after* corresponding to the patriarch's power. The mythologizing construction disregards, of course, the chronology of events. The patriarch had witnessed the landing of Columbus, but he is also one of the generals of the wars of independence and a partner in the American invasion. He is an archetypal figure of power and therefore a model of its historical meaninglessness. The interminable parade of American ambassadors parodies the stability of this model. The origin is thus only a projection of the present, in other words, a draining of historical meaning and its occupation by power.

The free scope of this model permits the manipulation of mythology by the established power, which seeks to incorporate the repertoires of popular culture. This free scope is disclosed in an unrestricted delirium of power that seeks to exert its will even on the natural order. It is here that the mythological code reveals its function. In the delirium of his love for Manuela Sánchez, the bewildered patriarch asks himself

> what was going on in the world because it's going on eight and everybody's asleep in this house of scoundrels, get up, you bastards, he shouted, the lights went on, they played reveille at three o'clock . . . and there was the noise of startled arms, of roses that opened when there was

still two hours left until dew time . . . and [they] replaced the flowers that had spent the night in the vases with last night's flowers, and there was a troop of masons who were building emergency walls and they disoriented the sunflowers by pasting gilt paper suns on the window-panes so that it would not be noticed that it was still nighttime in the sky and it was Sunday the twenty-fifth in the house . . . while he opened a way lighted by the day through the persistent adulators who proclaimed him the undoer of dawn, commander of time, and repository of light.

The comic license of the patriarch readily exposes a mythological code adapted to the hyperbolic demands of his will, although it is based on an inversion: the carnivalesque apparatus that his servants construct also reveals the will to reorder the natural order, to convert the repository of power into a manipulatable source of reality. Thus, whereas popular culture proceeds by a system of conversions, the mythology of power acts by a process of inversions.

The same process is at work in the episode of the eclipse, which the patriarch interprets as an example of his power, in the incident in which in the process of imposing martial law "he declared a state of plague by decree" and "Sundays were suppressed," or when "he stopped time by his orders on the abandoned streets." The mythological code operates beneath the hyperbole, illustrating a crazed will to power and also reconstructing its own cosmology as the reformulated origin.

This is why the people see in the dictator the signs of the beginning and also of the end of time; in other words, they convert to their own code the threats, derisiveness, and delirium of the tyrant. Thus when the patriarch makes his son a major general the omens begin again: "That unprecedented decision was to be the prelude of a new epoch, the first announcement of the evil times in which the army cordoned off the street before dawn and made people close balcony windows and emptied the market with their rifle butts so that no one would see the fugitive passage of the flashy automobile with armored plates of steel." Leticia Nazareno presides over the new, evil times by her abusive and, in the end, punished plunder of the public markets. Elsewhere we read that "even the most incredulous of us were hanging on that uncommonly large death which was to destroy the principles of Christianity and implant the origins of the third testament." Beneath the hyperbole we find once again the mythical rebirth of a new age, in this case with the shudder of the future.

Thus these inversions construct in the text the mythology that sustains *a world inside-out*. In effect, starting with the mythological origin of power we perceive that the inversion has modeled the historical reality; the world is continually being formed through the cycles of power, but its model of distortion is an unavoidable determinism. The world is inside-out at its very origin: violence and political oppression occupy its foundation and distort it. The mythology of the origin is, therefore, a loss of the origin.

This inside-out reality has a corresponding "inside-out" man, a dictator whose mythological dimension is "totalizing" but whose individuality is reductive. Thus, when he decides to go near the people, he leaves a series of catastrophes in his wake because his power is disruptive: "he was not aware of the string of domestic disasters that his jubilant appearances brought on."

This dimension also includes a physical caricature. His origin is uncertain, and his sex is a stigma, as the "camp follower" declares, "she let go of it with fright, go back to your mama and have her turn you in for another one, she told him, you're no good for anything." The apology for his condition is brutally illustrated in his displaced orgasm. The agony of an inordinate old age is also indicative of this condition.

The exact dimensions of this mythological power, which death reveals in its final derision, are defined at the end of the text, when the tensions are resolved. The summary judgment is finally a speech of consciousness and the myth yields to the evidence: "he had learned of his incapacity for love in the enigma of the palm of his mute hands . . . and he had tried to compensate for that infamous fate with the burning cultivation of the solitary vice of power"; "he had known since his beginnings that they deceived him in order to please him, that they collected from him by fawning on him, that they recruited by force of arms the dense crowds along his route"; and "[he] discovered in the course of his uncountable years that a lie is more comfortable than doubt, more useful than love, more lasting than truth." The sweeping response of the text emerges in this final revelation: "he was condemned not to know life except in reverse, condemned to decipher the seams and straighten the threads of the woof and the warp of the tapestry of illusions of reality without suspecting even too late that the only livable life was one of show, the one we saw from this side which wasn't his general sir, this poor people's side." This response is grounded in the popular culture, in the full awareness of its liberation. The mythology of the inside-out world dissolves at this point in a surge of consciousness that affirms the real social existence and rejects the confiscating and substitutive power. The patriarch now becomes "a comic tyrant who never knew where the reverse side was and where the right of this life which we loved with an insatiable passion that you never dared even to imagine out of the fear of knowing what we knew only too well that it was arduous and ephemeral but there wasn't any other, general, because we knew who we were while he was left never knowing it forever." The reaffirmation of an enduring popular and communal existence enhances these final pages with the almost epic breath with which writing conveys the birth of consciousness.

Having confronted from within the repertoires of popular culture and of power, the mythological code, which induces the hyperbolic expansions of the text, yields to the last evidence of the text, to the production of a consciousness deriving from the action of the speakers, an act that propitiates the judgment of all times in the dialogical scene of this writing. This final evidence takes us back to the beginning of the text, but only after confirming on the last page the popular jubilation over this final impeachment: "the good news that the uncountable time of eternity had come to an end." With the death of the "patriarch" an entire people arrive at the adulthood of recognition; with the destruction of a mythological model the inside-out world collapses and the popular culture recognizes its creative social dimension; with the disappearance of the distorting power based on this model an age without history comes to an end and a new age is announced. The end is thus a new beginning because it returns us to the point of departure of this debate, to the collective narrator.

THE CODE OF THE COLLECTIVE NARRATOR

The first page of the text opens on the "vast lair of power" and on the vultures that announce the patriarch's death. "Only then did we dare go in," the narrator says. A people deprived of a written history reconstruct their past starting from this first scene in their oral history. It is in their own narrative that they learn, face themselves, and discern. One of the triumphs of this novel is its construction on a scheme of alternating the speakers who give evidence; in other words, the account unfolds from the perspective of a collective narrator whose code is developed as the central productive system of the text. This code forms the circuit of communication, and through it the information transmitted gives account of its sources, indicating the instances of direct evidence and those of hearsay, inferential, and indirect knowledge that construct the semantic space of the communication. This is where historicity is produced in opposition to a history seized by power, in the debate that will liberate a shared consciousness.

The first death of the dictator also marks the first day of consciousness, the narrative of what has been seen unleashing the sum of what has been heard in order to reset the stage of what has been lived. Whereas the unwritten response of the people is to survive the dictatorship, to live longer than the tyrant, their wisdom lies in their capacity to discern, formulated in this case as the extensive process of relating. The collective narration is established, therefore, as the privileged space of knowing. Even in this elaboration of the text, which corresponds to a peculiar modeling of the Latin-American *text of culture*, García Márquez achieves a poetic result of remarkable persuasive power because the textual model he produces resolves the tradition of a formal debate that is characteristically our own, that of the founding text that constructs a narrative system in which literature reformulates culture. This tradition is encountered, among others, in the textual drama of the chronicles of the Indies (especially in the cultural text of Inca Garcilaso), in the discursive elaborations of Sarmiento, and in the reordering song of *Martín Fierro*.

And among the camellias and butterflies we saw the berlin from stirring days, the wagon from the time of the plague, the coach from the year of the comet, the hearse from progress in order, the sleep-walking limousine of the first century of peace, all in good shape under the dusty cobwebs and all painted with the colors of the flag.

This museum of power confirms the false, silenced carnival. The accumulation of this collective evidence adds credence to the information about the patriarch's death, which is then put to its first test: "Only when we turned him over to look at his face did we realize that it was impossible to recognize him, even though his face had not been pecked away by vultures, because none of us had ever seen him." This crisis of information, then, demands verification:

and even though his profile was on both sides of all coins, on postage stamps, on condom labels, on trusses and scapulars, and even though his engraved picture with the flag across his chest and the dragon of the fatherland was displayed at all times in all places, we knew that they were copies of copies of portraits that had already been considered unfaithful during the time of the comet, when our own parents knew who he was because they had heard tell from theirs, as they had from theirs before them, and from childhood we grew accustomed to believe that he was alive in the house of power.

The information is thus lost in the origins of the narrative, at the point where the mythologized dimension of the patriarch begins. But we can already sense that the perspective of the debate of the narrative is what will place all the cycles of information within the holocaust of power produced by this collective narrator.

In the realm of myth, the code of the collective narrator formalizes the communication, processing it in its own ambiguity: "The second time he was found, chewed away by vultures in the same office, wearing the same clothes and in the same position, none of us was old enough to remember what had happened the first time, but we knew that no evidence of his death was final, because there was always another truth behind the truth." Whereas different versions and alternatives support the construction of a myth, the narration of a text that is being produced collectively requires thorough verification because the communication emitted returns from the addressee as certainty, and it is through this dialogue that the speakers take shape. This certainty is what organizes knowledge: "None of us was old enough to have witnessed that death of Bendición Alvarado but the fame of the funeral ceremonies had come down to our times and we had trustworthy reports that he did not go back to being what he had been before for the rest of his life. . . ." This is why the myth reaches a crisis point when it is confronted with the evidence of an information that reduces it to its real measure: "Shortly before nightfall, when we finished taking out the rotten husks of the cows and putting a little order into that fabulous disarray, we were still unable to tell if the corpse looked like its legendary image."

The collective narrator is, then, the *collective I* of the popular culture. Its work shapes a cyclical series of information: the messages are emitted by an addressor (us) to an addressee (us). The information is thus circular and shifts as it processes and formalizes the messages in new circles of incorporation. The place of the addressor is constantly occupied by a momentary "I" that is part of a plural narrator, to which he delivers his message before returning to the latent collective chorus. Writing is thus mobilized by opening a syntagmatic space that expands as an articulated and, at the same time, free montage. The different codes alternate, confront each other, and interact, connoting the polyphony of an extraordinary enriched writing capable of achieving a supple dynamics in its broadly designed rhythms. In the process of alternating the speakers who comprise the collective narrator, as the messages are reiterated they go through different codes and thus take on different connotations and tensions. It is also through this reiteration that the meanings emerge as forms of the expression, creating the spectacle of a text that reveals its own semantic unfolding as a completely free and, unquestionably, rigorous game. Therefore, the narrators' perception of the critical information they received and emit also goes through the carnivalization of the writing of speech, in other words, through the feast of the names of the world that write the fullness of consciousness.

Actor and author of the information, the collective narrator is, in the broadest sphere of the textual carnivalization, the executant of the transgressive word because the official law is dissolved by the conversions of the popular culture as it moves between the addressor and the addressee in the cycle of communication.[13] Dissolving laughter and critical consciousness are mutually generated in this manner.

In addition to the collective narrator, who begins and ends the novel, reinitiating the critical communication in both instances, the place of the narrator is occupied by the patriarch himself, by a second person that detaches itself from the narrative as a dialogue inserted in the rhythm of the account, and by the third person of the text, as the open space of the chronicle. This narrative encounter is also a kind of textual theatricality of the communication.

The point of view in this novel is structured around the following series of narrators within narrators: a third person, which sometimes reverberates as the other part of an "us" seen in a mirror and which must be viewed as the space of the reference objectified by the text; a first person plural, a "we" that sustains the greatest amount of information and unfolds in different speakers; a first person that is occupied, for example, by the patriarch himself and confronts the collective narrator as a decoded referent and, alternately, as a curt public speaker or a deranged private speaker agonizing in his speech; and finally, a circulating second person of the communication that updates the event and the account of it.[14] Where, then, does the narration originate? What sustains this theater of voices? The answer is, of course, the book, or rather, the Book. Because here, as in *One Hundred Years of Solitude*, the beginning and the ending are articulated in the enigma of the book as the space that by replacing reality gives back to it a revealing center. But this is yet another code.

THE CODE OF WRITING

If, as Barthes suggests, the code is a system of the commonplace,[15] then the code of the commonplace par excellence is writing resolved in the book, there where the enigma of language is reestablished as a material space, in a language that refers to itself, in the "pure book" proposed by Derrida.[16]

In *The Autumn of the Patriarch*, before this final remittal to the act of the book, there is still an intimate debate on oralness and writing. Writing, it is true, occurs as the oralness of an expansive narration sustained by the polyphonic duration of the phrase. But it is also true that the speakers from the popular culture have an oral notion of language: the communication recognizes this dialogical nature. And, nevertheless, in the production of the narrative we encounter a plural writing: the names of the world are recorded time and again from each code to substantivize a realm whose meaning has been distorted by authoritarianism. This writing is, therefore, total. It writes the world with the names of the world in order to remake it as the original space of certainty, the joy and enigma of language. This is also true in *One Hundred Years of Solitude*, but now it carries a different risk: to reestablish in a world inside out the systematic conversion of a different world, a world liberating names starting from the subversion of its historicity.

The debate between oralness and writing is resolved, therefore, in a liberating text, but it is dramatized in the experience of a cultural conflict. Lacking a history of themselves, the people are also faced with a corresponding lack of documentary writing: "Although all trace of his origin had disappeared from the texts, it was thought that he was a man of the upland plains because of his immense appetite for power, the nature of his government, his mournful bearing, the inconceivable evil of a heart which had sold the sea to a foreign power and condemned us to live facing this limitless plain." Phrases such as "it was thought," "it was conjectured," or "it was known" denote referred information. This oral information replaces the texts and contradicts the false image of the patriarch's grandeur given by the school texts. For the tyrant, writing is another repressive mechanism, and its use to protest his rule is forbidden. During one period of his rule the patriarch is illiterate, but he later learns to read, inspired by Leticia Nazareno. Even so, there is no difference between the written and oral law of his government, although writing the law exposes the dependent nature of his rule: "Previously, during the occupation by the marines, he would shut himself up in his office to decide the destiny of the nation with the commandant of the forces of the landing and sign all manner of laws and decrees with his thumbprint." This thumbprint, this body writing, exposes the colonial condition. And when the ancient patriarch becomes a shadow of his former power and begins to lose his memory of writing: "[he] tore the margins off ledgers and in his florid hand wrote on them the remaining residue of the last memories that preserved him from death, one night he had written my name is Zacarías, he read it again under the fleeting light of the beacon, he read it over and over and the name repeated so many times ended up seeming remote and alien to him, God damn it, he said to himself, tearing up the strip of paper, I'm me, he said to himself, and he wrote on another strip that he had turned a hundred." This broken writing discloses the patriarch's increasing loss of control, even though his authority is still proclaimed by the bureaucratic writing of his newspapers in yet another distortion: "splashing about in the reading of his own news . . . he learned of historic phrases that his ministers of letters attributed to him." But he is not blind to the facts ("he checked the facts on paper against the tricky facts of real life"), and writing becomes the evidence of his final defeat, "until the last nostalgia trickled away through the fissures in his memory and all that remained was the image of her on the strip of paper where he had written Leticia Nazareno of my soul look what has become of me without you."

In this novel, writing is recorded writing and read writing. It is a spectacle that transmutes oralness, an inscription of the world in the restoring rhythm of the text. It is a discontinuous writing that resolves a configuration of critical and celebrative experience and whose material manifestation is a narrative of language itself. This also accounts for the importance of the "men of letters" in the novel.

The appearance of a "warrior from other lands and other times . . . a withdrawn young man, troubled by haughtiness . . . who wanted arms and assistance for a cause which is also yours, excellency, he wanted logistical support and political aid for a war without quarter which would wipe out once and for all every conservative regime from Alaska to Patagonia" incites the patriarch to declare that "he's got a fever in his quills." This censure of the young, romantic revolutionary is also applied to the writers: "he proclaimed a new amnesty for political prisoners and authorized the return of all exiles except men of letters, of course, them never, he said, they've got fever in their quills like thoroughbred roosters when they're moulting so that they're no good for anything except when they're good for something, he said, worse than politicians, worse than priests, just imagine, he said." The first parallel is between the young revolutionary and the "committed" writer; the second is between the gamecock and the men of letters: they all participate, in effect, in a struggle. Everything else follows from this recognition of the impugning aspect of writing. To the antipopular authority this impugning quality is its most certain threat, its negation. This underlines the subversive capacity of a writing that denounces the very root of underdevelopment: the colonial condition.

In the same vein, at the Rubén Darío poetry recital the patriarch cannot but acknowledge the fascination of a poetry that evokes "the eternal splendor of an immortal nation larger and more glorious than all those he had dreamed of during the long deliriums of his fevers as a barefoot warrior." This nation is nothing other than the poetic language conquered by Darío, that "heavy minotaur" who leaves the patriarch "excited by the revelation of written beauty." The revealing and impugning power of writing is thus inscribed in the debate on the discernment of the language of critical consciousness. This debate generates, in turn, the political meaning, its production as a liberating practice, and this practice confronts the machinery of domination, the political oligarchy of authoritarianism and dependency, the mark of colonialism. This political meaning is illustrated also by the anticolonial rebellion of General Lautaro Muñoz, an event that exposes the extent of the antinational plunder. Writing takes us back to the beginning, to its history as denunciation. In other words, it returns us to its appeal to revolt, there where writing itself is a work of impugning meaning. Thus the book that transforms history into a revealing self-consciousness is also an evidence of that other rebelling world: the memories of its liberated potentiality.

We have witnessed, therefore, a complex textual process. The codes as well as the narrators act in the "totalized" elaboration of a history that models reality as a myth, usurping its meaning. In this way, the communication of the speakers accumulates the information that makes of the patriarch and of power the mythological figure of a Latin America occupied by dictatorial rule. The entire novel is the encompassing construction of this tragic determinism, and therein lies the strength of its bitter political denunciation. But at the same time we have confirmed throughout the novel the deconstruction of this mythology of absolute power. The death of the archetype of power is the perspective of the narrative, carnivalization and criticism are its practice, and in this process the codes and narrators have dislocated the codification of absolute power. This novel is the deconstructed construction of power: the myth and its deconstruction occur at the same time, and writing has produced a book of the history of the beginning as a history of the end, that is to say, the book of the subversion of language, its accession to meaning in the foundation, once again, of the liberating consciousness.

Notes

1. See Graciela Palau de Nemes, "Gabriel García Márquez, *El otoño del patriarca*," *Hispamérica* 11–12 (1976): 173–183; Angel Rama, *Los dictadores latinoamericanos* (Mexico

City, 1976); Julio Ramón Ribeyro, "Algunas digresiones en torno a *El otoño del patriarca*," *Eco* 187 (May 1977): 101–106. Domingo Miliani has constructed an interesting typology of the dictator in a study titled "El dictador: Objeto narrativo en *Yo, el supremo*," *Revista de Crítica Literaria Latinoamericana* 3 (Lima, 1976): 55–67; and Jaime Mejía Duque, *El otoño del patriarca o la crísis de la desmesura* (Medellín, n.d.).

2. "Kundera on the Novel," *The New York Times Book Review*, 8 January 1978.

3. On the semiology of culture see Janvan der Eng and Mojmir Grygar, *Structure of Texts and Semiotics of Culture* (The Hague, 1973); Ecole de Tartu, *Travaux sur les systèmes des signes* (Brussels, 1976); Umberto Eco, *A Theory of Semiotics* (Bloomington, 1976).

4. Sarmiento's well-known comparison between Rosas the dictator and Rosas the *estanciero* [rancher] in *Facundo*, as well as the populist and autocratic measures taken by Dr. Francia, seem to have generated some of the hyperbolic images in this novel. Graciela Palau de Nemes has advanced a revealing account of the historical sources of the text and has even documented the supposedly inordinate hyperboles in the novel: "The sale of the sea is a consummate hyperbole and an unmatched allegory of a dictatorship. It feeds on a perfidious historical reality: the schemes of the Dominican caudillos Pedro Santana and Buenaventura Báez, who between 1845 and 1878 were ready to sell their country to the highest bidder, whether Spain, France, England, or the United States. Santana annexed the country to Spain; Báez negotiated a loan with English bankers in 1869; Samana Bay, on the northeastern coast of the island, in the Atlantic, became a booty. During his provisional government (1866), General Cabral proposed sharing with the United States the sovereignty of the waters of the bay in exchange for its defense. Báez later proposed the annexation of the entire country to save himself from ruin. During the dictatorship of General Ulises Hereus (1822–1899), the bay and the peninsula of Samana continued to be the booty with which foreign powers were tempted; the foreign debt increased and payments steadily declined. Confronted with the threat of English intervention, the United States intervened and took over the collection of customhouse duties to insure the payment of the foreign debt, which was settled with another loan from the United States in 1907. Between 1916 and 1924, using as pretext the continuous civil disorders, the United States again intervened and American marines occupied the country. The era of Trujillo followed this occupation and the rest is contemporary history" [Graciela Palau de Nemes, "Gabriel García Márquez," p. 178).

5. "Ainsi, le mythe et le nom sont, par leur nature même, inmédiatement liés. D'une certaine façon, ils peuvent chacun être determinés par l'autre, l'un se ramène à l'autre: le mythe personnifie (il nomme), le nom est mythologique" ["Thus, the myth and the name are, by their very nature, immediately connected. In a certain way, they can each one be determined by the other, one leads to the other myth personifies: [names], the name is mythological"] (Y. M. Lotman and B. A. Uspenski, "Mythe-Nom-Culture," in Ecole de Tartu, *Travaux*, p. 23). The lack of a name leads him to demand and usurp all names: thus, the mythological inversions of the name.

6. Louis Althusser has shown that, from a critical point of view, as "conceptions of the world" ideologies constitute an illusion; however, under their imaginary representation of the world they also allude to reality. In *Pedro Páramo*, for example, the popular Catholic ideology is represented as truth, as a natural order. In *The Autumn of the Patriarch* we also find a deconstruction of the ideology imposed as a world view by an authoritarian political model. See Louis Althusser, "Idéologie et appareils idéologiques d'Etat," in *Positions* (Paris, 1976), pp. 67–125.

7. See Max Horkheimer, "Authority and the Family," in his book *Critical Theory: Selected Essays*, translated by Matthew J. O'Connell and others (New York: Herder and Herder, 1972).

8. "From the semiotic point of view culture may be regarded as a hierarchy of particular semiotic systems, as the sum of the text and the set of functions correlated with them, or as a certain mechanism that generates these texts. If we regard the collective as a

more complexly organized individual, culture may be understood by analogy with the individual mechanism of memory as a certain collective mechanism for the storage and processing of information. The semiotic structure of culture and the semiotic structure of memory are functionally uniform phenomena situated on different levels: being in principle the fixation of past experience, it may also appear as a program and as instructions for the creation of new texts" (B. A. Uspenski et al., "The Semiotic study of Cultures," in Janvan der Eng and Mojmir Grygar, *Structure of Texts*, p. 17).

9. "At one time Tylor defined culture as the aggregate of tools, technological equipment, social institutions, faiths, customs, and languages. Today one could give a more general definition: the aggregate of all non-inherited information and the means for organizing and preserving it. From this emerge very diverse conclusions. Above all it substantiates the concept of mankind's need for culture. Information is not an optional indication of, but one of the basic conditions for man's existence. The battle for survival — both the biological and the social one — is a struggle for information" (Jurij Lotman, "Culture and Information," *Dispositio* 1 [1976]: 213–215).

10. Mikhail Bakhtin, *Rabelais and His World*, translated by Helene Iswolsky (Cambridge, Mass.: M.I.T. Press, 1968).

11. J. R. Ribeyro: "In short, I would have wanted García Márquez's dictator to be not only likeable, but also detestable." Angel Rama: "The ignominy or the perversion can only be measured from it [the reader's consciousness], and this should serve to temper the series of somnambulistic narrative inventions by interposing a protective shield to the fascination they exert."

12. "Dans une perspective sémiotique, on peut représenter le processus historique comme un processus de communication durant lequel l'afflux d'information nouvelle ne cesse de conditioner des réactions-réponses chez un destinataire social (le socius). . . . Ainsi les événements reçoivent un sens: leur *texte est lu* par le socius" ["In a semiotic perspective, one can represent the historic processus as a processus of communication during which the flow of new information does not cease to condition reaction responses in a social 'destinataire' (the 'socius'). . . . Thus the events receive a meaning: their text is read by the 'socius' "] (B. A. Uspenski, "Historia sub specie semioticae," in Ecole de Tartu, *Travaux*, p. 141).

13. On the carnivalesque author-actor see Julia Kristeva, *El texto de la novela* (Barcelona, 1974).

14. On the functions of the point of view of the narrator see Percy Lubbock, *The Craft of Fiction* (New York, 1921); Wayne C. Booth, *The Rhetoric of Fiction* (Chicago, 1961); Ludomir Dolezel, "The Typology of the Narrator: Point of View in Fiction," in *To Honor Roman Jakobson* (The Hague, 1967).

15. Roland Barthes writes that the code is a supratextual organization of the order of the "déjà-vu, de déjà-lu, de déjà-fait." ["already seen, already read, already done"]. See his "Analyse textuelle de un conte de Edgar Poe," in Claude Chabrol, ed., *Sémiotique narrative et textuelle* (Paris, 1973), pp. 29–54.

16. Jacques Derrida, "Force et signification," in *L'écriture et la différence* (Paris, 1967).

The Sleep of Vital Reason in García Márquez's *Crónica de una muerte anunciada*

Arnold M. Penuel*

> Fate is unpenetrated causes
> — Ralph Waldo Emerson

A masterfully-told murder tale with all the essential ingredients of the genre, Gabriel García Márquez's *Crónica de una muerte anunciada* [*Chronicle of a Death Foretold*] is based on an actual murder that occurred in Colombia in 1951.[1] Initially, this short novel begs to be read as just a murder tale. Its widely-publicized factual basis and narrative techniques discourage a perception of transcendent meaning in its pages. Although the narrator, supposedly the author himself, was a witness and a marginal participant in the action, his method is primarily that of an investigative reporter who describes the actions and the views of the numerous witnesses and participants, however contradictory they may appear. He does intersperse his own opinions about the events, which though significant, by no means preempt the reader's interpretive role, especially in view of the myriad perspectives and possibilities structured into the novel. Withal, the point of view leaves the impression of a scrupulous objectivity, born of the narrator's intelligent and extremely diligent efforts to re-create and understand what happened a quarter of a century earlier. The narrator imaginatively likens his task to ["trying to put back together so many scattered fragments of the broken mirror of memory"] (p. 13).[2] The strong impression of journalistic objectivity, involving multiple and often contradictory views, contributes decisively to the monopolistic hold the surface events exert on the reader's attention.

Nevertheless, a close reading of *Crónica* reveals that this novel, like most of García Márquez's other fiction, possesses a strong infrastructure of symbolic meaning, integrating a rich mixture of mythical, religious, social, psychological, and historical elements.[3] For various reasons, however, this infrastructure is more camouflaged and farther from the surface than in the novelist's other fictional works.[4] The novel abounds with evocative names and other allusive elements suggesting a symbolic mode of writing. Yet these elements so strongly resist being integrated into larger patterns of meaning that the reader may be tempted simply to drift along with the surface flow. The primary source of resistance lies in the novelist's technique of radical dissociation or displacement of many allusive elements from their referents. This technique, combined with the novel's factual basis and journalistic point of view, works constantly against the reader's tendency to search for transcendent meaning. Grasping the

*Reprinted from *Hispania* 68, No. 4 (December 1985):753–66. Reprinted by permission of the journal.

novel's symbolic meaning requires an effort resembling the piecing together of a jigsaw puzzle. The pieces are scattered about and must be
placed wherever they fit. The narrator's metaphor comparing his task to
that of fitting together the scattered shards of the broken mirror of
memory provides an appropriately dissociated clue to the nature of the
reader's task.[5] For the moment a few examples of dissociation will have to
suffice to illustrate the technique. Dr. Dionisio Iguarán exhibits few
characteristics associated with his mythological namesake, yet the Dionysian side of human nature is thematically central in the novel. Nor is there
any clear connection between General Petronio San Román and the
author of *The Satyricon*, but there are meaningful similarities between the
general's son and a major character in the Roman writer's masterpiece.
The names of other characters, such as Pedro and Pablo Vicario, are
transparently allusive, but turn out to have an ironic relationship with
their referents. Such a varying of the nature of the relationships throughout the text complicates even further the deciphering of the novel's more
abstract meanings.

One of the primary functions of literature is to define in changing
times and circumstances what it means to be human. When myths,
religious beliefs, moral codes, institutions, and social conventions thwart
rather than serve human needs, good writers take their readers back to
their common human roots, showing them how they fall short of — or
fulfill — both their elemental and noblest human potential. While *Crónica*
can certainly be read as an absorbing murder tale, it also undertakes a
humanizing mission. Indeed, one may well suspect that the murder tale
serves as an exciting means of enticing the reader into a recognition of
certain realities ordinarily difficult — and perhaps threatening — to perceive.[6]

The action of the novel revolves around a matter of honor. When
Bayardo San Román, a wealthy newcomer to a small river town near the
Caribbean coast of Colombia, discovers that his bride, Angela Vicario, is
not a virgin, he returns her to her home the very night of the wedding.
Pressured by her family to reveal the identity of the man who deflowered
her, Angela blames Santiago Nasar, a handsome young man of a wealthy
family, whom no one had ever associated with her. Immediately, Angela's
brothers, Pedro and Pablo, resolve to restore the family honor by killing
Santiago. Hog butchers by trade, the twin brothers sharpen their knives in
a butchershop and await Santiago in a store within sight of his home. They
announce their intention of killing him, and the reason, to dozens of
townspeople in both places. Despite the widespread knowledge of their
intention, for a variety of reasons, not only does no one prevent the
murder but virtually the whole town witnesses the gory, hair-raising event
in the town square.

Clearly, a principal object of criticism in *Crónica*, as reviewers and
critics have noted, is a set of communal values embracing a primitive code

of honor.[7] Moreover, these values presume the guilt of the man accused of violating the code. The Vicario brothers' reluctance to carry out their intention to kill Santiago Nasar is patently clear by the way they publicly announce this intention and by the way they conduct themselves in Clotilde Armenta's store. Just as evident is the more or less tacit complicity of their fellow citizens in the crime. In a sense, the failure of the townspeople to prevent the murder when the brothers provide them every opportunity to do so transforms the twins into unwilling tools of the town's collective will. The novel is replete with passages demonstrating the role the townspeople's observance of the strict code of honor plays in Santiago's death. The following passage, however, best sums up their attitude and the moral discomfort they feel considering the fateful consequences of the code: ["But most of those who could have done something to prevent the crime and did not consoled themselves with the pretext that affairs of honor are sacred monopolies, accessible only to those who take part in the drama"] (p. 127).

Complaining of the scarce development of the major characters, one reviewer has compared them to film characters.[8] The reason for the relative lack of development is that the town itself is the protagonist of the novel. The novel's chief interest lies in exploring the town's collective psyche or communal values. Moreover, it is likely, for reasons that will be made clear later, that the characters' relative lack of individualization is a part of the novel's message. The communal values determine the course of events in the town. What are the town's values? How did they develop? How are they maintained? What is their psychological conformation? What are their consequences? These are the principal issues explored in the novel and addressed in this study.

The novelist's ultimate target in *Crónica* is the ideal of instinctual renunciation in human conduct. The principal manifestation of this ideal is the cult of virginity. This ideal gives substance to the town's code of honor. There are omnipresent signs that the ideal and the code are in decline, yet they still hold sufficient sway over the collective psyche to bring on the death of Santiago when he is accused of having violated them.

Several circumstances provide evidence of the code's decadence. The most obvious evidence is the Vicario brothers' announcement of their intention to all comers, in hope that they will be stopped. Clotilde Armenta sees their reluctance very clearly. When the mayor does nothing more than take away their knives without trying to dissuade them from their purpose, she expresses her disillusionment in the following manner:

["It's to spare those poor boys from the horrible duty that's befallen them.

Because she had sensed it. She was certain that the Vicario brothers were not as eager to carry out the sentence as to find someone who would do them the favor of stopping them."] (p. 77)

The brothers' feeling that they will have discharged their duty by demonstrating the proper intention indicates a greater fear of "el qué dirán" or gossip than a conviction of the validity of the code. In their tacit hope that a symbolic gesture will suffice, they miscalculate their neighbors' reactions. The townspeople's ambivalence both before and after the crime further demonstrates the decline of the ideal of instinctual renunciation. While the collective obsession with the crime decades afterwards probably corresponds to a natural, human tendency to relive the most exciting event of their lives, it suggests also the need to relieve guilt feelings. Hence, the narrator speaks of a consoling pretext. This ambivalence is clear both in numerous individual reactions and in the spectators' spontaneous cry of revulsion in the plaza: ["They didn't hear the shouts of the whole town, frightened by its own crime"] (p. 153).

The double standard for men and women in sexual matters and the popularity of María Alejandrina Cervantes' house of prostitution provide additional evidence of the halfhearted devotion to the cult of virginity. Divina Flor, a servant's daughter in the Nasar household, is said to be destined to wind up in Santiago's bed, and he pursues her relentlessly. Nor does he miss an opportunity to deflower any virgin who crosses his path. It is possible that the difficult ideal of instinctual renunciation provokes a rebellion in men that makes a double standard inevitable or at least exacerbates it?

The juxtaposition of a marriage without love and the love of virginity reveals yet another facet of the decadence of the ideal of virginity. Bayardo San Román explains that he has been going from town to town in search of a wife. The pejorative of the two meanings of the novel's epigraph probably applies to him: ["The pursuit of love is like falconry."] Speaking of her first impressions of Bayardo years later, Angela confesses: ["I detested arrogant men, and I had never seen one so conceited . . ."] (p. 41). For the Vicarios, Angela and Bayardo's union is a marriage of convenience. Angela harbors no illusion of love for her prospective husband, and Bayardo's interest in this most spiritless of women appears enigmatic.[9] It is scarcely accidental that the description of the Vicarios' decision to marry (sell?) Angela to Bayardo is immediately followed by that of her fiancé's purchase of the widower Xius's house. In neither arrangement does Bayardo demonstrate but minimal regard for the feelings of Angela and the widower Xius, who is loathe to part with a house which has so many happy associations. Bayardo's disregard for Angela's feelings easily matches that of her own family.

[The parents' decisive argument was that a family dignified by modest means had no right to disdain that prize of destiny. Angela Vicario scarcely dared hint at the inconvenience of a lack of love, but her mother demolished it with a single sentence:
"Love can also be learned."] (p. 48)

Eventually Angela does learn to love, but the lessons come at an extremely high cost to her and others. Moreover, the reader has already been predisposed against marriages of convenience when the narrator tells him that Santiago ["was the only son of a marriage of convenience that didn't have a single moment of happiness"] (p. 14). The following passage underscores the commercial nature of Bayardo's wedding plans: ["Bayardo San Román, for his part, must have married with the illusion of buying happiness with the enormous weight of his power and fortune, for the more the plans for the festival grew, the more delirious ideas occurred to him to make it still bigger"] (p. 53). This passage subtly insinuates that Bayardo is attempting to compensate for his lack of love with a show of wealth and power.

A final indication of the weakness of the ideal of virginity is found in Bayardo and Angela's total indifference to this consideration when they finally learn to love each other. Although the narrator says that Angela became a virgin again for Bayardo when she fell in love with him, virginity here becomes a metaphor for her psychological fidelity to her husband. Within the context of her all-consuming love (the intense *quality* of which is expressed by the sheer *quantity* of letters she writes), the matter of physical virginity is an insignificant detail.

Crónica contains a subtle and indirect yet strong and persistent attack on the Catholic Church. The strength of this attack, which is unmistakably clear once the pieces fall into place, partially explains the novelist's relatively greater concealment of the tale's symbolic implications. The novel presents the Church as the author of the doctrine of instinctual renunciation, the root of all the trouble in the town. In its insistence on this doctrine the Church has set up an impossible ideal of conduct for humanity and has therefore undermined and betrayed the mission of love and fulfillment preached by Christianity's founder. The centerpiece of this doctrine is the cult of virginity, which in turn occupies a central place in the town's code of honor.[10] What appears to be a casual detail early in the novel foreshadows the identity of the novelist's chief target. When a maid accidentally dropped a pistol Santiago's father had concealed in a pillowcase, the pistol discharged and destroyed ["a life-size saint on the main altar of the church"] (p. 12). What for the maid was a frightening but meaningless accident is no accident at all within the novel's symbolic context. García Márquez has aimed the weapon directly at an important aspect of the Church's ideal of sainthood, that is, its advocacy of instinctual renunciation.[11] More than anyone else the Vicario family epitomizes the Church's ideal for family life. The family name itself suggests the Vicarios' pivotal role as representatives or intermediaries of the Church: *vicario* means both "church official" and "indirect." It was Poncio Vicario's (the father) namesake, of course, who handed Christ over to the Romans for crucifixion. Here, he hands his daughter over to San Román (to a Roman?), not for crucifixion but indeed for a long martyrdom. The easy symbolism of the twins' names is confirmed in the sequence of their acts. It is Pedro who takes the initiative in restoring Angela's honor. But when they return home to replace the knives the mayor had taken away from them, it is Pablo who must persuade the unenthusiastic Pedro to persist, reflecting thus the biblical sequence of the two saints' work. Appropriate in one sense, it is ironic in another that it is Pedro and Pablo who carry out to the extreme the implications of the Church's cult of virginity by killing a violator of that cult.

As the superlative form of her name suggests, the mother, Purísima del Carmen, attempts to exemplify the Church's doctrines in their purest forms. A psychological relative of Amaranta and Fernanda in *Cien años de soledad*, Pura also exhibits strong affinities with Galdós' Doña Perfecta and Lorca's Bernarda Alba. Also, according to Mercedes, the narrator's wife, ["She looked like a nun"] (p. 43). Products of the same small-town Hispanic catholicism, she and Bernarda Alba, as the following passage makes clear, would have understood each other perfectly.

> [In addition to the twins there was a middle daughter who had died of nighttime fevers, and two years later they were still in a period of mourning that was relaxed inside the home but rigorous on the street. The brothers were raised to be men. The girls had been reared to get married. They knew how to do screen embroidery, sew by machine, weave bone lace, wash and iron, make artificial flowers and fancy candy, and write engagement announcements. Unlike other girls of the time, who had neglected the cult of death, the four were mistresses in the ancient science of watching over the ill, comforting the dying, and enshrouding the dead.] (pp. 43–44)[12]

The narrator's mother makes remarks leaving the impression that the townspeople view this strict, old-fashioned upbringing as an admirable model:

> [The only thing that my mother reproached them for was the habit of combing their hair before sleeping. "Girls," she would tell them, "don't comb your hair at night; you'll slow down seafarers." Except for that, she thought there were no better-reared daughters. "They are perfect," she was frequently heard to say. "Any man will be happy with them because they've been raised to suffer." Yet it was difficult for the men who married the two eldest to break the circle, because they always went together everywhere, and they organized dances for women only and were predisposed to find hidden intentions in the designs of men.] (p. 44)

Such perfection enjoys the same ironic status as that of Doña Perfecta, whose fellow citizens consider her "un ángel."

The phrase ["the cult of death"], which applies *par excellence* to Pura's philosophy of "life," applies also, with somewhat less rigor, to the town's ethos. Pura simply embodies in an extreme form the more or less tacit values of her neighbors. She has the strength of character to live as many of her neighbors feel they should live. The narrator continues to describe Pura's actions with images of death even after the tragedy occurs. In a phrase that could have been used to apply to virtually all of Angela's life, the narrator states that Pura ["had tried to bury her alive"] (p. 115) and, again, that ["She had done more than what seemed possible so that Angela Vicario would die in life . . ."] (p. 118). Of course Pura's and the town's cult of death produces its expected (announced) victim. What surprises us (convincingly in my judgment) is Angela's rebirth — of which more hereafter.

The cult of virginity is an integral part of the cult of death. Here, as in *Cien años de soledad*, the obsession with virginity becomes a substitute for love and the ability to live positively. For García Márquez the cult of virginity is a vestige of taboo morality and symbolizes sterility in human relations and, ultimately, death. Santiago's death is the end-product of this cult.

The Church's role in the novel places it in clear contradiction to its original mission of promoting faith, hope, and charity among men and at variance with Christ's promise of fulfillment: "I am come that they might have life, and that they might have it more abundantly" (John 19:10). Although the Church's betrayal is multifaceted, the bishop's arrival symbolizes its failure most clearly. The flurry of activity and the expectations surrounding the arrival of the highest Church official that could be expected to visit the town symbolically demonstrates the townspeople's faith in the Church. Eager for the bishop's arrival, Santiago remains in town that fateful Monday instead of going as usual to his ranch el Divino Rostro (p. 11). Father Amador gives as a pretext for his failure to prevent the murder his distraction with the bishop's arrival (p. 93). In refusing to disembark, as Santiago's mother had predicted, the bishop betrays the townspeople's faith and hope:

["He won't even get off the boat," she told him. "He'll give an obligatory blessing, as usual, and go back to where he came from. He hates this town.

Santiago Nasar knew that it was true, but church pomp had an irresistible fascination for him. "It's like the movies," he'd told me once] (p. 15).

This interesting passage is packed with meaning. What appears as cynicism on the part of Plácida Linero proves to be simple realism. Hoping against all odds, Santiago remains in town chiefly out of love of excitement. The passage further suggests that though the Church still has the power to mold conduct, this power is seriously undermined by incredulity and doubt; the perfunctoriness of the people's faith matches that of the bishop's blessing as he passes by without stopping: ["It was a fleeting illusion: the bishop began to make the sign of the cross in the air opposite the crowd on the pier, and he kept doing it mechanically, without malice or inspiration, until the boat was out of sight and all that remained was the noise of the roosters"] (p. 27). There is no explanation of why the bishop hates the town, but if he does — and his passing by reveals at least indifference — such an attitude is at odds with the Christian doctrine of love and forgiveness. The town's perfunctory faith and the bishop's perfunctory performance of his duties are but two of many details revealing the Church's decadence. The decline of the Church's hold on the townspeople's imagination underlies their ambivalence, with regard to the cult of virginity and the code of honor.

Both humorous and ironic, the cocks prepared for the bishop's arrival play a significant role in the novel's symbolism. The townspeople, including Santiago, go to considerable trouble to gather scores of cocks and wood to prepare a coxcomb soup of which the bishop is so fond. When the bishop fails to stop, even to indulge in his favorite repast, the cocks, in seeming protest and provoked by the tooting of his boat, raise a cacophony of crowing. In a more serious vein, however, what the cocks really symbolize, echoing Peter's betrayal of Christ, is the bishop's, and by extension, the Church's betrayal of Christ's mission of love. In a sense, the cocks *announce* the Church's decadence, that is, its moribund status as an institution. Of course the Church's emphasis on the denial of the body contrasts sharply with the bishop's voluptuous refinement of taste and the ["Church pomp"] which so fascinate Santiago.

As if it were not clear enough that the Church's ideal of instinctual renunciation, exemplified directly in the Vicarios and indirectly in their fellow citizens, was a sufficient cause of Santiago's death, the novel presents additional evidence in the autopsy. The twins' gruesome murder of Santiago involving mutilation and seven major wounds, any one of which could have been mortal, symbolizes the Church's hostility toward the body, and in the last analysis, toward life itself. Father Carmen Amador performs the autopsy in the absence of Dr. Dionisio Iguarán. Notwithstanding the fact that he performs it reluctantly, at the order of Mayor Lázaro Aponte, it cannot be accidental that the town priest, whose dereliction of duty contributed in the first place to Santiago's death, should perform the autopsy. This fact and the manner in which the autopsy is performed clearly symbolize the Church's hostility toward the body, and its cult of death. Speaking of the autopsy, Father Amador exclaims: ["It was as if we had killed him again after he was dead . . ."] (p. 95). The space dedicated to the descriptions of the mutilations of Santiago's body during the murder and afterward during the autopsy is pointedly large (pp. 95–102, 151–55). Of the autopsy, the narrator says: ["It was a massacre . . ."] (p. 98). He later adds: ["They returned to us a different body. Half of the cranium had been destroyed by the trepanation, and the lady-killer face that death had preserved ended up by losing its identity. Moreover, the priest had pulled out the sliced-up intestines by the roots, but in the end he didn't know what to do with them, and he gave them an angry blessing and threw them into the garbage pail"] (p. 100). Finally, the narrator describes his own thoughts regarding Santiago's fate: ["I was thinking about the ferocity of Santiago Nasar's fate, which had collected twenty years of happiness from him not only with his death, but also with the dismemberment of his body and its dispersion and extermination"] (p. 102).

Although the descriptions of Santiago's murder and autopsy have additional literary functions, only indirectly unrelated to this analysis, the length of the descriptions, the insistent focusing on the gruesome mutilations, and the loss of identity and extermination are designed to present the Church's extreme denial of the body.[13] Not content with killing the body, the Church feels compelled to destroy it completely until it loses its identity through dispersal. In a way the novel constitutes a *reductio ad absurdum* of the Church's traditional mortification of the flesh. Of course such a metaphorical exaggeration is also characteristic of García Márquez's other fiction.

A final ironic twist delivers the bitterest of the messages of the Church's betrayal of its mission. Several circumstances associate Santiago with Christ. If valid, this interpretation means that the Church is presented as having strayed so far from its original teachings that it has symbolically slain its own founder. But what evidence do we have that Santiago is a Christ figure?[14] First the religious and biblical associations of many characters' names set the stage for such an interpretation. Moreover, some of these names possess, as indicated above, symbolic significance within a religious framework. Consider the following names: Pedro, Pablo, Poncio, Angela, Vicario, Cristo Bedoya, Lázaro Aponte, Magdalena, and Escolástica Cisneros. More importantly, consider the name Santiago Nasar. Ironically, Santiago's namesake is the patron saint of Spain, whose name was invoked by the Christians who battled his Moorish ancestors.[15]

Not only is Santiago, like Christ, of semitic origin, but his surname, Nasar, suggests *Nazarín*. Although there appear to be many coincidences in the sequence of events, some of which undoubtedly reflect the role chance plays in human affairs, it is no coincidence that Santiago's constant companion almost to his last moments of life, is Cristo Bedoya. Cristo's role as *alter ego* explains why he knows Santiago's house so well when he enters to see if Santiago has returned: ["Cristo Bedoya not only knew the house as well as his own, but was so much at home with the family that he pushed open the door to Plácida Linero's bedroom and went from there into the adjoining bedroom"] (p. 138). As Santiago and Cristo approach the square, the onlookers stare at the two as if they were to share the same fate: ["Cristo Bedoya also remembered a strange attitude toward them. 'They were looking at *us* (italics mine) . . . as if we had our faces painted' "] (p. 134). Moreover, the walk toward the square and the public nature of the murder emulate the circumstances of Christ's crucifixion: ["The people were dispersing and going toward the square in the same direction that they were headed. It was a thick crowd, but Escolástica Cisneros thought she noticed that the two friends were walking in the center of it without any difficulty, inside an empty circle, because everyone knew that Santiago Nasar was about to die and they didn't dare touch him"] (p. 134).

Additional details confirm Santiago's status as a Christ figure. The insinuations throughout the text that he is innocent of the violation imputed to him are reinforced by the narrator's judgment: ["My personal impression is that he died without understanding his death"] (p. 132). Another supporting bit of evidence is a detail in the autopsy report: ["He had a deep stab in the right hand. The report says: 'It looked like a stigma of the crucified Christ.' "] (p. 99). This detail fits with the impression the brothers create momentarily during their attack that they are nailing Santiago to the wooden door. The twins are surprised at how long it takes their victim to fall: ["Actually, Santiago Nasar was not falling because they themselves were holding him up with stabs against the door"] (p. 154). Also, the crowing of the cocks, discussed above, clearly relates Santiago's death to that of Christ.

It should be noted, finally, that both Christ's and Santiago's premature deaths are foretold, albeit in different ways. Christ's death is said by many interpreters to have been prophesied in the Old Testament, as well as by Christ himself in the New Testament. Santiago's death is announced or foretold in myriad ways. Both were victims of the multitude's ignorance and fear of life. Both deaths were announced in the sense of being the logical consequence of perverted values.

The strong Dionysian element in *Crónica* contributes in a complex manner to the novel's meaning. Representing the instinctual and unconscious side of human nature, which seeks expression in an uninhibited and spontaneous fashion, the Dionysiac is the primary source of human vitality. It can be constructive or destructive depending on how its energies are channeled. Nietzsche viewed it as complementary to the Apollonian side of human nature, which consists of intellectual and rational strivings. The Apollonian element is conspicuous for its absence in the novel. For good or evil the Dionysian element dominates the townspeople's individual and collective psyches.

My chief concern at this point is the role the positive manifestations of the Dionysiac plays in the novel. Reflecting the novelist's technique of dissociating clues to the novel's meaning from their referents, the name of the town physician, Dionisio Iguarán, as indicated above, serves to alert the reader to the importance of the novel's Dionysiac element. The positive aspects of this element are found in subtle, but unmistakable juxtaposition to its negative forms throughout the novel.

As a substitute for their waning faith, the men of the town find a new faith in what at first appears to be mere hedonism. The high priestess of this hedonism is María Alejandrina Cervantes who, as the narrator says, ["put an end to my generation's virginity"] (p. 87). María Alejandrina offers precisely what the Church would deny: instinctual fulfillment, tenderness, and consolation. Like the bad women in *Cien años de soledad* and García Márquez's other writings, María Alejandrina symbolizes fertility and the fullness of life, but, unlike the other bad women, her functions take on a quasi-religious significance. The first inkling of this religious context appears early in the novel when the narrator explains his whereabouts at the time of Santiago's murder: ["I was recovering from the revelry of the wedding in the apostolic lap of María Alejandrina Cervantes . . ."] (p. 11).[16] If the word "apostólico" is not sufficiently convincing, it should be noted that both her baptismal names possess strong religious associations. María, of course, represents the care and tenderness of the loving mother in Catholicism. Alejandrina, the feminine equivalent of Alexander, suggests (especially because of the adjective "apostólico") the seven popes who early in the history of Christianity assumed the name of Alexander.[17] The surname Cervantes is not religious, but the author of *El Quijote* is venerated in a quasi-religious fashion as representing the highest spiritual accomplishment of Hispanic civilization. Each of her names could be considered ironic or parodistic given her profession, but such an interpretation would be in utter disregard of the evidence that she plays a positive role in the novel.

While the church officials are shown as inept, trivial, uncaring, and, ultimately, destructive of human fulfillment, María Alejandrina is shown meeting human needs (not solely sexual). The following passage reveals some of her beneficent qualities:

> [María Alejandrina Cervantes, about whom we used to say that she would go to sleep only once and that would be to die, was the most elegant and the most tender woman I have ever known, and the most serviceable in bed, but she was also the strictest. She had been born and reared here, and here she lived, in a house with open doors, with several rooms for rent and an enormous courtyard for dancing lit by lantern gourds purchased in the Chinese bazaars of Paramaribo. She was the one who ravaged my generation's virginity. She taught us much more than we should have learned, but she taught us above all that there is no place in life sadder than an empty bed] (pp. 86–87).

The witticism about María Alejandrina's going to sleep only once refers on the first level of meaning, of course, to her profession. Does it also suggest the eternal vigilance of a deity? It is interesting — and perhaps meaningful — that while María Alejandrina seems never to sleep, Santiago's mother remains sleeping almost up to the moment of his death.

Significantly, after murdering Santiago, Pedro and Pablo Vicario go directly to the church (the parish house) where they surrender to Father Amador. In hot pursuit is ["a group of infuriated Arabs"] (p. 66). The priest recalls the surrender ["as an act of great dignity"], though the brothers arrived soaked in sweat and fresh blood (pp. 66–7). Showing no remorse or repentance, the twins tell Father Amador that they killed Santiago deliberately, but claim innocence because it was a matter of honor. The priest virtually absolves them then and there for guilt before God (p. 67). Father Amador's exculpatory reception is decisive in determining the type of defense they use in the trial: ["They were the ones who gave a hint of the direction the defense would take (based on honor) as soon as they surrendered to their church a few minutes after the crime"] (p. 66). The brothers never show the least conscious signs of repentance during the three years they spend in jail awaiting trial.

The narrator, on the other hand, overcome with grief after witnessing the autopsy, takes refuge and seeks consolation in ["the apostolic lap"] of María Alejandrina Cervantes. He and María Alejandrina are as inconsolable for the loss of their friend and the brutal manner in which his life was taken as the Vicario brothers are unrepentant. María Alejandrina can express her grief only through overeating. When the narrator, after observing the autopsy, entered her house, María Alejandrina ["was seated like a Turkish houri on her queenly bed in front of a Babylonic platter of things to eat: veal cutlets, a boiled chicken, a pork loin, and a garnishing of plantains and vegetables that would have been enough for five people. Excessive eating was the only way she could ever mourn and I'd never seen her do it with such grief. I lay down beside her with my clothes on, barely speaking, and weeping also in my way"] (p. 102).

The narrator falls asleep and dreams; he is awakened by María Alejandrina:

> [I dreamed that a woman was coming into the room with a little girl in her arms, and that the child was chewing without stopping to take a breath, and that half-chewed kernels of corn were falling into the woman's brassiere. The woman said to me: "She crunches like a nutty nuthatch, kind of sloppy, kind of slurpy." Suddenly I felt the eager fingers that were undoing the buttons of my shirt, and I sensed the dangerous odor of the beast of love lying next to my back, and I felt myself sinking into the delights of the quicksand of her tenderness. But suddenly she stopped, coughed from far away, and slipped out of my life. "I can't," she said. "You smell of him] (pp. 102–3).

This dream expresses María Alejandrina's inability to console herself by eating. She appears in the dream as a helpless child anxiously (breathlessly) chewing hard kernels of corn, which she cannot swallow; her grief is overwhelming. ["The anxious fingers"] which awaken the dreamer are the "real-life" equivalent of the anxious child in the dream. María Alejandrina's intention is to console herself and her friend by making love. In mourning, María Alejandrina has closed her house to the public and her mulattoes have dyed their clothes black as a sign of mourning.[18] From the Church comes the cult of virginity, tacit approval of the crime, excuses for failing to prevent it, and a horrible mutilation of the victim's body during the autopsy. Associated with María Alejandrina, on the other hand, are authentic grief, humane feelings, and an effort of tender consolation. This juxtaposition of values is meaningful. It is also meaningful that these values are associated with a woman who ministers to the needs of the body, and symbolically to the needs of the whole person. The fact that María Alejandrina is completely naked (as she usually is when no stranger is present) and her attempts to assuage her grief first through eating and then by making love demonstrate the primacy of the body and its inseparability from the human spirit.[19]

The widower Xius's role in the novel places the opposition between denial and celebration of the body in historical perspective. The name Xius appears to be a transformation of "Zeus," the Greek god who dwelt on Mt. Olympus. Like his presumed namesake, Xius resides in a choice location: high on a hill with a magnificent view. The house is suggestively described as commanding a view of a paradise: ["It was on a windswept hill, and from the terrace one could see the limitless paradise of the marshes covered with purple anemones, and on clear summer days one could make out the neat horizon of the Caribbean and the tourist ships from Cartagena de Indias"] (p. 49). Xius's glory, like that of the Greeks, lies in the past, in memories of his happy life with his wife, Yolanda, in this house on the hill. His role is to evoke Hellenic civilization or perhaps, because of the Latinate form of his name, Graeco-Roman culture and the pagan glorification of the body. When Bayardo buys the house from Xius and occupies it, he, however, cannot find happiness there. It is there that he discovers that his bride is not a virgin and returns her to her home. Symbolically, Roman Catholicism with its emphasis on instinctual renunciation has proved in this respect an unworthy replacement for the pagan religion of ancient Greece. While the pagan gods no longer inspire admiration and belief, their respect for and celebration of the body is worth salvaging. For this reason Xius's happiness lies in memories of the past and Bayardo cannot find happiness in the present.

A possible indirect contribution to the polarity of denial vs. celebration of the body is the reference to Nietzsche. Commenting on the presiding judge's marginal notes, the narrator says of him that ["he knew Nietzsche well, that he was the author in vogue among the judges of his time"] (129). This allusion should not be taken lightly since the judge is a very learned man and has meditated long on the events surrounding the crime. The allusion to Nietzsche serves as a clue to the importance of the denial-celebration dichotomy: the most insistent theme in Nietzsche's philosophy is the desirability for man of the uninhibited expression of his instincts. Anticipating Freud, he illuminated the consequences and implications of instinctual renunciation. Moreover, he viewed Christianity as the chief advocate of instinctual renunciation and the originator of a "slave morality."[20]

If, as I submit above, the town itself is the novel's collective protagonist, it makes sense to clarify the nature and consequences of the town's communal values. The discussion above of the Church's contribution to the formation of the townspeople's values and the alternative values symbolized in the portrayal of María Alejandrina Cervantes has in large part accomplished this task. Here, my concern is to analyze further the psychology of these communal values and the mythical context in which they appear. The analysis above clearly reveals the presence of conflicting values in the town and, as will become evident, this split is reflected within individual characters. Since Santiago's death is the main event in the novel, the focus will remain on the values that translate into his murder. Clearly, these values are under attack, despite all the camouflage about fate and coincidences. The opposing values are important too, serving by contrast and comparison to throw in relief the values under attack and also to point the way to positive alternative modes of living and being.

The wedding and the anticipation of the bishop's arrival coincide to produce a high level of excitement in the town. Manifestly a communal event, the wedding creates great excitement partly because of its magnitude and the fact that everyone participates in it. So fascinated is Santiago with its size that he spends many of his last hours calculating the costs: ["He said that they had sacrificed forty turkeys and eleven hogs for the guests, and four calves which the bridegroom had set up to be roasted for the people on the public square. He said that 205 cases of contraband alcohol had been consumed and almost two thousand bottles of cane liquor, which had been distributed among the crowd. There wasn't a single person, rich or poor, who had not participated in some way in the wildest fiesta the town had ever seen"] (p. 28).

The wedding party gives outlet to positive Dionysian energies, providing healthy and innocent pleasures: music, fireworks, abundant food and drink, dancing, and camaraderie. Even Santiago's pleasure of calculating the wedding costs seems innocent enough. Confessing to only a confused recollection of the party before retrieving it from other people's memories, the narrator specifies two memories kept alive in his household: ["For years they went on talking in my house about the fact that my father had gone back to playing his boyhood violin in honor of the newlyweds, that my sister the nun had danced a merengue in her doorkeeper's habit . . ."] (pp. 59–60).

On the other hand, Bayardo's motives for planning such a prodigal wedding cast little favorable light on his character. The passage cited earlier about his attempting to buy happiness discloses that his conspicuous consumption is owing not only to an attempt to buy admiration and friendship but also is a compensation for the absence of love. It is likely that the novelist meant for the reader to perceive Bayardo's wedding through the prism of "Trimalchio's Banquet" in Petronius's *The Satyricon*.

The dissociated clues here are Bayardo's father's name, Petronio, and the narrator's opinion, based on his reading of the presiding judge's marginal notes, that the latter knew Latin literature (p. 129). A *nouveau riche*, Trimalchio tries to win and impress friends with an exorbitantly expensive banquet featuring a great variety of human pleasures. The banquet ends on a morbid note with the host entertaining thoughts of death. Bayardo's status as a newcomer in the town, the exorbitant expenditures on his wedding, and his efforts to win friends and impress the townspeople with his wedding all echo Petronius's satire of the vulgar Trimalchio. Presenting Bayardo's wedding against the perspective of "Trimalchio's Banquet" not only enriches Bayardo's characterization but also adds to the significance of the wedding by revealing its universal archetypal dimensions.[21]

Several circumstances suggest that Santiago's death is intended to be perceived as a communal sacrifice, containing both Christian and primitive elements.[22] The cult of virginity, the symbolic role of the Church, and Santiago's status as a Christ figure are the principal Christian elements. For the most part the psychology and the form of the sacrificial rites are primitive. The atmosphere of almost orgiastic excitement occasioned mainly by the wedding, but intensified by the anticipation of the bishop's arrival, prepare the multitude psychologically for the culminating and most exciting event of all: the sacrifice of Santiago. Ironically, Santiago cannot include the incalculable value of his own life in his calculations of the wedding costs. Santiago's probable innocence corresponds to the need in such rites for an innocent or pure victim (the scapegoat of primitive Dionysian rites). The public nature of Santiago's death, the widespread announcement, the public complicity through tacit acceptance of its inevitability, the dense multitude accompanying Santiago as he walks to the place of his death and witnessing his death, and the consensus after this death that honor has been restored and equilibrium regained (except for Bayardo) all point to the sacrificial nature of the event. Moreover, both the execution of the murder and the performance of the autopsy suggest a frenzy of blood-lust characteristic of primitive sacrificial rites. Finally, the eagerness of the townspeople to view Santiago's mutilated body (p. 96) and their insistence on certifying their presence at his death by appearing as witnesses at the trial (p. 121) suggest the communal nature of the sacrifice.

What appears to be an act of solidarity from one perspective, more closely viewed, metamorphoses into symbolic self-immolation. Santiago, with his promising youth, his Hispano-Arabic heritage, his elevated position in the community, and his status as a Christ figure, symbolizes the future of his race and culture. What the town achieves with its twisted values, culminating in the sacrifice of Santiago, is the sacrifice of its own best future. This is the meaning of the narrator's anguished reference to the ferocity of Santiago's destiny ["with the dismemberment of his body and its dispersion and extermination"] (p. 102). Mutilation and dispersal of the body symbolize disunity.[23] The chief message here is that the inhumane and barbaric values underlying this disunity (or solitude) will lead to the extermination of the race—as they do in *Cien años de soledad*.

Fear of [gossip] is a potent force in the town, insuring that the townspeople adhere to their traditional values.[24] This fear colors nearly all the Vicarios' acts. Two years after a daughter's death, they observe, as noted earlier, a relaxed mourning at home and a rigorous mourning in public (p. 43). When Pura has the twins return the music box Bayardo gave to Angela, she times the return so that everyone who knew about the gift also witnesses its return (p. 42). Pura's attempt to bury Angela in life after the tragedy further illustrates this fear. The advice Angela's friends give her to deceive her husband about her virginity reveals the importance of appearances in the town: ["They insisted that even the most difficult husbands resigned themselves to anything provided that nobody knew it"] (pp. 52–53). Even though Angela would have been glad had Bayardo not shown up at all for the wedding, she refused to put on her wedding dress until he did appear: ["Her caution appeared natural because there was no public misfortune more shameful than for a woman to be jilted in her wedding gown"] (pp. 56–57). Of course the brothers' observance of the code of honor initially is due obeisance to appearances. In view of their obvious reluctance to carry out the murder and the hypocrisy in the townspeople's values, honor becomes little more than an institutionalization of the fear of ["gossip"]. One of the most revealing passages describes the return of Bayardo's mother and sisters to take him out of the town after the tragedy:

[They came on a cargo boat, dressed in mourning up to their necks because of Bayardo San Román's misfortunes, and with their hair hanging loose in grief. Before stepping onto land, they took off their shoes and went barefoot through the streets to the top of the hill in the burning dust of noon, pulling out strands of hair by the roots and wailing loudly with such high-pitched cries that they seemed to be shouts of joy. I watched them pass from Magdalena Oliver's balcony, and I remember thinking that distress like theirs could only be put on in order to hide other, greater shames] (pp. 111–12).[25]

Attempting to establish Santiago's innocence deductively, the narrator makes the following remarks which serve also to characterize the townspeople and Bayardo: ["On the morning of his death, in fact, Santiago Nasar had not had a moment of doubt, despite the fact that he knew very well what the price of the insult imputed to him was. He was aware of the prudish disposition of his world, and he must have understood that the twins' simple nature was incapable of resisting an insult. No one knew Bayardo San Román very well, but Santiago Nasar knew him well enough to know that underneath his worldly airs he was as subject as anyone else to his native prejudices. So the murdered man's refusal to worry could have been suicide"] (pp. 131–32). Remember also the presiding judge's marginal note: ["Give me a prejudice and I will move the world."] (p. 131).

The townspeople, to use David Riesman's terms, are an other-directed, lonely crowd: As weak as their traditional values are they do provide standards to live by, but the forces for change and renewal are even weaker. Their conduct revolves around negative axes; it is based on taboo morality. They have no positive center; nor is there positive leadership in the town. Unable to act, they can only react to events. Though chance does play a part in their lives, what they consider fate or destiny is principally a projection of their own passivity. The feeling of inevitability displayed by the crowd accompanying Santiago to the plaza reflects this passivity. The references to fate and chance mainly serve an ironic intention. The closer one examines the forces producing Santiago's death the smaller the role one assigns to chance. The town's collective character is its fate as well as Santiago's.[26] As the judge and the narrator's perceptions suggest, the town's traditional values are unexamined, which means they are prejudices. Naturally they are prejudices of origin, and their origin is amply documented above.

The community's indulgence of its prejudices paradoxically occasions the disclosure of a repressed set of values which, had they found timely expression would have avoided the situation that cost Santiago's life. If the town's unquestioning acceptance of ready-made values signifies its enslavement to unconscious forces, or forces of which it is only half conscious, this healthier potential set of values exists at an even greater remove from their consciousness. Exceptions are the characters who either do not know of the threat or are ineffectual, despite worthy efforts, to prevent the murder. While the superior, humane values signal their presence in various ways, their chief manifestations are psychosomatic and involuntary. All the signs of reluctance to carry out their announced intention that Clotilde Armenta observes in the Vicario brothers originate in their instinctive aversion to taking the life of another human being. Expressing no repentance of their crime and comforted by the feeling that they have fulfilled their duty, the twins nevertheless reveal an unconscious revulsion to the murder through the psychosomatic disorders they suffer. In jail awaiting trial, they cannot rest because each time they fall asleep they repeat the crime in dreams (p. 103). They are unable to rid themselves of the odor of Santiago's body until they wash themselves thoroughly (p. 104). Pedro is overcome by pain extending from groin to neck, and he cannot urinate (p. 105). Pablo is afflicted with a case of cholera so severe that he cannot stop urinating and thinks, consequently, that the Arabs may be poisoning him (p. 105).[27] The tone of the description is hyperbolic, but the psychosomatic nature of the disorders clearly signals to the reader, though not to the brothers themselves, their revulsion on a deeper psychic level at what they have wrought. Their inability to perceive the meaning of these symptoms is a product of a combination of their simplemindedness and the pressure of communal values. The body nonetheless repents of what the mind cannot repent of. The mind has become dissociated from the body's elemental wisdom. The twins cannot believe what they feel because their feelings are at odds with the communal values they have assimilated.

Other examples of psychosomatic or involuntary reactions to the murder include ["the cries of the entire town frightened by its own crime"] (p. 135), the death of Clotilde Armenta's husband, don Rogelio de la Flor, on witnessing the murder (pp. 127–28), Lázaro Aponte's conversion to vegetarianism after witnessing the autopsy, and Hortensia Baute's sudden insanity after seeing the murder weapons (p. 127).[28] In a general way the weakness and the belated expression of these healthy tendencies in individual townspeople parallel their weakness and belated expression in the town as a whole. Logically enough, the denied body, whose rejection has led in the first place to the perversion of values, points the way back to sound values rooted in an understanding and acceptance of the primacy of the body, but which (nota bene!) by no means reduce to bodily needs.[29]

Angela's rebirth years later, triggered by a sudden insight into her mother's character, marks the clearest path to the development of sound values. The insight comes when Angela observes her mother's trivial, but quite human vanity about her new glasses:

> [Pura Vicario had finished drinking, dried her lips on her sleeve, and smiled at her from the bar with her new glasses. In that smile, for the first time since her birth, Angela Vicario saw her as she was: a poor woman devoted to the cult of her defects. "Shit," she said to herself. She was so upset that she spent the entire trip back home singing aloud, and she threw herself on her bed to cry for three days.
>
> She was born again. "I went crazy over him (Bayardo)," she told me, "completely out of my mind"] (p. 121.).

This is the moment she begins writing the two thousand letters to Bayardo, which he never opens but whose writing culminates in their reunion. Angela's rebirth takes the form of a psychological awakening; dependent upon and submissive to her mother, who still beats her, she becomes independent and self-reliant. The following passage describes her transformation and her new understanding of love:

> [Mistress of her fate for the first time, Angela Vicario then discovered that hate and love are reciprocal passions. The more letters she sent the more the coals of her fever burned, but the happy rancor she felt for her mother also heated up. "Just seeing her turned my stomach," she told me, "but I couldn't see her without remembering him." She became lucid, overbearing, mistress of her own free will, and she became a virgin again just for him, and she recognized no other authority than her own nor any other service than that of her obsession.] (p. 122).

Angela's awakening to autonomy occurs in two stages. First, she recognizes the illegitimacy of her mother's authority and breaks that authority. Second, now the lucid, self-conscious mistress of her own fate, she replaces her mother's stifling authority with that of the man she loves.[30] Her love of Bayardo reinforces her independence from her mother and all that she represents. Passionate, concrete, and creative, her love makes possible the reunion with Bayardo and both exemplifies and symbolizes positive human fulfillment.

Angela's rebirth demonstrates what the town needs. Her submission to her mother's values parallels the town's submission to the perverted values of its culture. Before her rebirth, Angela possessed what Erich Fromm calls an "authoritarian conscience," that is, a conscience whose content is composed almost wholly of the largely unconscious "do's" and "don'ts" of parents and other authority figures.[31] Her real autonomy begins only with the development of a "humanistic conscience," that is, a conscience which takes into account individual circumstances, individual needs, and the probable consequence of an act. Angela's passage from dependence and submission to autonomy illustrates Fromm's concepts in exemplary fashion.

The town's crime is principally the result of its subjugation to the collective conscience of its forebears. Liberation from this authoritarian conscience requires recognition of its inadequacy and its destructiveness. It requires a larger role for the Apollonian side of man's nature. Like Angela, before her awakening, the town's collective behavior is largely determined by unconscious forces.[32] The town is asleep and, to combine the insights of Goya and Ortega, the "sleep of vital reason brings forth monsters."

Notes

*A brief version of this article was presented at the International Symposium on Gabriel García Márquez at Mississippi State University in April 1984.

1. Gabriel García Márquez, *El olor de la guayaba: Conversaciones con Plinio Apuleyo Mendoza* (Barcelona: Bruguera, 1982), p. 38.

2. Gabriel García Márquez, *Crónica de una muerte anunciada* (Bogotá: Oveja Negra, 1981). Subsequent references are to this edition.

3. See Graciela Maturo, *Claves simbólicas de García Márquez*, 2nd ed. (Buenos Aires: Fernando García Cambeiro, 1977), for a sound and insightful discussion of the symbolic function of literature and the ample cultural contexts of García Márquez's fictional worlds (pp. 13–14, 68–72).

4. The novelist makes remarks in *El olor* that can only encourage his readers to search for cryptic meanings in his works: "—Sí, creo que la novela es una representación cifrada de la realidad, una especie de adivinanza del mundo" (p. 48).

5. This sort of displacement is frequent in dreams. For a convincing comparison of the novelist's fictional world to the world of dreams, see Carlos Martínez Moreno, "Paritorio de

un exceso vital: Psicoanálisis y literatura en *cien años de soledad*," *Cuadernos de literatura*, 14 (1969), 59–76.

6. See Simon O. Lesser, *Fiction and the Unconscious* (New York: Random House, 1957), chs. IV & V, and *passim*. Lesser's brilliant analysis of the psychology of reading illuminates how fiction appeals to all three psychic functions: id, ego, and superego.

7. See Richard Predmore, "El mundo moral de *Crónica de una muerte anunciada*," *Cuadernos Hispanoamericanos*, 390 (1982), 703–12; D. Keith Mano, "A Death Foretold," rev. of *Chronicle of a Death Foretold*, by Gabriel García Márquez, *National Review*, 10 June 1983, pp. 699–700; Jonathan Yardley, "García Márquez and the Broken Mirror of Memory," rev. of *Chronicle of a Death Foretold*, by Gabriel García Márquez, *Book World*, 27 March 1983, p. 3; R. Z. Sheppard, "Where the Fiction is *Fantástica*," *Time*, 7 March 1983, p. 79; Peter S. Prescott, "Murder and Machismo," rev. of *Chronicle of a Death Foretold*, by Gabriel García Márquez, *Newsweek*, 1 November 1982, p. 82; Leonor Alvarez Ulloa, rev. of *Crónica de una muerte anunciada* by Gabriel García Márquez, *Crítica literaria*, 4 (1982), 183; Nina M. Scott, "Destiny and Causality," rev. of *Crónica de una muerte anunciada*, by Gabriel García Márquez, *Américas*, Jan.–Feb. 1982, p. 60.

8. Mano, p. 700.

9. In view of Bayardo's strong feelings about virginity, it seems feasible that he chooses Angela because she appears to be one of the most virtuous women in town. Impressed when he sees Angela and her mother dressed in mourning crossing the square in the heat of the day, Bayardo declares then and there his intention of marrying the young woman.

10. The cult of virginity has, of course, appeared in numerous cultures throughout history; the focus here is on its manifestation in a particular religion and a specific culture.

11. It is quite possible that the remarks on the wisdom of keeping the pistol and its bullets separated provide a subtle clue to the novelist's technique of radical dissociation of allusion from their referents. After all, only when the pistol is loaded with the bullets does it become possible to hit the target. Only by bringing together dissociated elements can the reader hit the critical target.

12. Remember Bernarda Alba's depressing remark on her daughters' prospects in life: ["Needle and thread for girls"], in Federico García Lorca, *Obras completas*, 15th ed. (Madrid: Aguilar, 1969), p. 1452.

13. Leonard Michaels, "Murder Most Foul and Comic," rev. of *Chronicle of a Death Foretold*, *New York Times Book Review*, 27 March 1983, views the murder as one of the most "powerfully rendered" in modern literature (p. 37).

14. Evoking mankind's first recorded murder (also of an innocent victim), Cristo Bedoya, frantically searching for the murdered Santiago, shouts to the narrator's mother: ["Luisa Santiago," he shouted to her, "where is your godson?"] (p. 144). The biblical prototype reads: "And the Lord said unto Cain, Where is Abel thy brother?" (Gen. 4:9).

15. The Arabs pursuit of Pedro and Pablo evokes the historical conflict between Christians and Moors in Spain (p. 66).

16. Michaels says that María Alejandrina Cervantes "is a magnificent, animalish whore whose lap is 'apostolic' in that it carries a message of erotic faith to the town, what García Márquez calls 'the disorder of love.' " (p. 36).

17. Predmore advances another opinion on the origin and moral implications of her name: ["It is likely that the name Alejandrina was chosen for the famous sinner of Alexandria who eventually became Santa María Egipcíaca. Thus between jokes and truths García Márquez begins to show us a world in which the moral is usually reversed"] (p. 707).

18. María Alejandrina's deeply-felt and privately-expressed grief contrasts markedly with the San Romans' ostentatious expressions of grief after Bayardo's misfortune (pp. 111–12).

19. García Márquez coincides in general with Freud in stressing the primacy of the body and in particular in the strength he attributes to the sexual drive. For both men excessive repression is the enemy.

20. Bertrand Russell, *A History of Western Philosophy*, (New York: Simon and Schuster, 1945), pp. 765–68.

21. Yardley thinks that the name Bayardo is part of a subtle tribute to Faulkner, since this "name recurs frequently in Faulkner's Yoknapatawpha County" (p. 3). While feasible, the name also has other associations. Its sound suggests *boyardo*, 'boyar,' a Russian feudal lord. Typically, the word *boyardo* is dissociated from its referent. The narrator tells us that Victoria Guzmán wakes up Santiago herself, ["since she never missed a chance to save her daughter from the clutches of the seigneur"] (p. 91). The rarity of both "Bayardo" and *boyardo* point to an intentional association in the novel.

22. In view of Santiago's fate, it hardly seems accidental that the account of the wedding costs evokes the image of a sacrifice: ["He said that they had sacrificed forty turkeys and eleven pigs . . ."] (p. 28).

23. J. E. Cirlot, *A Dictionary of Symbols*, trans. Jack Sage (New York: Philosophical Library, 1962), pp. 79–80.

24. The novelist's comparison of Soviet and Spanish village morality in *De viaje por los países socialistas*, 15th ed. (Bogotá: La Oveja Negra, 1980), is germane to this analysis: ["In an objective way, nothing so much resembles Christian morals as do Soviet morals. Girls in their relationship with men have the same manoeuvers, the same prejudices, the same psychological cunning as are proverbial with Spanish girls. It is understood at a glance that they manage the affairs of the heart with the conflicting simplicity that the French call ignorance. They are preoccupied with gossip and they enter into regular, long and supervised engagements"] (pp. 160–61).

25. The San Romans' theatrical mourning is comparable to Amaranta's theatrical death in *Cien años de soledad*, 15th ed. (Buenos Aires: Editorial Sudamericana, 1969), in which she demands of Ursula a certification that she is dying a virgin, a certification which also conceals shameful acts (p. 240).

26. The affinities of *Crónica* with Lope de Vega's *Fuenteovejuna* are sufficiently strong to suggest that the novelist consciously moulded elements of the Spanish Golden Age classic into the novel. This influence is the likely significance of the narrator's remark that the judge had read Spanish classics (p. 129).

27. The disappearance of the twins' major symptoms when they take a concoction recommended by the centenarian Arabic matriarch, Suseme Abdala, suggests that they unconsciously feel forgiven by the Arabic community through this merciful act (pp. 107–8).

28. For further examples, see pp. 127–28.

29. Lest the impression be left that the novelist's implicit advocacy of greater sexual freedom is only metaphorical, consider these remarks in *El olor*: ["We are all captives of our prejudices. In theory, as a liberal-minded man, I believe that sexual freedom should have no limits. In practice, I can't escape the prejudices of my Catholic upbringing and of my bourgeois society, and I am at the mercy, like all of us, of a double standard"] (p. 161). The presence of such a conflict within the novelist himself and his perception of its presence in his society — and undoubtedly others — provides a clue to the importance of the sexual element in his fiction.

30. In *La casa de Bernarda Alba*, in similar circumstances and for similar reasons, Adela replaces her mother's authority with that of Pepe el Romano.

31. See Erich Fromm, *Man for Himself. An Inquiry into the Psychology of Ethics* (New York & Toronto, Rinehart, 1947), pp. 143–72. The term "humanistic conscience" is also Fromm's.

32. The frequent images of and references to sleep reinforce the impression of a town

asleep, that is, a town driven by unconscious forces. The dreams, the Vicario brothers' drunken, somnambulistic state (pp. 24–5), Bayardo's semiwakeful state when he decides to marry Angela (p. 40), the dreamlike atmosphere which envelopes him when he returns Angela to her mother (p. 63), and the fact that Plácida Linero was sleeping almost up to the time of her son's death, all symbolize the role the unconscious plays in determining what happens in the town. It is interesting that while María Alejandrina is reputed never to sleep, Santiago's mother sleeps in more than one way. Perhaps her name, Plácida, suggests that she is too complacent about her son's welfare. Her failure to notice the ill omen in the dreams and her inadvertent closing of the door to the house when Santiago was trying to enter suggest the torpor of sleep. In passing, it should be noted that, according to Cirlot, both house and door are feminine symbols (pp. 81 and 146). Does her failure to provide for the security and welfare of her son symbolize Hispanic culture's failure to provide for the security and welfare of its sons and daughters — its complacent torpor?

García Márquez and the Novel   Gene H. Bell-Villada*

There are narrative works after whose publication the universe of novel-writing — its known inventory of accepted practices and possibilities — seems suddenly altered. These works expand the formal and technical means available to prose narrative; they redefine its range and limits as well as its problematic relationship to real life; and they establish an agenda for works currently in progress and to come. In the early twentieth century there were what we now see as the grand old classics of Modernism: Joyce's *Ulysses*, Faulkner's *The Sound and the Fury*, Proust's voluminous social and spiritual chronicle, Kafka's fantastical inventions. Another, large stage was set with the landmark texts of post-Modernism: Borges's *Ficciones* (1944), Beckett's *Molloy* (1951), Nabokov's *Pale Fire* (1962). Still another phase in the development of the novel was to begin with the spectacular success of Gabriel García Márquez's *One Hundred Years of Solitude* (1967) and, to a lesser extent, with the six-part extravaganza of *The Autumn of the Patriarch* (1975).

García Márquez's 1982 Nobel Prize comes in official recognition of many things, including his global readership, notably in the Third World, and also his radical humanitarianism, a key criterion in Alfred Nobel's legacy. At the same time the Swedish Academy's statement respectfully acknowledges that "each new work of [García Márquez] is received by expectant critics . . . as an event of world importance." Because of his having conceived an entire world fully inhabited by an array of characters who reappear from book to book in a variety of situations, the Nobel Committee compared the breadth and stature of García Márquez to that of Balzac and Faulkner, and they praised the Colombian's "wild imagina-

*Reprinted from *Latin American Literary Review* 13, no. 25 (January–June 1985):15–23, by permission of the journal.

tion" for having fashioned an art that "combines the fantastic and the realistic."

One normally doesn't turn to the press releases of prize committees as a starting point for literary reflections, but in this case the Nobel people did raise pertinent issues by evoking the distinctive aspects of García Márquez the man and the writer — such items as his broad literary canvas, his creative use of fantasy, his political leftism, his immense popularity, and of course his undeniable artistic greatness. This is a specific combination that, in advanced capitalist as well as communist cultures, has long been in scarce supply. Today there are but a handful of North Atlantic novelists of whom it could be said that they exhibit enduring artistry, produce an *oeuvre* of totalizing vision, enjoy worldwide readership, participate in progressive causes, and crystallize new ways of applying the fantastical imagination to human experience.

It was only some fifteen years ago that critics like Leslie Fiedler were making pronouncements to the effect that "the Novel is dead." And indeed at the time a relatively barren narrative panorama in the West (Germany excepted), along with the electronic paradise then being sung by media soothsayer McLuhan, did apparently suggest that the glory days of prose fiction were over. In retrospect, however, the doomsayers seem to have misconstrued their poor home harvests as a universal drought, for during that same decade the Latin Americans were beginning to demonstrate the formal and cultural renewability of the novel and its resources. And it is García Márquez who has done the most so far to save the novel from itself, to rescue it from the narrow impasses and byways into which it had taken refuge and set up shop.

It might be helpful to recall the world situation of the novel in 1967, the year when the tale of Macondo was being typeset and bound by its lucky Argentine publisher.

In the United States, prose fiction was in a state of directionless anomie. Norman Mailer had proved as yet incapable of replicating the grandeur of his first book, *The Naked and the Dead* (1948). Nabokov, our other novelist of record, was sliding into the onanistic, cranky self-indulgences of *Ada*. Meanwhile both WASP and Jewish novelists had fully restored traditional realist narrative, though none seemed able or inclined to enrich that nineteenth-century form with the social knowledge and vision of the nineteenth-century Europeans. Instead they concentrated on suburban *Angst* and on minutiae of the Self, producing a quasi-claustrophobic art best characterized as "solipsist realism." Bellow's one attempt at total narrative in *The Adventures of Augie March* had suffered from a pervasively flat, gray lifelessness, and Updike's portrayal of an entire town, in *Couples*, was to focus on a matter so trivial as spouse-swapping in exurbia, veiled through the mists of New England religiosity. Clearly, from the heights of Hemingway, Dos Passos, Faulkner, or even Henry Miller's *Tropics*, a lapse had taken place. The richest and most powerful nation on earth was producing novels that were materially weak and formally impoverished.

In Soviet aesthetics and among its intellectual apologists on the Western left the problem was precisely the reverse. There was one resemblance, however; what we know as "socialist realism" amounted alike to a restoration of nineteenth-century genre, revived in this case through State dictatorship, a rigidified social code, and a bastardized Marxism reflecting the narrow intellectual limits of Stalinism. With its search for a "positive hero," socialist-realist fiction worked from a conception of a character portrayal the very opposite of fine-grained subjectivism: a simplified psychology appropriate less for realism than for romance. This aesthetic came best argued, of course, via the programmatic critical writings of Gyorgy Lukács, who, for all his awesome erudition and Middle-European *Kultur*, remained ever obstinate in his distaste for Modernist experimentation, his negation of narrative "inwardness," and his dogmatic preference for fully-rounded and historically-rooted characters *à la* Balzac. On the other hand those "critical realist" attempts with which Communist-inspired Latin American authors had hoped to denounce social ills resulted only in novels that nobody reads and that never overthrew a single dictatorship (as García Márquez himself once put it). In sum, Soviet-style novelistics offered neither relief from nor alternatives to the wispy apolitical introspectiveness of U.S. Cold War narrative.

In the British Isles and France only Beckett, the last of the great avant-garde purists, could be said to have broken genuinely new ground in the novel. And it is no mean irony that this he achieved by fiercely paring down his material and experiential range, by rejecting the Dublin of *Ulysses* for the sealed jar of *The Unnameable*, by reducing fiction to the haunted voice and melodious murmurings of an isolated old man. Granted, there was the absolute perfection and beauty of his form and prose style, as well as an emotional register that masterfully encompassed everything from comic bawdy to painted nostalgia: the word "tragicomedy" describes his slender fictions as aptly as it does the *Godot* to which it serves as subtitle. Nevertheless, the Malones and Morans and Mahoods of this Franco-Irish minimalist — with their ramshackle bites and crutches and their travels through the mud — lead an existence that is as vividly and physically textured as it is slim, desolate and scanty. The remnants of reality in *Watt* and *Molloy*, while far more memorable than most anything to be found in Updike or Bellow, only helped to underscore the profoundly solipsized nature of the world of Beckett's choosing.

Not a few observers in the 1960s were wondering what kind of up-to-date fiction could be possible in the wake of *The Unnameable* or *Texts for Nothing*. The sense of narrative art run aground in its straits seemed additionally confirmed by postwar literary developments in France, where the spirit of vanguard exploration was being carried on by the so-called *nouveau roman* movement. Working under the double shadow of Joyce and especially Beckett, practitioners such as Robbe-Grillet, Sarraute, and Butor considerably expanded the arsenal of novel-writing and in turn exerted a decisive influence on emerging Latin Americans such as Cortázar and Sarduy. At the same time the New Novelists expressly set out to narrow still further the human content — the characters and feelings, the simple raw pleasures and the "soul" as it were — of the novel form, looking upon such circumscription as a progressive advance. Confronted by what they saw as general loss of novelistic authority and by widespread incapacity to believe in literary characterization, in response they contrived elusive shadowy beings or highly restricted first-person narrations, together with a flat, cool, colorless prose and a descriptive objectivism aimed at transcending such obsolete notions as "humanism" and "tragedy." Convinced that they had found an alternative both to the withered values of bourgeois classicism and to the shrill dictates of *engagé* art, they carved out their working space in a self-conscious technicism, a neat and brittle formalism that, in retrospect, seems terribly precious, quietist, and cold.

By 1967 there were informed readers who were aware that in Latin America something new was taking shape. Already the work of Alejo Carpentier and Julio Cortázar had been proving that the diverse exquisite corners into which the novel had painted itself were neither final nor necessary. But it was *One Hundred Years of Solitude* that was to make the difference. Breaking from the claustrophobic atmosphere that had permeated French and American writing, García Márquez reopened the doors and windows and took on the life of the streets, giving us a vast panorama in which every grand historical situation — from utopian harmony and dizzy prosperity to flaccid decadence and class war — was fully conjured up. The book came written with utter authority, had the voice of a wise yet involved and caring speaker who — like an African *griot*, or a super-narrator of folk epic and fairy tale, or an ancient Biblical scribe — truly knows everything about and everyone in a society, from its high notables to its sullen rejects, and moreover sees fit to tell the whole world about them.

Further, instead of those novels with four or five select characters typical of Updike or Butor, the Colombian author evoked a total world in which every conceivable human type played some role. Here were enterprising pioneers, heroic revolutionaries, calculating merchants, moralistic clerics, rigid monarchists, ruthless conservatives, fiery syndicalists, shallow opportunists, wild visionaires, sober scholars, old-fashioned prudes, earthy voluptuaries, exotic nomads, sensitive aesthetes, bureaucrats and imperialists, fops and swingers and more. Here there was maternal warmth, personal hauteur, filial piety, mature friendship, marital stability, lonely isolation, and a moving instance of tragic true love. Here one found bittersweet liaisons without a trace of the maudlin, casual sex without any forced contrivance. Here were growth and decay, high seriousness and low comedy, sadness and joy. *One Hundred Years of*

Solitude reminded the literati that such things as eroticism and humor and love and struggle all form part of human variousness and can once again belong to literature itself.

It was nonetheless clear that this was no conventional family saga of the commercial sort. Any reader sensitive to certain twentieth-century issues could see the "progressive" turn of mind that coexisted with the highly sophisticated artistry: here was a man of the left who had learned and assimilated many a lesson from Kafka, Faulkner, Virginia Woolf, and other Modernist figures. Indeed, what is most notable about *One Hundred Years of Solitude* is that it remains in the leftist camp even as it breaks with Stalinist "rules." Realist dogma was now effectively superseded by a visionary imagination rooted as much in Afro-Caribbean folklore as in Western technique, was challenged by a verbal magician capable of conjuring up with supreme ease such items as a levitating priest, a rain of yellow flowers, a beautiful young virgin rising up to heaven, and a military massacre which the authorities erase from memory literally overnight.

In the same way, the Lukácsian demand for rounded characters was discarded in favor of what are mostly a series of cartoon-like stereotypes. Straight linear narrative was replaced by a conception of time that, while developmental and evolutionary enough to be "Marxist" in its general contours, was also structured and rearranged into a myriad subtle flash-backs and foreshadowings — such as the opening sentence of the book, with its effortless evocation of three separate moments, or the concluding page, with its vision of simultaneity. Finally, the intricate web of parallel-isms, congruences, and repetitions in *One Hundred Years of Solitude* gave evidence of a meticulous craftsman who took quite seriously the formal aspect of his art — which aspect is the ultimate criterion, as it were, for all art. Form-conscious without being formalist, García Márquez proved to his leftist brethren once and for all that literary experimentation need not be escapist or subjectivist, and that established realism is neither the final word nor the sole means available to the progressive imagination.

García Márquez's wide gamut of sentiments needs no further men-tion. In the countless discussions of fantasy, politics and sex in his work, however, what often goes overlooked is the determining presence of that most complex of structures of feeling — namely, tragedy, in the specific Hegelian sense of a clash between equally valid though mutually irrecon-cilable opposites. Inasmuch as we have cast a previous glance at French writers, it may be fruitful to note a couple of contrasting views of tragedy from the Paris of the 1950s: while Robbe-Grillet in *For a New Novel* summarily dismissed "tragedy" as one of the many perverse maneuvers of bourgeois humanism, Sartre in *Search for a Method* regretted that contemporary Marxism hadn't yet found a way to incorporate the sense of tragedy into its worldview.

It took a self-taught and anti-academic Third World leftist like

García Márquez to furnish striking instances of Sartre's desideratum. For a few such tragic conflicts one may cite José Arcadio Buendía's contradictory penchants for village leadership and pure science, or Colonel Buendía's monumental heroism and his enormous human failings, or Amaranta's powerful vocation for incest versus the socially necessary prohibitions, or in particular the final couple's foredoomed conflict between their blissful and intense passion and Amaranta Ursula's mundane but crucial house-keeping chores. And there is in *No One Writes to the Colonel* the stubborn opposition between the need for food and the family honor symbolized by the fighting cock, or in "Tuesday Siesta" the clash between criminal laws and a mother's devotion to her son, or in "Artificial Roses" the struggle between young Mina's broken heart and her grandmother's tough solici-tousness, or in *Chronicle of a Death Foretold* the probable innocence of Santiago Nasar versus the Vicario clan's need for a sacrificial victim. These are all recognizable as the basic stuff of tragedy, and it is no accident that among the classic works most cherished by García Márquez are *Oedipus Rex* and the *Antigone* of Sophocles.

Oceans of ink have flowed in commenting on the use of fantasy in García Márquez — why and how it works and the like. For our purposes, it should suffice to say that the fertile commingling of the fantastical with the realistic stands as García Márquez's most momentous single innovation in narrative art. After *One Hundred Years of Solitude* it became possible to write "serious" novels that incorporate the unreal without spilling over into sword-and sorcery and other kinds of escapism. For paradoxically the unreality in García Márquez, while intended for the delectation of readers who do in fact enjoy the wild invention for its own sake, actually has the hidden job of underscoring and enhancing the realities under depiction. Hence the priest levitates because he seeks contributions for a brand-new church and knows that a miracle will impress the villagers. The rain of flowers befits the universal sense of mourning caused by the death of founder and patriarch José Arcadio Buendía. And the magical exorcising of the fruit workers' massacre by the ruling apparatus is a masterful "Orwellian" instance of that notorious tendency on the part of all states to conceal their less than savory pasts. García Márquez himself, it should be noted, dislikes the term "fantasy" and sees his writings as essentially realistic — a perception recently confirmed by Joan Didion in *Salvador*.

And indeed the paradox can be taken still further. It can safely be said that the most significant and immediate contribution to novel-writing and novel-reading by the tropical visionary García Márquez is his having led the art of fiction back to real life and thereby restoring to prose narrative the hurly and burly of reality in all its rich and contradictory manifesta-tions. García Márquez once quipped that "reality isn't restricted to the price of tomatoes." Though meant as a reply to the orthodox left and its economic *idées fixes*, the aphorism could just as well be aimed at any of the novelists in the U.S. or France who had restricted their sights either to the insides of middle-class heads or to outside objects like centipedes and Venetian blinds, even as they remained oblivious to most everything else. What Arthur Miller deplored about the American theatre in the 1950s was perfectly applicable to the fiction of that decade: he complained of a "narrowing field of vision," an "inability to put the whole world on the stage and shake it down to its foundations," and an incapacity to distinguish "between a big subject and a small one, a wide and narrow view."

One Hundred Years of Solitude has as its big subject and wide view not only the full spectrum of human diversity but also some three centuries of Colombian and by extension Latin American history. This total edifice García Márquez built in great degree by rooting his account in concrete, verifiable data. From the attack by Sir Francis Drake on Riohacha (a real incident that occurred in 1596), which traumatizes Ursula's great-great-grandmother, to the bitter banana workers' strike and army massacre (based closely on the bloody United Fruit events of 1928), which signals Macondo's decline, García Márquez is scrupulously faithful to his collective past, reinvent and embellish it though he may. The fact that *One Hundred Years of Solitude* is required reading in many Latin American history and political science courses in the U.S. goes a long way toward demonstrating the essential truth of García Márquez's novel, its over-all correspondence to a broad social and historical reality.

The strike scenes in themselves are worth a close look. In the hands of a less seasoned author, it would have been all too easy to bungle these episodes, to lapse into solemn preachiness and propaganda, to draw excessive attention and make them the book's reason for existence. García Márquez shuns this trap by subordinating the strike materials to the overarching narrative plan, treating them as simply one episode among many and never once raising his voice in the process. Moreover he provides comic relief via Fernanda's prissiness, and further lightens up the actual strike narrative with jokes concerning Virginia hams, portable latrines, the blue pills which the infirmary dispenses for all ailments, and the children who rip off the pills and use them as bingo markers. The horrors of the massacre itself—one of the most hair-raising scenes in modern fiction—are soon offset by the aftermath, with its dark magic and collective amnesia.

This is García Márquez the prestidigitator deftly at work. Less visible, however, is the hand of García Márquez the meticulous historical researcher. In 1928—coincidentally the year of García Márquez's birth—the United Fruit Company plantations across the length and breadth of Caribbean Colombia were hit by massive labor unrest. The military were called in, and there is evidence that the Company brazenly paid them off to gun down the strikers. A national political crisis ensued, with extensive hearings and grisly eye-witness testimony in the Colombian Senate, the published record of which García Márquez apparently depended on for his Macondo strike scenes.

Both in the Senate hearings and in the novel we read of workers protesting against the poor sanitation, the lack of toilets, the Company commissaries, the payment in credit slips instead of hard cash. Military orders to shoot were handed down by a General Cortés Vargas; his name and his decision are specifically retained in *One Hundred Years*. A survivor and Senate witness was to recall having heard a distant voice crying out in pain, "AY MI MADRE!"; the heart-rending cry and its circumstances found their way into García Márquez's narrative. (The set phrase, a common interjection in Spanish, is rendered by Gregory Rabassa as "Aaaagh, Mother.") Figures for casualties inevitably varied according to source. General Cortés Vargas put them at a low 40 dead and 100 wounded. Strike organizer Alberto Castrillón, by contrast, calculated them at 1500 dead and—significantly—3000 wounded. Plainly, García Márquez's own approach in his account of the slaughter in Macondo plaza was to cite the highest *reported* casualty figures from the 1928 repression.

The instant brainwashing that follows, García Márquez likes to tell his interviewers, is but an exaggeration of what actually did happen, the government and media have convinced most everybody that the strikers simply went home satisfied. Far-fetched as this recollection may seem, I accidentally confirmed it first-hand during the summer of 1982, when I visited Aracataca, the novelist's birthplace and also the principal model for Macondo. There I saw many vivid reminders of García Márquez's imagined world—in the town cemetery, for example, the very first tombstones I saw were for a couple of ladies with the family name of Ternera. The highest point of my visit, however, was a brief conversation with a senior citizen, a short, wiry, crusty sort with rugged Basque features and thinning gray hair. He had worked as a timekeeper for United Fruit, and he recalled with wistful joy the good old days of Company wealth.

When I asked about the strikers, however, he turned grumpy and replied, "Look, those strikers only made a mess of things. And I'll tell you something: all that talk of massacres just isn't true. It never happened. The most *I* ever heard of was a couple of guys dead. Really, if so many died, then where did they put the corpses?" Those were the man's words, pretty much. García Márquez, as we know, imagined a 200-car train for the disposal of his 3000 corpses, though this too may have its source in history: a Company foreman at the Colombian Senate hearings testified to having seen a fourteen-car train chock-filled with imprisoned field workers, being transported to Aracataca.

From this sketchy account it should be clear that García Márquez the visionary fantasist is also, to a degree that is not generally recognized, a poet of reality. As a neat little capstone one might mention that destructive five-year rainstorm — caused by the company — in relation to García Márquez's prophetic strain: in 1972, on the floor of the U.S. Senate, a committee chaired by Claiborn Pell (D-R.I.) disclosed that U.S. military forces in Southeast Asia had been seeding clouds so as to generate hurricanes and floods in Vietnam.

The same mix of formal exploration and extravagant fantasy that builds on history can be noted in García Márquez's other great novel, *The Autumn of the Patriarch*. Itself an ambitious experiment from the most minute aspects of its delirious syntax to its daunting edifice of six long paragraphs, it spans anywhere from 107 to 232 years. Each of its six chapters starts out by picking up on a moment in the multitude's discovery of the dictator's rotting corpse in the Presidential Palace, followed thereafter by an extended flashback that focuses on episodes chosen from the man's long existence, these serving to highlight his larger-than-life idiosyncrasies, manias, and of course crimes. Once again García Márquez experiments with point of view, in this case giving us not the supernarrator of *One Hundred Years* but an almost audible and ever-shifting voice that ranges from the plebeian and ribald popular citizenry of "we" to the many "I" narrators, comprising the lowbrow Patriarch and his comical mother and his many varied loves and political lackeys, together with long snatches of first-grade reading books and popular songs and the poet Rubén Darío — all of these constantly coming and going in mid-sentence. A technique that Faulkner seemed to have exhausted in *Absalom! Absalom!* has been broadened and then distilled to its utmost creative limit.

The hyperbole of the book, while unforgettable, again exaggerates from real-life facts. Two major examples will suffice. The 107-to-232 years of the Patriarch's power are a threefold and fourfold version of the forty- and fifty-year autocracies of such grotesque figures as Juan Vincente Gómez, Trujillo, and the Somozas. And the climactic scene in which the Yankees carve up the Caribbean Sea and ship it off to Arizona suggest the many like if lesser instances of U.S. business imperialism — such as the French cloisters, Italian palazzi, and London bridges which from time to time have been disassembled and carted off to select urban and desert locales in this vast Republic. Perhaps García Márquez's most striking artistic contribution is his discovery that the best way for literature to approach U.S. imperialism is not to fulminate and rage against it but to do the reality one better by magnifying it to almost cosmic, and comic, extremes, thereby satirizing it in the grandest possible manner.

After years of the novel narrowing its sights and subject matter, this trans-Caribbean bard has come along to rejuvenate its ties with reality and widen its format and purview. His influence, moreover, is growing steadily. His mixture of the fantastical and the prosaic can be found in the work of his U.S. admirers John Nichols and Robert Coover; and his amplifying effects are discernible even in John Updike, who ventured for the very first time outside of the mental turf and geography of suburban realism with *The Coup* (1978), a novel about an African dictator. Whereas at one time American authors used to look to France for their models and mentors, they are now taking vital lessons from their South American writing kin.

In his highly learned, fervently reasoned, and loyally Russian polemic *On Socialist Realism* (1960), the dissident Soviet writer Andrei Siniavski once noted the many problems inherent in the reigning Communist aesthetic — *i.e.* its irreconcilable demands for realistic format, romantic effects, and visionary consequences. In its stead Siniavski pinned his hopes on "a phantasmagoric art . . . in which the grotesque will replace realistic descriptions of ordinary life. Such an art would correspond best to the spirit of our time. May the fantastic imagery of Hoffman and Dostoevsky, of Goya, Chagall, and Mayakovski . . . and of many other realists and nonrealists teach us *how to be truthful with the aid of the absurd and the fantastic*" (emphasis added). Only a few years after this passionate literary plea a writer from an impoverished tropical small town, on a continent whose social conditions recall those of nineteenth-century Russia, delivered a phantasmagoric book that fits precisely the terms of what Siniavski had so ardently (and perilously) advocated. With the aid of the absurd and the fantastic, Gabriel García Márquez has been truthful to his land, his people, and his art.

INDEX

219